THE ECONOMIC PROBLEM OF
THE DANUBIAN STATES

THE ECONOMIC PROBLEM OF THE DANUBIAN STATES

A Study in Economic Nationalism

by

FREDERICK HERTZ

NEW YORK

Howard Fertig

1970

Copyright 1947 by Frederick Hertz

HOWARD FERTIG, INC. EDITION 1970
Published by arrangement with Victor Gollancz Ltd.

Library of Congress Catalog Card Number: 68-9662

PRINTED IN THE UNITED STATES OF AMERICA
BY NOBLE OFFSET PRINTERS, INC.

CONTENTS

I. General Aspects of the Problem

II. The Development of the National Income in Austria-Hungary in the last ten years before the World War

III. Economic Nationalism between the two World Wars

IV. The Balance-Sheet of Economic Nationalism

A. Changes in the Structure of the Population

B. Structural Changes in Agrarian Conditions

C. Structural Changes in Industrial Conditions

I. GENERAL ASPECTS OF THE PROBLEM

1. An Historic Experiment in Economic Policy

Our age has in many fields witnessed great revolutions. One of these arose in economic policy and thought, and it is still in progress. Almost all the principles which only a few decades ago had been considered unshakeable truths were challenged and declared old-fashioned superstitions. The attacks came from different political quarters and were inspired by widely divergent ideals. To a great extent, however, they converged in discrediting economic internationalism, which was exposed to a cross-fire from all sides.

The majority of economists for some time opposed these attacks, but later the champions of the new faiths gained considerable ground in their ranks also. The arguments of the economists, however, had little influence on public opinion. Many critics of the old dogmas were not affected by their objections because they did not share the underlying belief in the great importance of economic considerations. To these critics some political ideal seemed of paramount importance—either the greatness of their nation, or the purity of their race, or the supremacy of a class, or the balance of the Corporate State, or the rule of an efficient *élite*, or the dictatorship of an inspired leader. The ideas of a world economy, of world trade, a world currency, freedom of migration, etc., seemed to many of them particularly suspect of impairing the national sovereignty or some other claim to power. The enhancement of power and prestige, territorial expansion, strategic frontiers, the keeping down of an hereditary enemy—such aims seemed immensely more important than economic co-operation between nations, and the claim of a party or class to power, and to the spoils of power, was more alluring than the aim of co-operation between all sections within a nation.

Most economists, moreover, used mainly the method of abstract analysis, assuming a simple constellation of forces for deducing

9

possible interactions. This method, though exceedingly illuminating, could not by itself settle complex questions of reality. Abstract economics resembles a subtle game of chess subject to strict rules, while economic reality—especially in our age—is like warfare, with all its unaccountable and imponderable factors.

The present study is intended as a contribution to the empirical analysis of a problem of great practical importance. The results will also have significant theoretical implications. But I have withstood the temptation to mix theory with statistics and the discussion of world problems with that of Danubian questions. This might have confused the readers and diverted their attention from the concrete problem. Neither does this study lead to the recommendation of some patent medicine for all possible illnesses, such as pump-priming, or free enterprise, or planning, or federation. Its object is more modest. A student of medicine must first have a thorough knowledge of anatomy, physiology, pathology and other disciplines, before he tackles therapy. In brief, this study is designed to contribute to the elucidation of certain structural and functional problems of fundamental importance.

The special field of the investigation is the Danubian area which once formed Austria-Hungary and was later divided into the Succession States. Italy, though one of the successors, is not included, nor are Bulgaria and Germany, though they are riverains of the Danube. The Austro-Hungarian Empire had in its western half, usually called Austria, a strongly federalistic and supra-national character, while in the Hungarian half the Magyars occupied a ruling position. This large area formed an economic unit with internal free trade, a common currency and a common customs tariff which in comparison with our time was moderate. After the break-up of Austria-Hungary, the new States, dominated by intense nationalism, surrounded themselves with high tariff walls and other economic barriers, tried to conquer foreign markets by subsidising exports, and in their economic policy often gave national prestige precedence of wealth. State interference in economic life greatly increased, owing partly to nationalism, partly to the political pressure of powerful parties and social sections. Some of the new States pursued also a progressive policy introducing beneficial social and other reforms. But seen as a whole the lack of external and internal co-operation led to a standstill, and even to a decline, in economic development, to impoverishment and unemployment, to the spread of corruption and violence, and to the rise of dictatorships, paving the way for Hitler. This process has often been called the Balkanisation of Central Europe.

The partition of Austria-Hungary may be regarded as one of the most instructive experiments in political and economic organisation. The most suitable objects for a comparative study are the three States, Austria, Czechoslovakia and Hungary, and our investigation will be centred upon these countries, and will only to a lesser degree be extended to the other Succession States. The reasons for this restriction are: (1) that the three States have been entirely formed out of territories of former Austria-Hungary, which fact greatly facilitates statistical comparisons; (2) that they were not, or were very little, exposed to the direct ravages of war, while the other States had to suffer great devastations; (3) that their historical and social background was essentially Central European, while the other States showed many East European features.

In the three States principally treated the damage caused by the war of 1914–1918 consisted in the loss of a certain number of the population, in the exhaustion of stocks of raw materials, in the postponement of replacement of machinery, in the diminution of livestock and so on. On the other hand, the war stimulated the extension of certain industries. For Austria proper the increase in capacity during the war has been estimated at 20%. It must further be taken into account that after the war the world experienced an extraordinary technological progress, such as the phenomenal rise of the automobile, the rapid expansion of the use of electricity, the systematic rationalisation of production symbolised by the conveyor belt, the introduction of broadcasting and many other important new processes.

It may therefore be assumed with assurance that in the three countries Austria, Czechoslovakia and Hungary the direct damages of war [1] were after a few years at least countervailed, and probably outbalanced, by factors of expansion. A standstill

---

[1] There were, of course, indirect damages, such as the certain increase in State expenditure. On the other hand the inflation after the war wiped out most debts.

or decline in the national income can therefore not be mainly ascribed to war damage, but must be traced to changes in political and social conditions, in particular to measures of policy.

The three other countries had much more to suffer by the direct ravages of the war. On the other hand, their national income was mainly the product of a rather primitive agriculture capable of comparatively quick reconstruction.

This study is by no means designed to give an exhaustive description of economic conditions in the Danubian States. It is primarily an analysis of certain fundamental problems. The League of Nations, the International Labour Organisation and other institutions have in their publications dealt with many questions of the Danubian States which have been excluded from our survey. The reader interested in them will, however, find references to the principal sources of detailed information.

Particular attention has been given to the comparison of the national income and its constituent parts before and after the First World War. The national income sums up all the positive and negative factors and enables us to form an opinion of the success or failure of the economic systems.

One of the most prominent statisticians of our time, Mr. Colin Clark, has also investigated "the vexed question of the alleged economic disadvantages consequent upon the break-up of the old Austro-Hungarian Empire ".[1] He comes to the conclusion that the "average real income per head over Central Europe as a whole, in spite of all, appears to be now distinctly higher than it was in 1913". He substantiates this statement with figures showing astounding increases of national income for Hungary, Yugoslavia and Czechoslovakia, while Austria and Roumania show moderate decreases. Our investigation will reveal a very different picture.

In comparing the development of the national income before and after the war it must be considered that after the war great changes took place in the monetary systems and the price levels. The comparison of national income figures therefore can only be carried out if the post-war figures are converted into pre-war currency and reduced to the pre-war price level. The method employed by us is that generally used by economists dealing with

[1] Cf. Colin Clark, *The Conditions of Economic Progress*, 1940, p. 135.

questions of this sort. But it is clear that the use of conversion co-efficients, like various price-index figures or the relation between the gold content of currencies, implies a certain margin of error. We have therefore taken great care to check comparisons of national income figures by two other methods, as far as the statistics available permitted. On the one hand, we have made parallel comparisons of quantities of production, such as the weights of crops or of industrial output, in order to check the agricultural or industrial income; on the other, we have also compared figures of consumption and investment. The national income is partly consumed, partly invested. The trend of consumption and investment must therefore reflect that of the national income. Lastly, other statistics also are symptomatic of the development of the national income, in particular figures showing the growth of wealth, of taxable income, etc.

In conclusion, it may be mentioned that we have avoided comparing income figures which were abnormally depressed by the world crisis. Even if such figures have been quoted for the sake of statistical continuity, no conclusions have been drawn from them. Certain statisticians have started from abnormally low levels, such as existed either in the last year of war or in the depth of the post-war depression, and they then showed the great increase in the subsequent years. An investigation of this kind may be useful to show how far a country has succeeded in overcoming the consequences of a catastrophe like the war or the world crisis. But it does not show whether the economic structure before the war or that after the war has proved more productive.

Since our study is to a great extent a comparison between conditions before and after the First Great War of 1914–1918, *it is clear that expressions like "the last war", "pre-war", "post-war", etc., refer to that war.*

2. THE DEFINITION OF NATIONAL INCOME

Before entering into the discussion of the Central European problem it must be made clear what concept of the national income will be employed in the course of this investigation. Both the concept of the national income and the method of its computation have recently been much disputed. A number of important

13

points were discussed at the Centenary Meeting of the Royal Statistical Society, April 17th, 1934, by Sir Josiah (later Lord) Stamp, Professor A. L. Bowley and others.[1] The tenor of this debate confirmed the general trend in the development of opinion on this subject which has taken place in recent times. The national income was formerly conceived mainly as the annual net production of material goods, including cost of distribution. The value of services not directly connected with production was regarded as derived income which was paid out of the income created by production and had therefore to be eliminated in statistical calculations in order to avoid duplication. House rent, too, was eliminated. This view, however, has been more and more abandoned in recent treatments of the subject. Many economists demanded the inclusion of all services, or at least of those which were paid for in money, and also the inclusion of house-rent. Other points, too, were raised which, however, need not be discussed for the purpose of this study.

Behind the different theoretical definitions of national income there are obviously different practical aims in defining it. Whether we use a wider or a narrower definition depends on the practical purpose for which the figure is wanted. Main differences are whether the income is to express the productive power of a nation, or its possible range of consumption, or its taxable capacity. The income and wealth of an individual, too, can be estimated quite differently. A man living in luxury may be regarded as very rich by his neighbours and by the income-tax inspector, while his banker may have formed a much more critical view of his wealth.

In the same way, the question whether certain items are to be included in the national income will depend on the aim of our question. If the national income is to express the productive

[1] Cf. *Journal of the Royal Statistical Society*, 1934, "Methods Used in Different Countries for Estimating National Income" (also reprinted as a separate publication). The general economic and statistical problems have, furthermore, been discussed at various sessions of the International Institute of Statistics (cf. its *Bulletin*, XIII, 1; XIV, 3; XX, 1; XXV, 3; XXVIII, 1), at a Congress of the Verein für Sozialpolitik (cf. its *Schriften*, vol. 172, 1926), and in a special Conference of the Hungarian Statistical Society (cf. *Journal de la Société Hongroise de Statistique*, tome 16, 1938, pp. 286–325); cf. further the address by A. W. Flux and the ensuing discussion in the *Journal of the Royal Statistical Society*, 1929. The most up-to-date and illuminating discussion of the problem, however, is A. L. Bowley, *Studies in the National Income, 1924–1938* (1942).

strength of a nation, then, for example, house-rent cannot be counted as a part of it, as it is merely the value of the use of an existing commodity.[1] If it is to indicate the amount of goods which a people may consume every year without diminishing its resources, then house-rent may be included.

Another point of dispute is whether the unpaid work of housewives shall be included in the national income. In my view it certainly belongs to it. There is no reason why washing done by a laundry should be counted as an increase of the national income and the same work done by a housewife not. But to estimate this sort of work in money is a matter of great difficulty, and the attempts made are open to grave objections. The only adequate method would be a careful investigation of a sufficient number of various types of households and the working out of averages. This also applies to other cases. Failing such studies, the best way seems to be either to omit certain minor items altogether, or to add at the end of the list those items which cannot be exactly estimated owing to lack of reliable data. Some part of the national income will always escape an accurate computation—for example, the wages paid for occasional work which is usually not recorded in labour statistics. The chief sources of income, however, can nowadays be ascertained with a great degree of accuracy, and it seems desirable, in summing up the various elements of the national income, to keep apart those figures which have been accurately ascertained and are recorded in the official statistics, from those which are merely vague estimates, or perhaps no more than arbitrary guesses.

A special problem is that of non-material values created mainly by the so-called liberal professions—*i.e.*, the Civil Service, the Churches, the schools, scientific institutions, lawyers, medical doctors, writers, artists, musicians and so on. Stamp in his abovementioned paper has strongly advocated the inclusion of all these services in the national income. He calls the adherents of this doctrine idealists and those in the opposite camp materialists. The conclusive argument is, in his view, that the creators of non-material things contribute to "total human enjoyment", and therefore to the national income, no less than those who make

[1] It is, besides, illogical to treat the annual production of new houses and the value of the use of old houses as items of the same kind, and to add them together.

material things. To this it can be replied that the so-called liberal professions comprise elements which must be judged quite differently. A State official employed on a State railway or in a State factory does economic work which is in no way different from the work in private enterprises of the same kind. Many other State officials, however, are not in this position. A lawyer who recovers claims for an industrial company and charges legal expenses for his work adds to the cost of production of the company, and his private income certainly increases the national income. But a lawyer who drafts the last will of a client or who pleads for a defendant before a court can hardly be said to contribute to the national income, though the results of his activities may be "enjoyed" by the heirs, the acquitted person and by himself.

Those economists who advocate the inclusion of all immaterial goods in the national income assume that the financial reward of their creators represents the amount of their contribution to the national income, just as the wages and profits paid in the production of material goods constitute its value in the national balance-sheet. This view seems to me a complete fallacy.

In a recent conference on the problems of national income an economist asked in what way the labour of a farmer who destroyed parasites damaging his crops was different from the work of a policeman who arrested a parasite of society—*e.g.*, a housebreaker. The answer obviously is that the result of the farmer's labour can be accurately estimated. A certain quantity of foodstuffs which have a fixed market price has been saved from destruction. The work of the policeman was quite different. If he had not arrested the house-breaker, the national income would not have been smaller. A certain part only would have been in the possession of the criminal instead of that of the lawful owner. The real value of the policeman's work—from a public point of view— was that he helped to maintain the reign of law and security, which has an inestimable value. It is certainly not expressed in the salary of the policeman. The same holds good for all officials not employed in economic enterprises of the State.

The work of the Army consists in preparing for a possible war, and in waging it, if it comes. The value of this work obviously has no relation at all to the pay of the soldiers. Two nations at war with one another may expend the same amount on their armies, and yet one wins the war and the other loses it. The value of the work of a clergyman will be estimated quite differently by a believer and by an unbeliever. Likewise, the work of an artist may appear very great to his admirers, and very small to his adverse critics. His income is certainly not a measure of the value of his work.

The significance of wages and other costs paid for the production of immaterial goods is entirely different from that of similar amounts paid in the production of material goods. The contribution of a cotton-weaver to the national income can be exactly stated in $£$ s. d.; the contribution of a teacher, scholar or artist can not. The expenses of the British Museum, according to the budget of 1938–1939, were £198,743, and the expenses of a big cinema company may have been ten times that amount. Should we say, therefore, that the cinema company contributed ten times as much to the immaterial national income as the British Museum?

If the salaries of public officials of every description form an asset, then we must admire the dictators who, by the introduction of big gangs of Blackshirts, Gestapo men, Storm-troopers, etc., greatly increased the national income. The "human enjoyment" of these individuals certainly increased. But was this not offset by a decrease in the "human enjoyment" of many others?

In my view Stamp was wrong when he identified the national income with "total human enjoyment". Not even the private income corresponds to the degree of enjoyment of its recipient. We may enjoy many things which are not income, such as health, love, friendship, trust, fame, power, knowledge, beauty and so on. My conclusion is that the real materialists are those who estimate certain immaterial goods in money and put them on the same level as other goods exchangeable on the markets.

Obviously various concepts of the national income are admissible, and the choice of the concept must depend on the specific object of the investigation. Estimates of the national income have usually been made for ascertaining the general economic strength of a nation for some practical purpose. For most purposes, however, the restriction of income to material goods is preferable. Farmers and workers can live without poets, but poets cannot live without those who produce bread. If the question is raised whether

17

a country can bear still further taxation, or whether it is capable of paying interest and amortisation on a loan, it is the material goods that matter, not the immaterial ones. No foreign banker would give a loan to a country which has plenty of officials or soldiers but insufficient material resources. In the case of countries in urgent need of foreign credit the bankers frequently even demanded a reduction of the expenses for the Civil Services as a condition of a loan. If we are to assume that the salaries of the officials constitute national income in the same way as the wages of industrial workers, this would mean that the bankers demanded the reduction of the national income, which is obviously absurd.

On the whole, three concepts of national income must be distinguished :—

(1) The produced income, consisting of the goods and services produced by economic means in a territory in a certain time. Goods accruing to its possessions without economic activity are not produced income—for example, a treasure found without effort in a hiding-place, the timber grown in a wood without being cut, or a tribute exacted from a vanquished enemy.

(2) The consumable income, consisting of all increases in wealth which may be consumed without diminishing the initial total of values.

(3) The taxable income, consisting of those values which the State may tax without diminishing the taxable capacity of the people. House-rent, for instance, is not, or only to a small degree, income produced in the period. One could as well include the value of the use of clothing or of public roads in the national income. But house-rent is as a rule a good index of the taxable capacity of an individual, whether landlord or tenant.

Another distinction cuts across all others—namely, that between real and nominal income. Income is expressed in money since its various elements must somehow be summed up. But the value of money is constantly changing, and several methods have been evolved to eliminate these fluctuations and to calculate the real income. One of the factors causing changes in the nominal income is taxation. Some taxes certainly raise prices, while others do not. It would be absurd, however, to say that the State, in introducing new taxes, increases the real produced, or consum-

18

able, income. The effect is only a change in the price level, and possibly in the distribution of income. We may also think of a mediæval robber-knight or an American gangster-chief extorting high ransoms from the people of his district. Nobody would say that he thereby adds to the national income, but he may make the price level rise and thereby increase the nominal income.

In our investigation various concepts of national income will be used according to the problem treated. Its main object, however, is not to estimate the absolute amount of income, but its increase or decrease, and the per cent rate of change. For this purpose any reasonable concept of national income may be used. The only conditions are that the figures form an index apt to express the wealth of the country, and that only such figures be used for comparison which are based on the same concept of national income, and are calculated in the same way. Whether or not certain minor items are included is not essential. In comparing estimates of national income a certain margin of error does not affect the validity of the comparison if the error was in each year compared of about the same size, because in this case it cancels out.

II. THE DEVELOPMENT OF THE NATIONAL INCOME IN AUSTRIA-HUNGARY IN THE LAST TEN YEARS BEFORE THE WORLD WAR

1. ESTIMATES OF THE NATIONAL INCOME IN FORMER AUSTRIA-HUNGARY

THE AUSTRO-HUNGARIAN EMPIRE consisted of two groups of States commonly called Austria and Hungary which were independent of each other but had the ruler and certain institutions in common. The word Austria, however, was not an official designation. The seventeen territories which were popularly called Austria were officially described as "the Kingdoms and countries represented in the Imperial Parliament". The structure of this group was to a great extent federalistic. The Hungarian group, called "the countries of the Crown of St. Stephen", was more centralised, though Croatia had her separate parliament and autonomy.[1]

The monetary unit in Austria-Hungary was the Krone or crown, which was based on gold. 24·02 Kronen (abbreviated K.) were equivalent to the pound sterling, though the actual rate in the last years before the war was 24·10.

The most careful calculations of the income and wealth of Austria and Hungary before the Great War have been made by an Hungarian economist, Professor Friedrich de Fellner. In various publications he estimated the income and wealth of Austria and of Hungary on the basis of the average figures of the years 1911–1913, and he also estimated Hungary's income for 1899–1901.[2] After the war Fellner furthermore calculated how the income and wealth of the Hungarian countries had been

---

[1] Cf. for particulars my book, F. Hertz, *Nationalgeist und Politik*, I, 1937.
[2] Fellner's principal study was published in the *Bulletin de l'Institut International de Statistique*, XX, 1915, and the *Statistische Monatsschrift*, edited by the Austrian Statistical Office, 1916. The estimate of Hungary's income for 1899 to 1901 was printed in the *Bulletin*, XIII, 1903.

divided among the Succession States.[1] Fellner's investigations have been criticised by some statisticians, and some corrections have been found advisable. On the whole, however, they have been recognised as fundamental for the problem of the national income in Central Europe. Fellner used for his work the objective method, and he excluded from the national income immaterial goods and domestic service as well as house-rent, though he gave estimates of the personal services separately. The followers of the opposite school, therefore, found his concept of the national income too narrow.

The total income of Austria before the war was estimated by Fellner at 12,565 million K., and that of Hungary at 6,742 million K.

We need not for our purposes enter into a detailed discussion of Fellner's figures. On the whole his estimate must be regarded as a minimum rather than as an over-statement. The value of forestal output, the contribution of commerce and transport to the national income, and other items have certainly been much underestimated by Fellner. Vienna's very great income from international trading and banking is completely ignored. The very large income from building and from restaurants, hotels, theatres, etc., is also ignored. Some income of the liberal professions should have been included because it formed part of the cost of industrial production. Account should also have been taken of excise duties increasing prices.

Ernst Waizner has checked the accuracy of Fellner's estimate by calculations of his own.[2] He worked out an estimate by means of the subjective method, and, moreover, tried to rectify Fellner's calculations, using the objective method. He based his estimates on a much wider concept of the national income. This must be kept in view when his figures are compared with those of Fellner. Lastly, Waizner has calculated how the national income of old Austria was divided among the Succession States.

The estimate which Waizner made by means of the subjective method agrees very well with Fellner's figure for Austria, provided that those items are eliminated which Fellner does not regard as part of the national income, while Waizner includes them.

[1] Cf. *Metron, International Review of Statistics*, III, 1, 1923.
[2] Cf. Waizner in *Metron*, VII, 4, 1928; pp. 97–182.

Waizner estimated that agriculture, forestry, mines, industry, trade, commerce and transport produced a total value of 12,124·4 million K., while Fellner found for the same items 12,214 million K.; Waizner put the income from commerce and transport considerably higher than Fellner, while he estimated the industrial income lower, though in our view on an erroneous assumption. In the other items the differences between Fellner and Waizner are not great. Waizner, furthermore, included in the national income that of the liberal professions, the Civil Service, the Army, the house-owners, the domestic servants, the people living on rents, and even that of people without any profession. The total amount for these professions is 2,827·7 million K. This shows that the use of the wider concept of national income gives much higher amounts than the use of the narrower one. This may in some respects be very misleading.

In an important point, however, Waizner's attempt at correcting Fellner's calculations certainly went astray, and it is advisable to devote some attention to this matter, as a general problem of great significance is involved. Fellner calculated the value of industrial output by means of two methods. For some industries exact data were available because these branches were subject to excise taxes and had to furnish detailed statistics of their output to the Ministry of Finance. For all the other industries Fellner calculated the output in the following way. He first ascertained the amount of wages paid in each branch according to the annual statistics of the Workers' Accident Insurance, which comprised all factory workers and some other categories. Then he ascertained the percentage which in each branch wages formed in the value of output. If, for example, in a certain industry wages formed 20% of the value of output, and if the amount of wages actually paid was 100 million K., the value of the output could be estimated at 500 million K.

Now, Waizner thinks that the percentages of wages in the values of output were in reality much higher than Fellner assumed, and that he therefore over-estimated the value of output in the different branches of industry. The only argument put forward by Waizner to support this statement is that the British Census of Production of 1907 showed higher percentages of wages. I had pointed out in one of my books that Fellner's calculations were

22

confirmed by the British Census. This Census showed that the value of net output of all industries [1] per head of personnel employed was in England and Wales £104 and in the whole United Kingdom £102. The corresponding figure for Austria, according to Fellner's estimate, was £107, or almost the same as in England. Waizner, however, regards this comparison of mine rather as an argument for the opposite conclusion. He says that it is very improbable that Britain, with her highly developed industries, should produce only as much per head of worker and employee as Austria, and that the estimate for Austria must therefore be too high. [2]

The Hungarian Industrial Census of 1906 shows a net output of £109 per worker. This would confirm Fellner's estimate, but Waizner refused to accept this as a proof, because he thinks that Fellner's calculations were based on that Census. Fellner's statement of his sources, [3] however, makes it clear that two-thirds of the total value were estimated from data furnished by well-known experts, mainly leaders of industrial organisations, and from official excise tax returns, though the rest was obviously taken from the industrial Censuses.

Waizner's arguments are based on a fundamental mistake. He forgets that the level of prices was higher, and the level of wages lower, in Austria than in Britain. For the years concerned the difference in the price level was at least 10%, and that in the wage level 35·7%. Now, if we assume that the British employer saved a part of the extra cost caused by higher wages by employing labour-saving machinery, etc., and that the increase in the cost of production was only 25%, and if we modify the Austrian figures accordingly, then the share of wages in the net output of Austrian

[1] The net output is found by deducting the value of all the materials, coal, etc., used in the production of the final product from the gross output. Sometimes an amount for depreciation is also deducted. The net output indicates the increase in the value of the materials resulting from the industrial process.

[2] Waizner obviously believes that the technical equipment of the Austrian industries was generally inferior to that in Britain. But this is a mistake. The output of pig iron per high furnace, for instance, was before the war twice as great in Austria as in Britain, and the Austrian cotton mills were, according to the statistics of the International Cotton-spinners Association, equipped to a much greater extent with modern ring-frames than the British mills. It must also be considered that the structure of industries was different in the two countries. Austria, for example, had a much higher proportion of food industries, and the British Census included mining and building, which were excluded by Fellner.

[3] Cf. the data in Fellner's paper in *Statistische Monatsschrift*, 1916, p. 556.

industries becomes 51·5%, or almost exactly the same as that of Britain, according to Bowley. This comparison is merely an illustration of the weight of the factors which Waizner overlooked, not an exact calculation. Waizner's only argument against Fellner's estimate is therefore a mistake. Many of Fellner's figures, moreover, can be checked by data from other sources, and on the whole accord with them. Waizner has decreased Fellner's estimate of industrial net output by 25%, though this suggestion was scarcely more than a guess. If Fellner's original figures are to be restored, Waizner's figures of industrial net output must be increased by a third. If it is assumed, however, that Fellner's estimates of industrial output should be reduced by 10% in order to avoid any possible over-estimate, then Waizner's figures must be increased by a fifth.

2. HUNGARY'S MONEY INCOME ROSE BY 92% AND HER REAL INCOME BY 75%

The national income of former Hungary has been calculated by Fellner both for the average of the three years 1911–1913 and for the average of the years 1899–1901. As in both cases he used the same method, the results can aptly be compared. The estimate for 1901 was 3,211 million K. and that for 1913 was 6,742 million K. The increase in these twelve years was 110%, and this would correspond proportionately to 92% in ten years. But there was also a considerable rise in the price level, which may be estimated at between 20% and 25%. *The real income therefore rose by about 75% on the average.* From 1900 to 1910 the population increased by 8·5%.

Fellner's calculation can be checked by the following data compiled by me from the official statistics. In the ten years 1898–1908 the number of industrial workers in Hungary increased by 75%.[1] In the period 1903–1913 the consumption of coal rose by 93%, that of pig iron by 83%, the value of imported raw materials and half-manufactured goods by 106%, the tons of freight transported on the railways by 87%, savings deposits (1902–1912) by 98·3% and the value of the life insurance policies by 96·4%.

[1] This figure was calculated on the basis of the Industrial Censuses of 1898 and 1906; cf. W. Offergeld, *Grundlagen und Ursachen der industriellen Entwicklung Ungarns*, 1914.

3. THE DEVELOPMENT IN AUSTRIA

The national income of Austria was estimated in 1898 by the Minister of Finance, Prof. Kaizl, a distinguished economist, and leader of the Czechs in Parliament, at 6,000 million K. If this figure is compared with Fellner's estimate for 1911–1913 the increase in the intervening fourteen years is found to have been about 100%, and this would correspond to an increase of about 71% in ten years. Our subsequent detailed calculations will lead to almost exactly the same result.

In Austria all income over 1,200 K. (£50) was liable to income tax. The assessment was made on the basis of the actual income in the previous year, so that for instance the figures for 1913 actually refer to the income for 1912. The following table shows the income assessed (in million K.).

Income from:	Land.	Houses.	Profits.	Wages and salaries.	Capital.	Sundry.	Total.
1903	254	349	946	1,232	492	47	3,319
1913	481	585	1,932	2,739	766	139	6,642
Increase	89%	68%	104%	122%	56%	196%	100%

This section of the national income in the ten years immediately before the war increased by exactly 100%. It formed more than 43% of the total national income as calculated by Waizner. But it did not comprise the bulk of the income of the peasants and the working classes. The income of these classes must therefore be estimated on the basis of other data.

4. THE AGRICULTURAL AND FORESTAL INCOME OF AUSTRIA

The average total agricultural and forestal income of Austria in the three years 1911–1913 was estimated by Fellner at 4,169 million K. This figure may be assumed to be fairly correct, and seems to have been generally accepted.[1] Agricultural statistics

---

[1] Fellner has on the whole been very careful in his estimates, and has supplemented the official statistics by a considerable amount of information supplied by experts. Nevertheless mistakes or miscalculations of minor importance sometimes occurred. In calculating the agricultural net income, for example, Fellner made obvious mistakes in regard to the value of the production of honey

provide such detailed data of crops, livestock, prices, etc., that it is much easier to ascertain the value of the agricultural output of a country than its industrial output. No calculations are available showing the development of agricultural income in Austria in the period under review. But Fellner has calculated that the agricultural income of Hungary in twelve years rose from 2,209 to 4,550 million K., or by 106%, which would correspond to 88% in ten years. It is probable that those parts of Austria which had large agricultural resources, such as Bohemia, Moravia, Galicia, parts of Upper and Lower Austria, and Lower Styria, could to some extent keep pace with Hungary. The mountainous parts, however, remained more or less backward.

In order to ascertain the development in Austria we have to calculate the average agricultural income in 1901–1903 by the same method which Fellner employed for calculating that for 1911–1912. The calculation shows that in 1901–1903 the value of crops, including fodder, amounted to 2,293·2 million K.[1] As regards animal production, the value of the livestock for 1902 can be estimated at 2,416 million K.[2] and, assuming that the annual yield formed the same percentage as established by Fellner, the value of the annual output of meat, milk, hides, wool and manure can be assessed at 855 million K. This estimate can be checked by an entirely different method. Animal production depends mainly on the quantity of fodder available, and Fellner has calculated that the value of the animal output was 26·5% above that of the fodder consumed by the livestock.[3] As the average fodder crop for 1901–1903 was 693·7 million K., the value of the animal production would have amounted to 877·5 million K. This figure agrees closely with the former one, and we may take the mean

and of carding thistles. If these are corrected, the agricultural net income is 4,143 million K. Surfaces of land are indicated in hectares (ha.). 1 ha. is 0·404 acres, and 1 acre is 2·471 ha.

[1] A number of prices were taken from the Hungarian statistics.

[2] The value of livestock was estimated on the basis of the average prices paid in 1902 at the great Hungarian livestock markets. On the basis of the previous Census of 1890, the value of livestock has been estimated at 1923·4 million K. Cf. *Geschichte der oesterr. Landwirtschaft*, vol. II, p. 804. It must be remarked, however, that the Censuses of livestock were taken on December 31st—*i.e.*, at a time when the livestock was at its lowest level.

[3] This fodder consisted of grass, hay, clover, fodder-maize, turnips, etc., and 80% of the oats produced, the rest of the oats being used for seeds and for human consumption.

between them. This would be 866 million K. This amount must furthermore be increased by the output of poultry, honey, wax and cocoons, which can be estimated at 49 million K. The total animal output thereby rises to 915 million K. The gross output of crops and animal products together was 3,208 million K. The net output can be calculated by deducting the value of the seeds, fodder, manure and depreciation of machinery. Fellner found that this amounted to 42·2% of the gross output. On this supposition the net output of agriculture for 1901–1903 can be estimated at 1,854 million K.

Account must further be taken of the value of certain minor products not included in the foregoing crops—namely, fruit (152 million K.), wine (130 million K.) and certain vegetables (6 million K.). This last figure is certainly greatly under-estimated, but data for an accurate estimate for 1901–1903 are lacking.[1] We may further add the yield of maritime fisheries (7 million K.) and the value of game (7 million K.). Certain minor items, like freshwater fish[2] and furs, may be ignored, as Fellner also takes no account of them.

The value of the output of timber has been estimated by Fellner at 106·7 million K. This estimate, however, does not include the cost of felling and also for other reasons appears too low.[3] It would amount to only 10·92 K. gross income per ha. of forestal land. Now, the accounts of the vast Austrian State forests show that in 1912 the gross income per ha. productive land was 27·28 K. and the net income 9·86 K.[4]

[1] Waizner points out that Fellner made a mistake in regard to the vegetables included in this item, and estimates the value at 68·1 million K. for 1913. Cf. *Metron*, VII, p. 142.

[2] Cf., however, data in *Statistische Monatsschrift*, 1907 and 1908.

[3] More than ten years before Fellner an estimate of Austria's forestal production was made arriving at a value of from 160 to 200 million K. Cf. *Geschichte der österreichischen Land- und Forstwirtschaft, 1899–1901*, IV, 336.

After the break-up of Austria the Czechoslovak Minister of Agriculture, Prof. Brdlik, one of the foremost agricultural economists, estimated the pre-war value of the forestal output of Czechoslovakia at 280 million K. The woods in Czechoslovakia, however, covered only half the surface which formerly belonged to Austria, and also the quantity produced was about half. Cf. the official publication *Tschechoslovakische Republik*, edited by Butter and Ruml, 1921, p. 58.

The prices assumed by Fellner were certainly too low. Cf. the prices quoted in A. von Engel, *Österreichs Holzindustrie und Holzhandel*, III, 359.

[4] These figures may be compared with the returns of the Bavarian State forests, as the two countries had to a certain extent similar natural conditions. But in Bavaria the gross income per ha. was 81·42 K. and the net income

The difficulty in estimating the total value of the forestal output is that the prices of wood varied enormously, according to local demand and local conditions of transport. The statistics for the period 1900–1910 show an increase of only 3·3% in the timber cut and a decrease of about 10% in the firewood produced.[1] The trade statistics show an average increase of 16% in the price of timber exported. But these data are not sufficient for an estimate. The demand for wood by the mines, the paper factories, building, the chemical industries, the furniture factories, etc., rapidly increased in the ten years before the war. A characteristic symptom also is that the net return of the State forests from the average 1899–1903 to the average 1911–1912 rose by 116·3%.

An accurate estimate of the development of the forestal income in the period under review would require many data which are not at present obtainable. We have therefore to accept Fellner's estimate for 1911–1913 as a makeshift, and assume that the corresponding income for 1901–1903 was about 80 million K. The real increase in the intervening period was probably much greater.

5. Rise of 87% in Agricultural Net Income—The Share of Large and Small Farms

If these figures are assembled, the result is as follows:—

Net Output of Agriculture, Forestry and Fishing
('000,000 K.)

	1901–1903.	1911–1913.	Increase.
Net output	2,236	4,143	% 85
Per head of working population [2]	358	633	77

[2] The wives, children and other relatives of peasants helping in the farm work were counted only as half-time workers.

44·10 K. The gross income was three times the Austrian one and the net profit more than four times. Cf. *Statistisches Jahrbuch für das Königreich Bayern*, 1915, p. 100.

[1] The decrease in the production of firewood was obviously due to the fact that the use of coal greatly expanded also in rural areas where wood had hitherto had very little value, and was therefore freely used as fuel. But if a part of the same wood was now used for paper-making, this meant a doubling or trebling of its price.

This net output included wages, taxes and interest on mortgages. The main taxes were those on land and on rural houses; their amount was fixed at about 62 million K. for the State, and the provinces and towns raised percentages of this amount as rates for their own revenues. Interest on mortgages can be estimated for 1902 at 112 million K. and for 1912 at 162 million K.[1] A large part of this interest, however, flowed directly or indirectly back to agriculturists. The main owners of mortgages were the savings banks and similar communal institutions which were practically only the trustees of many millions of small savers.

If interest on mortgages is deducted the net income was:—

('000,000 K.)

1902.	1912.	*Increase.*
2,124	3,981	87%

We may also try to give an approximate idea of the distribution of income between large and small farms by means of the income-tax returns.

Income tax was paid only by those whose income was 1,200 K. (£50) or more, and in 1903 only 80,000 persons engaged in agriculture were liable. Of the total agricultural income estimated for 1911–1913 only 11·6% appears in the income-tax returns as income from land. Comparing the number of agricultural taxpayers with the statistics of farms according to size, we come to the conclusion that in 1903, on the whole, only farmers cultivating more than 40 ha. or 100 acres of productive land were liable to the tax—except, of course, very efficient ones, small growers of particularly remunerative crops, or owners of very fertile land. The bulk of the peasantry was practically exempt from income tax, as their assessment would have been too difficult and expensive.[2] The income from land assessed can therefore be practically

[1] Estimated by me on the basis of the statistics of mortgages, cf. *Statistische Rückblicke aus Österreich* (a handbook dedicated by the Austrian Statistical Office to the International Statistical Congress, 1913), p. 22, and R. Mully von Oppenried, *Die Hypothekaranstalten in Deutschland und Oesterreich-Ungarn,* 1911, p. 184.

[2] It is probable, however, that many peasants who actually had an income of 1,200 K. or more were not assessed for income tax owing to a clause in the law exempting peasants with a certain low cadastral return from the liability to make a statement of their income.

identified with that from large and middle-sized farms. It should be increased by a certain percentage—perhaps 10%, considering the difficulty of checking the calculation of individual agricultural incomes, the pricing of products consumed by the farmer and his family, etc.[1] The result is:—

('000,000 K.)

	1901–1903.	1911–1913.	Increase.
Income of large and middle-sized farms . . .	279	529	% 89
Income of small farmers and wages of labourers . .	1,845	3,452	87

The first category comprises those landowners who had an assessed income of 1,200 K. (£50) or more, the second those who earned less,[2] and the agricultural labourers. As a rule there was in the same place little difference in the standards of life of a small peasant and a labourer.

The Census of farms of 1902 showed that the total number of farms was 2,856,349, and that, of these, 2,693,260 did not exceed 20 ha. The Census of occupations of 1910 showed that there were 2,589,842 independent farmers (owners and tenants). It may be assumed, therefore, that the peasants proper numbered about 2·5 million and that they were helped in their work by 3·9 million members of their family. The number of agricultural labourers proper, on farms of every size, was 2 million. The average income of a peasant or labourer was therefore 767 K.[3] A peasant family on the average consisted of 4·6 members, of whom 2·6 were working on the farm, not including hired labour.

[1] No addition is, however, required in regard to the total income, as this was not calculated from income-tax statistics, but from the statistics of crops, livestock, etc., which were probably more accurate than the income-tax statistics based on the statements of the taxpayers.
[2] The first category was assessed after deduction of land tax plus rates. We could not deduct these items from the income of the second category, as the amount of provincial and local rates paid could not be ascertained.
[3] In Moravia the annual wage of an agricultural labourer was before the war 564 K. for men and 514 K. for women, in lower Austria 604 K. on large estates. The average income of a peasant given above (767 K.) was really the wages of 2·6 persons. If the family helpers are counted as half-workers the earnings of a peasant family per full worker were 426 K., or less than those of a labourer.

6. Progress of Agriculture—Rise in the Value of Land

The increase in the national income was due partly to the improvement of methods of production and the increase in output, partly to the great rise in prices which took place on the world's markets, and it was enhanced by the Austrian protectionist tariff which came into force in 1907. From 1900 to 1906 the fallow land decreased from 943,705 to 342,002 ha. and by 1913 had fallen to 320,697 ha.[1] The slow ox before the plough was largely replaced by the faster and stronger horse, and the number of farms and labourers compulsorily insured against accidents through agricultural machines almost doubled. From 1901–1903 to 1911–1913 the average yield per ha. increased in wheat by 16%, in rye by 24·3%, in barley by 21·2%, and in oats by 33·9%, and the weight and quality of livestock rose. A significant symptom was the development of agricultural co-operative societies. The number of credit societies for peasants (*Raiffeisenkassen*) rose between 1903 and 1914 from 4,155 to 8,516. The savings deposits at the *Raiffeisenkassen* increased between 1903 and 1913 from 283 to 796 million, or by 181%.

The estimate of the development of the agricultural income may be compared with the rise in the value of land, though it must not be overlooked that this price is not determined by the total agricultural income, inclusive of wages, but by the net income of the farmers. The price of land has also the tendency to move inversely to the rate of interest. The average rate of the Austro-Hungarian Bank rose between 1904 and 1913 from 3·5% to 5·95%, and this rise must to some extent have checked the increase in the price of land. The 4% Austrian Loan fell between 1902 and 1912 from 99·54 to 87·68.

Most large estates were entered in a special land-roll—the so-called *Landtafel*. The average value of an estate of this kind transferred by sale, inheritance, etc., rose between 1900 and 1910 from 64,1866 K. to 117,224 K., or by 80·7%.

All the other rural property, of which the bulk was formed by peasant farms, was also registered separately. The average value

---

[1] Strakosch (*Grundlagen der Agrarwirtschaft in Österreich*, 1916, p. 228) ascribes this to the increase in protective duties on grain. But his own table on page 223 shows that it took place in the years before the new tariff came into force.

of this kind of rural property rose in the eight years between 1902 and 1910 from 2,040 K. to 3,220 K., or by 57·8%. The value of property transferred by inheritance rose from 2,095 K. to 3,244 K., or by 54·8%.

The difference between the increases for large and small farms was due to the fact that the estates were usually valued according to the market price of land, while the peasants valued their farms according to traditional standards. When a peasant died or retired the farm had to be valued for the settlement between the eldest son and his co-heirs. In a great part of Austria, however, the traditional rule was that a very low price was fixed—often only a third or a half of the market price—in order to avoid overburdening the successor with debts.[1] These traditional values did not follow the fluctuations of market prices, and the statistics therefore showed smaller increases in the price of peasant land than in that of estates. Another reason was the splitting up of peasant farms. From 1900 to 1910 the number of farmers increased by 20%. The average size of a farm was therefore smaller in 1910 than in 1900, and this must have affected the prices of land as shown by the statistics.[2]

The conditions of the peasants, moreover, differed greatly in various parts of the Empire. In some parts, like Galicia, Slovakia and Croatia, the nobility possessed large tracts of land, whereas the peasants had not enough of it, and this gave rise to a swelling tide of emigration to America. In the Alpine parts of Austria proper and in other territories the bulk of the land was in the hands of small peasants, who for the most part did not sell much, but consumed most of their products themselves. These peasants had little or no profit from the rise in prices, which increased their income only on paper, while their cost of living rose at the same pace. Many of the Alpine peasants were even hard hit by the high tariffs on grain, as they had to buy cereals.[3] In the Bohemian countries and in the flatter parts of Austria the peasants seem to

[1] Cf. the detailed data in K. Schmidt, *Die Vererbung des ländlichen Grundbesitzes in Österreich* in *Schriften des Vereins für Sozialpolitik*, vol. 178, II.

[2] Cf. also the data on the rise in farm prices given by Professor Spiethoff, then of the University of Prague, in *Schriften des Vereins für Sozialpolitik*, vol. 155, III, p. 109.

[3] Cf. Ferdinand v. Pantz, *Die Hochschutzzoll-Politik Hohenblums und der oesterreichische Bauernstand*, 1910. The author strongly criticises the policy of high tariffs on grain. The opposite point of view is defended by Strakosch in the book quoted above.

have profited most from higher yields and prices. Many of them could greatly improve their situation. But the large increase in agricultural income expressed in money must not obscure the fact that the conditions of the peasantry and the progress of agriculture were by no means entirely satisfactory.

The statistical result of our investigations is that the agricultural and forestal net income increased by 85·3%, the agricultural income alone by 87·2%, the agricultural income assessed for income tax—*i.e.*, that of large and middle-sized farms—by 89%, and the value of an average large farm by 80·7%, while the value of peasant farms rose by only about 57·8%.

7. The Income of the Workers in Industries and Trade

In estimating the non-agricultural income we shall first ascertain the amount of wages and salaries in industries, trade, transport and the liberal professions, exclusive of public service. For this purpose we have compiled the wages of the principal sections of the personnel employed according to the statistics of the Accident Insurance and the statistics of mines. It must be noted that the Accident Insurance did not take account of wages exceeding 2,400 K. (£100). A number of insured persons had such earnings, especially among the salaried persons who formed 8% of the insured. But the income-tax statistics, covering all incomes from 1,200 K. upwards, show that this number was not so great as to have an appreciable effect on the calculation of an average wage. The development of the wages of the four largest groups was as follows:—

('000,000 K.)

	1902.	1912.	Increase in amount of wages and salaries.
			%
Factory workers . .	758·9	1,458·8	92·2
Transport workers . .	305·7	561·8	83·8
Building trades . . .	140·3	353·1	151·6
Miners (1903–1913) . .	117·7	178·0	51·2
Total of wages . .	1,322·6	2,551·7	93

The number of workers in these four groups, their average wage and the total number of all the workers employed were :—

	1902.	1912.	Increase.
Workers, etc., employed in the four groups ('000's) . . .	1,871	2,639	% 44
Average wage per head .	707 K.	948 K.	34
Total of all workers employed (health insured, yearly average) ('000's)	2,766	3,843	39
Percentage of workers included in the above calculation of wages .	67·6%	70·1%	

As about 70% of all workers employed were included in the above calculation of average wages, it may safely be assumed that these averages applied also to the rest of the workers. These comprised workers and employees not liable to accident insurance, such as persons employed in small handicrafts without motor power, in shops, bureaux, in home work, domestic service, etc. Apart from domestics, who will be treated separately, these classes probably received about the same average wages as the workers included in our calculation. To them must further be added the small independent workers and traders whose income was so low that they were exempted from income tax. Their standard of life was on the whole the same as that of a factory worker. They can be identified with the small independent workers and traders in the lowest (IV) class of the Trade Tax. In 1902 716,078 persons were in this class. In the same year the Industrial Census showed 732,272 workshops with only one worker—namely, the owner. Shortly before the war the Ministry of Finance estimated the average income in this class at 1,000 K., which was little more than the average wage calculated above.

Before multiplying the average wages by the numbers of all workers employed, we must, however, deduct the number of employees with an income of 1,200 K. or more, and therefore liable to income tax. Their income is shown in the income-tax statistics, and will be added later. Their number for 1903 is indicated in the detailed statistics of the occupations, etc., of income-tax payers published by the Ministry of Finance,[1] and the number

[1] Cf. *Beiträge zur Statistik der Personaleinkommensteuer in den Jahren 1903 bis 1907*, I (1908).

for 1913 may be calculated by assuming that the rate of increase was the same as in the preceding period covered by the statistics just mentioned.

The figures are as follows:—

	1902.	1912.	*Increase.*
All employees (exclusive of agricultural and domestic workers and public employees) ('ooo's)	2,766	3,843	% 38·9
Less those paying income tax (who are added later) ('ooo's) . .	321	500	—
Plus small independent workers (class IV of trade tax) ('ooo's) .	2,445	3,343	—
	716	881	—
Average wage (as calculated above from insurance statistics, etc.) ('ooo,ooo K.) . . .	3,161	4,224	—
	707	948	—
Total wage income ('ooo,ooo K.)	2,234·8	4,004·4	79·2

The wage income of all employees (exclusive of agricultural and domestic workers, of public employees, and of those earning more than 1,200 K.) increased from 2,234·8 million K. to 4,004·4 million K., or by 79·2%. The workers with a wage of 1,200 K. or more appear in the income-tax statistics, and will be added later.

We have now to ascertain the income of the domestic servants. A careful study of their conditions has been made by Dr. Hugo Morgenstern, and the results were published in 1902 by the Office for Labour Statistics in the Ministry of Trade.[1] The number of domestic servants was in 1900 478,756, and in 1910 470,072. Their number was therefore stationary, and it is hardly necessary to calculate separate figures for 1902 and 1912. We may instead use the figures shown in the Censuses for 1900 and 1910. Most domestics were employed by persons belonging to branches of industries, commerce and the liberal professions. Few domestic servants were employed by agriculturists. The reason obviously was that in agriculture the housework was usually done by the

[1] Cf. Hugo Morgenstern, *Gesindewesen und Gesinderecht in Österreich*, 1902. A large part of this book deals, however, with agricultural workers living in the farmer's house, not with domestic servants proper.

same persons who worked on the farm, except on large estates, which, however, were not so numerous as to employ a large proportion of the total. It is to be noted further that by far the greater part was employed in the advanced and wealthy Western provinces, and only a small part in the backward regions. Lower Austria, with Vienna, alone employed about a quarter, and the German and Czech territories together about three-quarters.

Most domestic servants received very low wages. When Morgenstern collected his data he found that a housemaid was paid about 24 K. a month in the great cities, and only 10 K. in the backward Eastern and Southern provinces. An experienced cook received between 16 and 40 K., a youthful beginner between 4 and 16 K. To this must be added food and lodging and customary gifts. We should estimate the average total earnings, both in money and in kind, at about 360 K. a year. The income of this group would, then, in 1902 have amounted to 172 million K. For 1912 an average wage of 40 K., including food, etc., would seem a moderate estimate. This would make an income of 226 million K. The increase in the average wage corresponded to the rise in the price level, but was below that in the general wage level.

The income-tax statistics have, further, a schedule "other income" in which earnings were classed such as directors' fees, and certain allowances to public functionaries. We assume that half these earnings were a remuneration for work, and half a profit on the possession of capital. This item, however, is very small.

The following table includes all categories of the personnel employed, except the agricultural workers—who have been

EARNINGS OF EMPLOYEES IN INDUSTRIES, COMMERCE, TRANSPORT
AND THE LIBERAL PROFESSIONS

('000,000 K.)

	1902.	1912.	Increase.
Wages and salaries from 1,200 K. (£50) upwards . . .	1,232	2,739	% 122·3
Wages and salaries under 1,200 K. . .	2,235	4,004	79·2
Domestics	172	226	31·4
Sundry (half)	24	70	196
Total	3,663	7,039	92·2

shown together with the small peasants—and certain classes of public employees who appeared neither in the Health Insurance statistics—since the State provided for them in case of illness—nor in the income-tax statistics, because their income was too low. Most of the workers and employees in public service or public enterprises are, however, included, and the number of the rest was not very great. We may therefore ignore it.

8. Income from Profits, Interest and House-Rent

The income of this kind can be approximately ascertained from the statistics of various taxes. How much of it shall be included depends on the definition of the national income. House-rent is

Income from Profits, Interest and House-Rent

('000,000 K.)

	1902–1903.	1912–1913.	*Increase.*
			%
House-rent (gross) . . .	736	852	16
Profits (except limited companies) .	946	1,932	104
Plus 10% for under-statement .	95	193	—
Profits of limited companies .	148	461	212
Interest on agricultural mortgages .	112	162	45
Other income (half) . . .	24	70	196
Total	2061	3670	—
Less 10% on rent . . .	74	85	—
Income	1,987	3,585	80

now usually included, though to us this does not seem very logical. Nevertheless, we follow the usage. A certain amount—say, 10%—must, however, be deducted for repairs and depreciation. Gross rent includes the interest on house mortgages. Interest on agricultural mortgages has already been indicated, and must be inserted here. But the interest on public loans paid out of taxes forms no true element of the national income. The interest paid to the banks on credits appears in the profits of the companies. There are other minor items of this kind, which may, however, safely be ignored, as they are probably counterbalanced.[1]

[1] An accurate calculation would, for example, have to include the interest charged by certain savings institutions on short-term credits. Their long-term

The national income comprises, furthermore, certain public revenues which are not included in the amounts hitherto considered, such as profits from public enterprises and certain taxes increasing the price level. As a rule it is assumed that customs and excise taxes fall under this category. The general Trade Tax must also be taken into account, as it was excluded from the income assessed for income tax. Special Trade Tax and Rent Tax are included in other items.

PUBLIC REVENUES TO BE ADDED IN THE CALCULATION OF NATIONAL INCOME

	1902.	1912.
Profits from State enterprises (railways, post, forests, mines, salt, tobacco, etc.) . .	56	220
Customs	105	195
Excise duties	334	408
Trade tax	34	37
Total	529	860

9. AUSTRIA'S NATIONAL INCOME INCREASED BY 86%

The foregoing tables cover all important elements of the national income, and these can now be assembled in the following table :—

TOTAL NATIONAL INCOME OF AUSTRIA

	1901–1903 (or 1902).	1911–1913 (or 1912).	Increase.
			%
I. Agriculture, forestry, fishing .	2,124	3,981	87
II. Industries, commerce, transport, liberal professions, public service :			
(a) Wages and salaries . .	3,663	7,039	92
(b) Profit, rent, interest . .	1,987	3,585	80
III. Public revenues raising price level	529	860	62
Total	8,303	15,465	86

credits and holdings of securities are, however, included, and these formed the bulk of their assets. On the other hand, the banks and other companies possessed shares, and their proceeds are shown twice. In 1912 the total balance sheets of all banks showed an income of 30 million K. from securities, and a part of this amount is duplicated in our table.

It is understood that this was the national income produced in Austria, not her consumable income. The table does not take account of amounts paid to Austria from other countries, or vice versa. Fellner has estimated that taking the average in the years 1911–1913 Austria received 596·7 million K. from abroad (mainly from Hungary) and paid 246·1 million K. to other countries. She had, therefore, a surplus of 350·6 million K.[1]

The figure of 15,465 million K. is a little larger than Waizner's estimate of 15,325 million K., and considerably larger than Fellner's figure of 12,565 million K. But Fellner based his estimate on a much narrower concept of the national income. In a previous chapter I have explained why I, too, would prefer a narrower concept than that employed here. The question is, however, irrelevant for our purpose, as we primarily wish to ascertain not the absolute amount of the national income, but its development in a given period. For this purpose our calculations offer fully reliable index figures.

10. THE SHARES OF THE SOCIAL CLASSES AND THE STATE IN THE NATIONAL INCOME

The total income can also be classified according to great social groups. The small peasants and traders whose income did not reach an amount equivalent to £50 a year, and who were therefore not liable to income tax, are for this purpose classed as workers, though many of them were to a modest extent also employers. On the other hand, the employers proper naturally owed their income not merely to their capital, but also to their work. Houses and other capital, lastly, were not exclusively in the hands of capitalists, but many small houses and very considerable amounts of savings deposits and other capital were possessed by the lower middle class and the workers, or by their associations, insurance institutions, savings banks, etc.

In calculating the share of interest on capital we must further include interest on public loans, which did not form part of our estimate, and which must therefore be added. In 1912 the interest paid by Austria on her loans was 427·5 million K., not including

[1] Data for the time before 1902 are available in the *Tabellen zur Währungsstatistik verfasst im Finanzministerium*, 2 Teil, 1900–1904.

a Hungarian contribution to a common loan. The interest paid by the provinces on their loans was 44·8 million K., and, allowing for loans of cities, etc., the total can be estimated at 500 million K. If this amount is added to the national income [1] the shares of the main classes were:—

(Average 1911–1913)

	%
Landowners with an assessed income of £50 or more . . .	3·3
Small peasants and agricultural labourers	21·6
Industrial workers, clerks, other employees, Civil Servants and independent workers	44·1
Employers, owners of houses and securities	25·5
State (only enterprises and price-raising taxes)	5·4
Total	100·0

It must further be noticed that the total public revenues were, of course, much greater than the last item. In 1913 the gross revenues of the State were 1,198·6 million K.; in 1912 those of the provinces 465 million and those of thirty-five larger cities and towns 420 million K. This makes a total of 2,084 million K. A certain amount would have to be added for the smaller towns. If the total of public revenues is compared with the national income, or with certain parts of it, it is clear that taxation was not excessive.

11. ALL NATIONALITIES SHOWED A GREAT RISE IN INCOME

It has often been contended by nationalist propagandists that in old Austria Vienna played the rôle of a great parasite battening on the sweat and toil of oppressed nationalities and subjected provinces. But the statistical data show a quite different picture. The rise in income assessed for income tax and that of wages of workers insured against accident can serve as a reliable index of economic progress.

From 1903 to 1913 the province of Lower Austria, which included Vienna, showed an increase in assessed income of 107%

[1] A more accurate method would require very complicated calculations and the result would be about the same.

The above table shows the distribution of the income produced in Austria, and no allowance has, therefore, been made for international payments. Nor has account been taken of the influence of taxation on the final distribution of income.

and in wages of 92%. In all the other, predominantly German-speaking, Alpine territories the assessed income rose by 95% and wages by 87%. In the three Bohemian territories, where the Czechs formed the majority, assessed income increased by 97% and wages by 94%. The predominantly Southern Slav territories on the Adriatic Sea showed an increase of 94% in income and of 92% in wages. In Galicia and Bukowina, which were mainly Polish, Ruthenian and Roumanian income rose by 91% and wages by 148%.

These data show that all nationalities and all parts of the Empire derived almost equal profits from the general development. If Vienna showed a greater increase in assessed income, this was due to her function as the economic centre, and the income assessed there subsequently to a great extent flowed back to the provinces in the form of investments and other outlay.

One of the numerous falsehoods spread by nationalistic propaganda is the view that the Austrian Government was responsible for the unequal development of industries in different parts of the Empire. Even an otherwise very careful and reliable British student of Central and Eastern Europe says: "Industrialisation was fostered by Government policy in some provinces, such as Bohemia, discouraged in others, such as Galicia." [1] But if we compare the statistics we find that from 1903 to 1913 the number of factories increased in Galicia by 39%, in Bohemia by 35%, the number of factory operatives in Galicia by 56%, in Bohemia by 39%, the wages in Galicia by 148%, in Bohemia by 94%. The idea that the Central Government in Vienna discouraged industrial development in Galicia shows also a complete misunderstanding of the federalistic structure of Austria. The wide autonomy of Galicia and the power of the Polish representatives in Parliament would have made such an interference impossible. If Galicia was backward in industrial development, this was due to natural and historical causes. The Austrian exchequer spent much more in Galicia and the other backward provinces than it received from them in revenues.[2] This policy greatly stimulated economic development in those parts.

[1] Cf. Doreen Warriner, *Economics of Peasant Farming*, 1939, p. 76.
[2] Cf. *Österreichisches Statistisches Handbuch*, XX, 372.

Of the revenue raised by the State in Vienna and the surrounding province of Lower Austria not more than 50% was spent in State expenditure in the same territory. The rest was spent mostly in the backward provinces.

12. The Great Rise in National Income Confirmed by Further Facts

Our calculations have hitherto mainly made use of the statistics of agricultural production, of income tax and of wages. But we can check the result by numerous independent data, and by a different method of estimating the increase in industrial production.

In the last ten years before the war[1] the number of factories increased by 41%, that of industrial workers (including the building trades) by 49%, and the fire insurance value of the factories by 87%.[2] A good index is the quantity of raw materials used in production. Consumption of coal rose by 54% and that of pig iron by 90%. The water-power installed rose considerably, and the capacity of the power-stations selling electricity increased in the seven years 1907–1914 by 220%. Austria had to import most of her raw materials, and the value of raw materials imported into the Austro-Hungarian Customs Union rose by 111%. Assuming a rise of 25% in the price level, this would correspond to an increase of 88·8% in quantity. The import of raw materials into Austria alone, both from Hungary and from other countries, rose in value from 1901 to 1911 by 70·3% and that of semi-manufactured goods by 92·6%.[3] In those branches of industries which used home-produced raw materials the rise of industrial production led to a decrease in the export of raw materials, or to its stagnation. The surplus of imports of raw materials over exports rose therefore by 149·5% in value, corresponding to 120% in quantity.

The following table gives some data on the increase in technical efficiency of industries and mines :—

Period 1903–1913, or 1902–1912.
[2] Cf. *Die privaten Versicherungsunternehmungen im Jahre 1912* (1916), p. 150.
[3] Cf. *Statistische Rückblicke aus Österreich*, 1913, p. 63.

	From:	*To:*	*Per cent.*
Coal (1901–1911) . . .	167 t.	194 t.	16·2
Lignite (1901–1911) . .	377 t.	460 t.	22
Iron ore (1900–1910) . .	3,487 mq.[2]	4,686 mq.	34·4
Salt (1900–1910) . . .	414·7 mq.	527·1 mq.	27·1
Pig iron (1900–1910) . .	1,573·4 mq.	2,635·9 mq.	67·5
Sugar (1900–1901 to 1910–1911)	102·3 mq.	143·1 mq.	40
Tobacco (1902–1912) . .	8·88 mq.	10·55 mq.	18·8
Cotton (1900–1910) . .	11·07 mq.	11·97 mq.	8·2
Wool (1900–1910) . . .	4·4 mq.	6·3 mq.	43
Cotton and wool (1900–1910) [1] .	5·37 mq.	7·13 mq.	32·8

[1] The Census also showed a number of weavers without indicating the material, and it is probable that they manufactured both cotton and woollen goods. [2] Metric quintals (t indicates metric tons).

The increase in the weight of output per operative is not, of course, a fully satisfactory means of measuring the progress of productivity. This may also consist in the growth of the degree of refinement and quality which is not expressed in weight. The ten percentages of increase shown in the above list make an average of 31%.[3] If the increase in the number of industrial workers (factories and building trades) is combined with one of 31% in productivity the rise in output would be 95·2%. If we compare this figure with the increase in the import of raw materials indicated and with the facts that the amount of wages of industrial workers rose by 101·5% and the industrial profits assessed for income tax by 104%, we come to the conclusion that the output of industries and building must have increased by a percentage of between 90 and 100.

Data showing the development of wealth confirm this estimate. Total savings deposits rose by 89·3%, the cheques, etc., passed through the Clearing House by 249%, the amount insured by life insurance companies by 82% and the annual value of estates paying death duties by 98%.

The development of agriculture was much less impressive than that of industries. The increase in the weight of the four great grain crops was only 34%, though the value increased by 75·5%.

[3] The rate of technical progress would therefore be about 3% per year. It is interesting to note that the same rate of technical progress was observed in Britain. Cf. W. Beveridge, *Full Employment in a Free Society*, 1944, p. 101.

The other crops and the livestock showed even smaller increases. If, however, one sums up the quantities of the principal sorts of fodder,[1] one finds that from 1902 to 1912, the aggregate increased by 30%. This means that the weight of the livestock must also have increased accordingly, and to this were added further improvements through the progress of agricultural technique like the introduction of high-class breeds.

A large section of the peasants, however, still stood outside the sphere of money economy, and as far as they had a money income it was extremely low. The wages of an agricultural labourer often amounted to but a third or less of the wages of a skilled industrial worker in the same province. The great increase in the number of industrial workers which took place in the period before the Great War, therefore, resulted in a rapid rise in the national income. On the other hand, the great migration from the agricultural to the industrial districts set limits to the rise of industrial wages.

13. THE COST OF LIVING ROSE BY 20% AND WAGES BY 34%

In order to estimate the real increase in the national income we must try to ascertain the rise of prices which inflated the money income. No official index was calculated at that time, but Austrian and Hungarian statistics contain much information about prices of specific commodities. In 1911 an Hungarian economist, Dr. Bela de Jankovich, Vice-President of the Hungarian Parliament, published a paper on the prices of forty-five commodities in Austria-Hungary from 1867 to 1909, and calculated a number of indices according to Sauerbeck's method.[2] For the period from 1899 to 1909 his figures show the following increases: cereals 47%, meat and fat 34·3%, sugar, coffee, tea 5·6%, all foodstuffs 36·3%, coal and metals 7·5%, textile materials 5·3%, other raw materials 13·8%, all commodities together 23·55%. The increase in the cost of food, therefore, was very considerable. The actual increase in the cost of living of the broad masses, however, was less.

Useful information about the actual rise in the cost of living can

[1] We included in this calculation oats, maize, sugar-beet (less the weight of the sugar extracted), turnips, hay, clover, vetches, and similar plants.
[2] Cf. Bela de Jankovich, in *Bulletin de l'Institut International de Statistique,* 1911, XIX, 3.

be gathered from statistics published by the Army commissariat about the cost of the daily food allowance of a soldier from 1863 to 1910, and about the prices of the foodstuffs used for feeding the soldiers, taking the average in 200 garrison places.[1] From 1900 to 1910 the cost of the food allowance rose in the single military districts as follows: Vienna 18%, Prague 20%, Josefstadt-Leitmeritz 15%, Graz 20%, Innsbruck 15·4%, Cracow 22·2%, Lemberg 14%, Przmysl 27·6%, Zara-Ragusa 20·4%.

I have calculated weighted indices of food prices by two methods. First, I valued the actual quantities of all foodstuffs consumed by an average Vienna working-class family[2] at average prices for 1902 and 1912, and found an increase of 24·6%. Then I calculated a weighted food index according to Zahn's method, and found an increase of 23·6%. As Jankovich's figures, quoted above, and many other statistics collected by me, show that industrial raw materials and prices of industrial products, and also houserent, rose far less than foodstuffs, and as foodstuffs amounted to 50·7% of the cost of living of the working families investigated, we may assume that the rise in the cost of living of the working classes scarcely exceeded 20%. The rise in the general price level may perhaps be estimated at 25% as the maxima. On the whole, therefore, the movement of prices seems not to have differed much from that in other countries. The price index of the *Statist* showed for the period from 1903 to 1913 a rise of 23·2%,[3] and Zahn estimated the rise of food prices in Bavaria in the period 1902–1912 at 21·75%.

Wages per head in all industries subject to the Workers' Accident Insurance (factories, building, transport) increased from 1902 to 1912 by 35·8%. If the miners are included the increase was 34%.[4] The increase in the money income of the workers was,

[1] Cf. *Statistische Rückblicke aus Österreich*, 1911, pp. 76, 77, and *Österreichisches Statistisches Handbuch*, 1912, p. 349.

[2] The quantities are contained in *Wirtschaftsrechnungen und Lebensverhältnisse Wiener Arbeiterfamilien in den Jahren 1912–1914, herausgegeben vom Arbeitsstatistischen, Amt.* 1916 (summarised in *Statistische Monatsschrift*, 1916). Zahn's method is described in *Bulletin de l'Institut International de Statistique*, XIX, 3, 126. The prices of industrial products can be seen from the annual estimate of all prices made by experts for the trade statistics, and published by the Ministry of Commerce.

[3] Cf. Sir George Paish, *Prices of Commodities in 1913*, cf. further Franz Eulenburg, *Preissteigerung des letzten Jahrzehnts*, 1913.

[4] The wage of miners per shift from 1901 to 1913 rose for hewers and haulers

therefore, to a great extent swallowed up by the rise of 20% in the cost of living. Nevertheless there was considerable social progress. The period shows a rapid development of the trade unions and co-operative societies.[1] The hours of work were shortened, working conditions improved, collective agreements concluded, and household expenses reduced by co-operative buying.

14. Rise in Consumption and Small Savings

The improvement in the living conditions of the masses expressed itself in the rise in consumption per head. The following figures refer to the whole Customs Union, including Austria, Hungary and Bosnia:—

	1902.	1912.	*Increase.*
			%
Coffee, kg.	0·94	1·08	15
Tea, gr.	21	33	57
Cotton goods, kg.[2]. . .	3·04	4·14	36
Woollen goods, kg. . .	0·70	1·01	44

[2] The imports of cotton and all cotton goods were summed up and the exports deducted. The same method was followed for woollen goods.

In Austria alone the consumption of tobacco in the same period remained almost the same; it was 1·37 kg. in 1902 and 1·35 kg. in 1912. Between 1901/2 and 1911/2 the consumption of beer rose from 74 l. to 81 l., or by 9·5%. A considerable increase took place in the consumption of sugar. The average of the two years 1900/1 and 1901/2 had risen by the years 1910/1 and 1911/2 from 14·7 kg. to 21·9 kg., or by 48·9%.

From 1905 to 1912 the consumption of meat in Vienna increased from 74·5 to 80·5 kg. After the war it was much lower: in 1935, for example, the figure was 58·3 kg.

by 37·4%, for other adult underground workers by 42·4% and for adult surface workers by 39·7%. Cf. Lukas Waagen, *Bergbau und Bergbauwirtschaft*, 1919, p. 322. The wages of bank clerks rose from 1904 to 1913 for those with ten years service by 36·2%, and for those with twenty years by 62·1%. Cf. Carl Morawitz, *50 Jahre Geschichte einer Wiener Bank*, 1913, p. 72.

[1] Cf. Julius Deutsch, *Geschichte der oesterreichischen Gewerkschaftsbewegung*, 1908, *Die Tarifverträge in Oesterreich*, 1908. The social legislation of Austria-Hungary in comparison with Germany has been described by Prof. Walter Schiff, *Der Arbeiterschutz im Deutschen Reich und in der österr. Monarchie*, in *Schriften des Vereins für Sozialpolitik*, vol. 155, I and II, 1916.

The annual increase in deposits in the Savings Banks is also an index of the earnings of the masses and the lower middle class. If we compare for Austria the four-year averages 1899–1902 and 1908–1911 we find an increase of 101%. The year 1912, however, brought a sharp setback, owing to the threat of war with Russia over the Balkan question.

15. EMIGRATION

In spite of these improvements wide sections of the population still lived under very poor conditions. This was one of the main reasons for the fact that there was a large emigration from Austria-Hungary to America.[1] In the five years 1908–1912 1,034,813 emigrants left Austria-Hungary for overseas countries. Of these 549,552 were Austrians. A large proportion of the emigrants, however, returned to Austria-Hungary after they had earned sufficient money to buy a plot of land in their home country or to establish a business. In the five years indicated the number of those who returned from the U.S.A. alone was 401,802. In addition, large numbers migrated annually to Germany and other European countries for seasonal work and returned when the season was ended.

16. UNEMPLOYMENT VERY SMALL

A favourable point in the pre-war economic system was, how-ever, that extensive and persistent unemployment was unknown. In 1900—a year of acute depression [2]—the number of unemployed in the principal towns was statistically ascertained, and the pro-portion of unemployed in the population was found to be very low. In Vienna 2·25% of the civil population were unemployed, and in the working-class districts the percentage varied between 2·28% in Meidling and 3·70% in Brigittenau. In Prague the percentage was 1·90%, in her industrial suburbs 2·09%. In other industrial centres it was: Reichenberg 1·11%, Pilsen 0·47%, Brünn 0·97%, Graz 1·29%, Trieste 0·52%.

[1] Cf. Leopold Caro, *Auswanderung und Auswanderungspolitik in Österreich*, 1909.
[2] Cf. W. L. Thorp, *Business Annals* (published by the National Bureau of Economic Research, New York, 1926, p. 227) says that the year 1900 was in Austria one of industrial depression, poor crops, severe coal strikes and dull bourse.

In 1907 the Federation of Austrian Industrialists was disquieted by the shortage of workers, and an inquiry was made as to its causes, in particular as to the possible influence of emigration.[1] The report confirmed that many manufacturers, especially in Bohemia and Moravia, complained of the insufficient number of workers, and their estimates of the percentage of their productive capacity unutilised for this reason varied between 10% and 30%.

The statistics of the Labour Exchanges show the relation between posts offered and posts sought. They begin in 1903, when there were 83·6 offers for 100 applications. By 1907 the percentage had risen to 99·6, and in the following years up to 1912 it was 96·4, 87·0, 91·1, 93·7 and 89·3. In 1913, however, the figure fell to 76·5%. In this year economic life was gravely disturbed by the shadow of the approaching war. The Balkan Wars depressed the export trade, there was acute tension with Russia, and both Russia and Austria mobilised a great part of their armies. In Austria the rate of interest was the highest for fifty years. It is clear that the drop in employment was not due to causes inherent in the economic system.

These statistics, moreover, tended rather to overstate unemployment. As there was no unemployment insurance, the workers did not need to inform the Labour Exchange when they had found a post, and many remained registered as unemployed long after they had again got work.

The absence of grave unemployment can also be shown by a comparison of the Census with the statistics of employment furnished by the data of the Health Insurance. The categories of workers liable to insurance amounted, according to the Census of 1910, to 3,808,153. In the same year the number of persons actually insured was, taking the average of the monthly figures, 3,665,996, inclusive of miners. This figure differed only by 3·7% from the Census figure. The actual figure of unemployed may have been slightly greater if voluntarily insured persons were omitted. Their number, however, was small. In any case the comparison confirms the conclusion that the number of unemployed was exceedingly low considering that the above percentage

[1] Cf. Arthur Friedmann, *Arbeitermangel und Auswanderung*, published by the Federation of Industrialists, 1907, p. 22.

includes many workers who were out of work only for seasonal reasons, or because of infirmity, etc.

17. The Real Income in Austria Rose by 69% and the Rise was Much Quicker in Austria and Hungary than in Germany and Britain

The figures quoted show that the general price level certainly did not rise by more than 25%. If this figure is assumed, the rise of the real national income was 69%. During the same time the population increased by 9·3%. The increase in the real income per head was, therefore, 63%.

It is interesting to compare the movement of the national income in various countries. For Britain the increase in the real national income from the average of the years 1894–1903 to the average 1911–1913 was estimated by Colin Clark at 34·5%.[1] This would be an increase of 2·65% per year, and the increase over ten years would be 26·5%, while in Austria the rise of the real income was 69%. For Germany Helfferich has estimated that in the sixteen years 1896–1912 the national income rose by 82·7%, or by 5·17% per year. In ten years this would be an increase in the money income of 51·7%, while in Austria the money income rose by 86% and in Hungary by 92%.[2] Nevertheless public opinion in most countries, particularly in Austria, regarded the rise in Germany's wealth as phenomenal, while the economic development of Austria-Hungary was belittled.

18. This Progress was Due to the Natural Division of Labour between the Austro-Hungarian Territories Made Possible by the Absence of Trade Barriers

The great industrial development of Austria-Hungary was especially remarkable because the natural conditions of the territories concerned were far less favourable to such a development than those of most other great States in Europe.[3] The extent of

[1] Cf. Colin Clark, *National Income and Outlay*, 1938, p. 232.
[2] A comparison of the real income would show about the same result.
[3] Cf. a detailed analysis of the foundations of Austrian industries in my book, *Die Produktionsgrundlagen der österreichischen Industrie vor und nach dem Kriege*, 1918.

natural resources like coal or iron ore was small. A large part of Central Europe lacks great navigable rivers and easy access to the sea. From an economic point of view the Danube flows in the wrong direction. The mountainous nature of wide tracts makes communication difficult and expensive. The social structure and historical factors added to the difficulties of industrial production.

The greatest asset which Austria-Hungary possessed was her large internal market. The internal Customs and trade barriers had been abolished in Austria-Hungary earlier than in many other countries. It was Maria Theresa and some of her enlightened Ministers, especially Count Philipp Cobenzl and Count Carl Zinzendorf, who overcame the stubborn resistance of vested interests against the abolition of internal trade barriers.[1] Most Austrian territories were made a common Customs area in 1775, Galicia joined in 1784, Tyrol in 1822 and Hungary in 1851. The reason why Hungary remained so long outside was that the Hungarian nobility refused to contribute adequately to the State revenues, and the Customs were intended to serve as indirect taxation. Austria was at that time more progressive than Germany. In Prussia the internal barriers were removed only in 1818, the principal German States formed a Customs union in 1832–1833, and others joined in the forties and fifties. Nevertheless many internal obstacles to trade between the German States subsisted till Bismarck founded the Empire and established economic unity. The early introduction of internal free exchange of goods in Austria led to the development of a natural division of labour between the provinces which was most beneficial to all of them.

One of the most important factors in the development of the national wealth was the rôle of Vienna as a great international centre of banking and trade. Her banks enjoyed the highest credit in the Western countries, and were, therefore, able to finance the economic development of all provinces on very favourable conditions. The currency was solidly based on gold, and its backbone was the Austro-Hungarian Bank, common to both countries,

[1] Cobenzl was far ahead of his time in his view that Free Trade should also be established between all trading nations and that this would greatly contribute to the general welfare. Cf. Adolf Beer, *Die Zollpolitik und die Schaffung eines einheitlichen Zollgebietes unter Maria Theresia* in *Mitteilungen des Instituts für Oesterreichische Geschichtsforschung*, 1893, XIV, 259.

which in 1913 had assets of 3,313 million K. or £138 million. The Austrian banks had in 1913 assets of 21,020 million K. or £876 million. The Hungarian banks had assets of 13,613 million K. or £567 million. The assets of the banks were about double the amount of the total national income of both States. These assets included, of course, the deposits and savings of many millions of small people.

It is an interesting sociological problem why this great economic achievement has never been adequately recognised in the literature on Austria-Hungary.[1] Quite the contrary. Most of the books in English, even by distinguished writers, convey the impression that the Empire was economically stagnating and politically rotten. The reason is that these authors got their views from a certain section of Austrian and Hungarian intelligentsia which had a great influence on public opinion. Many of these intellectuals were brilliant writers, but they lacked a sound economic knowledge and political judgment. It was the tragedy of Austria-Hungary that the fierceness of the national struggles had induced many of the best elements of all nations to withdraw from public life. A large part of the German–Austrian intellectuals had Pan-German sympathies and deprecated Austria in order to extol Germany. Business men knew that wealth was increasing. But they seldom said so publicly, lest taxes might be increased too. They more frequently described their own situation as an unfavourable one.

19. IN AUSTRIA LITTLE STRIVING FOR ECONOMIC SEPARATION

The nationalists of all nationalities naturally liked to employ also economic arguments for their propaganda. But in Austria no serious economist or responsible politician would have dreamed of demanding the disruption of the economic unity. The advantages of the economic community were overwhelming. In 1908 Dr. Eduard Benesh, later co-founder and president of Czechoslovakia, published a book in which he advocated a federalisation of Austria.[2] In this book he said :—

[1] Except in my book on the foundations of Austrian industries, published 1918.
[2] Cf. Eduard Benesh, *Le problème Autrichien et la question Tchèque*, 1908, p. 307. R. W. Seton-Watson rightly says in his *History of the Czechs and Slovaks*, 1943, p.

"One has often spoken of a dismemberment of Austria. I don't believe in this at all. The historic and economic bonds between the Austrian nations are too powerful to make such a dismemberment possible. The introduction of the manhood suffrage (1907) and the democratisation of Austria, especially of Bohemia, prepare the soil for national appeasement."

The book ends with the statement that the Austrian question was on the way to solution.

The only serious movement for economic separation was that of the Hungarian nationalists who called themselves the Independence Party, and demanded a Customs barrier around Hungary, a separate national bank, and in general the abolition of all common institutions, though they did not reject a common monarch provided he was willing to fulfil the aspirations of Hungarian nationalism. The development of the national income, however, showed that Hungary derived greater profits from the economic union than any other part of the Empire. The demand of the Hungarian nationalists, therefore, was actuated merely by motives of power and prestige, and it shows that aspirations of this kind pay no regard whatever to the real economic interests of the nation.

285, that none of the Czech leaders was for separatism before the war of 1914. This fact by itself disposes of the propaganda slogan that the Slavs were oppressed in Austria.

III. ECONOMIC NATIONALISM BETWEEN THE TWO WORLD WARS

1. THE WORLD BACKGROUND

IT WOULD be misleading to regard conditions in the Danubian countries without close reference to world conditions. The fate of those countries was to a very great extent determined by the course of development in other parts of the world. The characteristic tendencies dominating the post-war period, in particular Economic Nationalism, could be found all over the world, though differing in the individual countries in strength and guise. But in the Danubian nations the world-wide tendency of mutual economic seclusion was greatly aggravated by political enmities. Political and economic nationalism were everywhere in close interaction. World conditions, moreover, not only shaped the Danubian development, but were also influenced by it. It is therefore advisable to begin with a glance at the background of post-war world conditions.[1]

The First World War caused unprecedented losses in lives, health and working power of the nations involved. The material and non-material damage was enormous, partly owing to direct destruction in the war zones, partly arising in various indirect ways. A large part of the direct material losses, however, was made good after the war in a comparatively short time through an extraordinary increase in technical efficiency. There was hardly ever a time when the pace of technical progress was so rapid and when so many new ways of producing wealth were made available. The introduction of methods of standardised and rationalised mass-production—for example, of the conveyor-belt—the rapid increase of the automobile, the radio, the aeroplane, the sound-film, the large increase in the use of artificial silk and other new materials, the harnessing of great water-powers, the electrification of transport, the development of much-improved methods in agri-

[1] An excellent survey is H. V. Hodson, *Slump and Recovery*, published under the auspices of the Royal Institute of International Affairs, 1938.

culture, and—last but not least—the much greater care for human life, health and working power by means of social hygiene and the mental advancement of the broad masses of the people by educational reforms—all these achievements seemed to promise the advent of an era of unparalleled prosperity. The scope and rapidity of the progress may be illustrated by the fact that the number of motor-cars in the United States was in 1910 less than half a million, but in 1920 $7\frac{1}{2}$ million and in 1930 27 million.

At the same time strenuous efforts were made to further the economic and financial reconstruction of the world by means of international co-operation. This implied to a great extent the return to the qualified liberalism characteristic of the pre-war era. The aim was by no means unadulterated Free Trade or pure Capitalism, but a serious attempt was made to combine the principles proved by long experience with ideas designed to serve new social aspirations. The League of Nations took the lead in these endeavours. Hardly a year passed without important international conferences and consultations inspired by the liberal belief that the prosperity of every people depended on that of all the others. States in financial distress received through the League not only expert advice as to ways of putting their budgets in order and of restoring their international credit, but also large loans raised under the guarantee of the financially strong States, and therefore granted on better terms than would otherwise have been obtainable.[1] Constant attempts were made to remove trade restrictions and similar obstacles to the revival of international trade. The International Labour Organisation devoted most valuable work to the amelioration of labour conditions. The Statistical Office of the League compiled a vast amount of data on the economic development of all nations, and numerous prominent economists were busy investigating the conditions of general prosperity and working out detailed proposals.

[1] Countries which raised loans under the auspices of the League of Nations were Austria, Greece, Hungary, Bulgaria, Estonia and Danzig, while other countries received valuable help from experts nominated by the League for investigating their conditions and giving advice.

The imposing work done by the League in the field of economic and financial reconstruction forms the subject of a long series of publications too numerous to be mentioned here. Their titles can be obtained from the League's *Catalogue of Publications on Economic and Financial Subjects*, which is an indispensable guide for every student of our problem.

The hopes placed on the economic guidance of the League seemed to be realised. After the violent fluctuations of the first post-war years a considerable boom set in, reaching its peak in 1929. Soon, however, a terrible financial crash, starting in America, shook the whole economic life of the world. In 1931 the collapse of the Austrian Creditanstalt aggravated the unfavourable conditions to a panic. In many countries great banks broke down and the currencies depreciated. Even in Britain financial conditions became critical, the Bank of England suspended payment in gold and the value of the pound fell. A long and severe industrial and agrarian depression set in, the number of unemployed rose to unprecedented heights, everywhere tariffs were raised, other trade restrictions were introduced or currencies devalued. International trade showed a catastrophic reduction. After a few years economic life slowly recovered and the menace of Hitler's ambition created a boom in the armament industries. At the end of 1937 a new downward tendency made itself felt, but it was checked by the outbreak of war.

It would be beyond the scope of this study to discuss the numerous theories put forward in the search for the causes of the great crisis. But it may be said that Economic Nationalism had a much larger share in the causes of its special severity than is allowed for by abstract speculations on the trade cycle.[1] To a considerable extent the crisis was the aftermath of the World War, which caused far-reaching and lasting changes in the structure of economic and political life. The World War itself sprang from nationalism, and its legacy was a fatal aggravation of nationalist rivalries and sentiment. Causes inherent in the economic system also played a part in bringing about economic fluctuations, but without the influence of political and economic nationalism the ups and downs would have been much more moderate.

2. THE DESTRUCTION OF ECONOMIC UNITY IN THE DANUBIAN AREA

The fundamental fact in the economic development of the Danubian countries after the war was the destruction of their economic community within the Austro-Hungarian Empire. The

[1] I shall give ample theoretical and statistical arguments for this statement in another study.

co-operation of ten nationalities, the division of labour according to economic reasons and their mutual exchange of products, labour and capital were superseded by a constant economic war of all against all, centred on the aim of a large measure of self-sufficiency, and on the ruthless exploitation of economic power at the expense of weaker nations. The war and pre-war events had left bitter memories in the minds of many nations, and they were now carried away by the longing for full national independence and for national aggrandisement and prestige. In framing the Peace Treaties for the Danubian countries the statesmen of the great victorious Powers did little to encourage economic co-operation and political conciliation. Some of their decisions were palpably incompatible with the principles of self-determination and the equality of nations, and were bound to arouse bitter resentment. True they permitted preferential tariffs between Czechoslovakia, Austria and Hungary for a period of five years, but no use was made of this clause. A prominent Czech economist, Prof. Basch, recently wrote: "It is clear to-day that these provisions should have been made compulsory and should have been extended to all Succession States." [1] But at that time public opinion was widely dominated by intense nationalism, which rejected any community with the neighbours regarded as enemies.

In particular, Vienna, the former seat of the Imperial Government and of the great banks and industrial companies, was the object of jealousy and animosity. A Dutch economist who came to Vienna as an expert of the League of Nations described the general feeling in the words: "Vienna was regarded as a gigantic parasite, the city of lotus-eating idlers. 'Vienna has ruined us all!' was the cry; we must make ourselves independent of Vienna." [2] But the antagonism of some nations to Austria was surpassed by the hostility of Hungary towards Czechoslovakia, Roumania and Yugoslavia, and vice versa, and that between Italy and the Southern Slavs. Czechoslovakia was on the brink of war with Poland. The relations of the Soviet Union with Poland and Rou-

[1] Cf. Basch, *The Danube Basin, etc.*, 1944, p. 32. J. M. Keynes made the still more attractive suggestion that a great Free Trade Union should be formed under the auspices of the League of Nations, comprising the whole of Central and Eastern Europe, the U.K., etc. Cf. Keynes, *The Economic Consequences of the Peace*, 1920, p. 265.

[2] Cf. J. van Walré de Bordes, *The Austrian Crown, its Depreciation and Stabilisation*, 1924, p. 7.

mania were bad. Bulgaria, too, harboured bitter feelings towards her neighbours. In the Southern Slav kingdom, later called Yugoslavia, the ruling Serbs were soon at loggerheads with the "liberated" Croats and Macedonians, and in other Succession States also the minorities raised bitter complaints. To all this was added a fierce social tension born of the sufferings of the great masses in the war, and intensified by Communist propaganda in the war-stricken countries.

3. AUSTRIA'S DEPENDENCE ON FOREIGN TRADE

Among all the new States, Austria was worst hit by the destruction of the former economic unity. Her neighbours were eager to destroy her position as the economic centre of the Danubian area, and to appropriate as much as possible of her trade by means of their political power. The high state of development of Austria's industries and her lack of sufficient fertile soil and natural resources, made her largely dependent on the import of foodstuffs, coal and raw materials. Former Austria-Hungary was to a remarkable degree self-supporting. As the experts of the League of Nations—Mr. Walter (now Lord) Layton and Professor Rist— pointed out in their report on Austria, Austria-Hungary imported and exported less per head of the population than any other important European State except Russia.

TRADE PER HEAD, 1913 (IN DOLLARS)

	Import.	Export.
Austria-Hungary	13·8	11·8
Germany	39·3	36·9
France	41·5	33·9
Great Britain and Ireland . . .	69·8	55·5
Russia	5·2	5·7
Switzerland	95·3	70·4

After the war conditions changed completely. New Austria belonged to the countries with a very high quota of international trade per head.

The following table shows to what a great extent Austria needed imports in order to live, and that she paid for them by exporting a very considerable amount of her products, though her

TRADE PER HEAD (IN DOLLARS)

			Imports.		Exports.	
			1924.	1929.	1924.	1929.
Austria	.	.	74	69	43	46
Czechoslovakia	.	.	34	40	36	41
Hungary	.	.	18	21	14	21
Yugoslavia	.	.	9	11	10	10
Roumania	.	.	8	10	8	10
Poland	.	.	10	11	9	10
Germany	.	.	35	50	25	50
France	.	.	54	54	55	47
Italy	.	.	21	29	16	19
Russia	.	.	—	3	—	3
Great Britain	.	.	113	118	79	77
Switzerland	.	.	116	127	93	99

balance of trade still showed a substantial deficit. Among the other Succession States only Czechoslovakia had also a considerable import quota per head, though it was much smaller than that of Austria, and was more than covered by export. Austria exported more per head than Czechoslovakia. The other Succession States had little foreign trade per head, and their imports were roughly equal to their exports. Only Austria, therefore, was faced with a serious problem in paying for her imports. She could achieve this only by exporting manufactured products.

4. AUSTRIA EXPORTED ABOUT 45% OF HER INDUSTRIAL PRODUCTION

An estimate of the amount of exports needed by Austria to pay for her import requirements can be formed on the basis of the trade statistics for 1928 and 1929. These years were the best in the period between the two wars, and their trade came nearest to the level which may be regarded as normal—namely, that of approximately full employment of the industrial capacity. In the subsequent years the world crisis, and the specific Danubian catastrophe, created a most abnormal situation. If we wish to estimate the capacity of an economic organism we must, of course, observe it in a state of comparative normality, though it may be questioned whether such a state ever occurred in the post-war period.

58

The prosperity of the late 'twenties was probably to a great extent a fallacious one.

The structure of Austria's foreign trade in 1928 and 1929 was as follows:—

('000,000 Schillings)

	Imports.		Exports.	
	1928.	1929.	1928.	1929.
Livestock . . .	270	259	23	19
Food, drink . . .	747	710	54	44
Coal . . .	226	265	4	2
Raw materials, half-manu-factured goods . .	713	731	501	481
Wholly manufactured goods . . .	1,283	1,290	1,627	1,627
Gold, silver . . .	78	55	41	32
Total . . .	3,317	3,310	2,249	2,206

This trade balance shows at a glance that Austria depends to a very great extent on the import of food, coal and raw materials, for which she has to pay mainly by the export of manufactures. But it is remarkable that Austria has also a very large import of wholly manufactured goods, which is equal to about 80% of her export of such goods. This state of things is deeply rooted in the natural and historical conditions of the country, and cannot be changed in a short time, if at all. Austria's soil and climate will never be able to produce all the food needed, and the country is poor in coal and raw materials. True, coal can to a certain extent be replaced by the harnessing of water-power, and this was done on a large scale in the period between the wars. It requires, how-ever, great investments of capital, which is very short in Austria. As regards the inadequacy of natural resources, it may be men-tioned that in 1928 the value of the mineral output of Austria was only 84 million S. (about £2.4 million), of which 63 million S. was that of coal.[1] Among other raw materials only wood is of great importance, and among the exports of raw materials and semi-manufactured goods timber and wood-products like paper-pulp, cellulose, etc., were the largest item. The fact that Austria

[1] Recently Austria has also become an oil-producing country.

had to import also a considerable quantity of manufactured products is also mainly due to Nature. Many industries are best located in regions where certain raw materials are produced, or where power and heat, or the cost of transport, are cheap; or they depend on a very wide home market. In all these respects Austria often cannot compete with other countries, and must for this reason import a large quantity of industrial products.

These circumstances make it clear that Austria can live only by exporting wholly manufactured goods, and in this regard she has not been lacking in technical and commercial efficiency. In the years between the two world wars many industries exported more than half their total output, and some even 80% or 90%. On the other hand, many industries are not suited for export. Articles like bricks or bread, or activities like building, nowhere contribute much to exports.

An approximate idea of the relation between industrial output and export can be formed in this way. For pre-war Austria Fellner estimated the net output of manufactured articles (exclusive of mines, smelting and handicrafts) at 4,193 million K. This estimate was obtained after deducting the cost of all materials used and allowing for depreciation, and amounted to 44% of the gross output. The share of post-war Austria was, according to Waizner, 29·5%, and the index of industrial prices was in 1928–1929 46% above the pre-war level.

The net output of all factories in post-war Austria in 1928 can therefore be estimated at 2,600 million S., assuming full employment of the existing capacity. The export of wholly manufactured goods was 1,627 million S. To this must be added manufactured goods listed under "food, drinks", such as margarine, flour, sugar, chocolate, beer, etc., amounting to about 20 million S., a further 40 million S.[1] "invisible exports", and about 90 million S. listed as "half-manufactured goods".[2] The total is 1,777 million S. If it is assumed that the net value was again 44% (which will presently be qualified) the net output was 782 million S., and the percentage of all manufactures exported 30%. This figure, however, can only be regarded as the

[1] According to the estimate of Dr. Friedrich Gebert, *Fremdenverkehr und Zahlungsbilanz, herausgegeben von der Handelskammer Salzburg*, 1928.
[2] Excluding pig iron and raw metals, as these were not included in Fellner's estimate of manufactures, but were listed under "mining".

minimum limit—the actual percentage must have been higher, partly because the net value of 44% was too low,[1] partly because it is doubtful whether the industries were employed at pre-war capacity.

We can check this calculation by a different one aiming at the comparison of gross values, including the value of the raw materials, etc., used, but excluding duplication. To this end we may start from the net values of industries, mining and forests in old Austria as estimated by Fellner, and assess post-war Austria's share by means of the quotas calculated by Waizner, and the percentage of the forests which fell to small Austria. To this must be added the Austrian quota in the surplus of imports of raw materials, etc., over exports, and the sum must be converted into Schillings at the price level of 1928. If this (incomplete) sum of industrial gross output is compared with the total industrial export, including raw materials and half-manufactured goods, one arrives at the figure of 58·8%. This figure, however, is certainly too high, and can only be regarded as the maximum limit. The reason is that the pre-war trade statistics naturally indicated only the raw materials, etc., imported from outside the Customs union and from Hungary, but not those imported from Austrian territories which later formed part of Czechoslovakia, Poland, Yugoslavia, Roumania and Italy. Moreover, certain raw materials produced by Austria's agriculture could not be estimated, nor the increase in value resulting from the services of commerce and transport. We can only assume that the percentage of post-war Austria's industrial output exported was somewhere between the minimum of 30% and the maximum of nearly 60%. The average would be 45%. Now, it has been estimated that in 1931 actually 45% of the industrial output was exported, but as I was unable to see this calculation I cannot say what method was employed.[2]

[1] It was estimated by Fellner that the value of all materials used in the production of industrial output, plus depreciation, amounted to 56% of the sum of the outputs of the various branches. But a material frequently went through different branches of industries, and was then counted several times. Cotton, for example, was converted into yarn, then into woven fabrics, then into printed or dyed calico, and lastly into women's dresses. In this case the value of the raw cotton appeared four times in the sum of all outputs. Now, in the sum of industrial export no such multiplications occur, and the deduction of 56% must therefore be too high.

[2] The figure of 45% is quoted in *Monatsberichte des österreichischen Instituts für*

5. The Austrian Balance of Payments

The extraordinary rôle of exports in Austria's economic life is also illustrated by the export quota per head already indicated. It is further significant that Austria's total exports amounted in 1928 to about 33% of the national income, while British exports were estimated at only about 17% of the British national income. Even that high proportion, however, was not sufficient to meet the requirements of foreign exchange for the import of food, raw materials and manufactures. Taking the average for the four years 1926–1929 the annual surplus of imports over exports was 1,055 million S. This large deficit was the dominant factor in the Balance of Payments.[1] A number of items increased it, while others decreased it. The largest negative item was interest and amortisation on State loans (108·6 million S.), and the largest positive ones were: tourist traffic 244–254 million, transit trade 120 million, transit traffic 71·3 million. But all the investigations of the most competent experts were not able to clear up how the deficit in the balance of payments was covered. After making all allowances, an annual amount of about 600 million S. remained for which no possible cover could be ascertained. It had not been paid for out of long- or short-term loans. In the seven years 1923–1928 the total trade deficits amounted to 6,775 million S. In this time the long-term indebtedness to foreign creditors increased by only about 1,000 million. The short-term liabilities increased by about 600–700 million, but this was counterbalanced by the increase in short-term assets held by the banks. It can only be surmised that a considerable part was covered by selling out Austrian investments abroad to foreign buyers, and by the return of flight capital. Payments of this kind, however, could not be regarded as regular income, and the

Konjunkturforschung, 1936, p. 262, but without indicating the source. The article gives some data about the export quotas of certain industries. Other data are given in the *Österreichischer Volkswirt* of 17.12.1927 and 21.12.1929. The first article estimates the share of the output exported at: iron ore 50–65%, steel alloys 70%, machines 60%, paper 75%, articles made of jute 70%. The second article adds: magnesite 85–90%, machines 50%, but certain machine factories 80–90%, cotton yarn 50%.

[1] Cf. on the Austrian Balance of Payments the data compiled by the Austrian Statistical Office in its paper *Statistische Nachrichten*, 1930, p. 44; 1931, p. 103; 1934, p. 120.

question arose how the deficit would be met after their exhaustion. When the great crisis broke upon the world a large part was, of course, wiped out by insolvency and by the depreciation of currencies.

Assuming that 500 million of the deficit in the Balance of Payment would be covered by additional exports, this would actually require an increase in exports of almost 1,000 million, because an additional import of raw materials would first be needed, and this could be paid for only by further exports of industrial goods. It is out of the question that the bulk of the necessary raw materials could be produced within Austria, though a small part might. The share of exports in output would be increased far beyond 50%. The industrial plant would also have to be greatly extended, and this would depend on the possibility of obtaining capital abroad.

These estimates cannot, of course, claim any accuracy. They only give an idea of the magnitude of the problem. In any case, they show that the employment of the Austrian workers and the standard of life of the Austrian people depend more than in most other countries on the accessibility of foreign markets. A wide scope of freedom of international trade is a question of life or death for Austria.

6. THE BLOCKADE OF AUSTRIA

When the war had ended the Austrian Republic was faced with appalling difficulties. She had neither food, nor raw materials, nor money, nor credit. Her new neighbours immediately stopped supplies and introduced the most rigorous trade restrictions, practically amounting to a blockade. Vienna was starving, industries could not work and the finances and currency were utterly ruined. The Great Powers came to the rescue, sending food and trying to persuade Czechoslovakia and Poland to provide Austria with the coal needed for restarting her industrial production. But all these efforts could not prevent the collapse of the currency. The value of the Austrian Crown fell to almost nothing, and the impoverishment of the middle classes prepared the soil for the growth of reactionary forces which later succeeded in destroying democracy. In 1922, however, the League of Nations arranged a large loan to Austria, her budget and currency were stabilised and the conditions thereby created for a more normal economic development.

7. The Idea of a Danubian Economic Union

From the beginning of the new era all those closely acquainted with the economic conditions of former Austria-Hungary had grave apprehensions regarding the consequences of the destruction of the economic unity. In Austria, in particular, the conviction was general that the country had no chance of economic survival without an economic union with some of the neighbouring States. Already when Austria-Hungary was in dissolution the Social Democratic Party—then the strongest party in new Austria—declared twice, on October 10th and 21st, 1918, their willingness to enter into negotiations with the other nationalities of the vanishing Empire with a view to the formation of a democratic federation of national States. If this should prove impossible they claimed self-determination for Austria also, and envisaged a union with Germany. All the other Austrian parties issued similar declarations. But there was no response, and it became ever more clear that the nascent new States were dominated by intense nationalism, and had not the slightest desire for close co-operation. This induced the Social Democrats to take the lead in declaring the union of Austria with Germany. This move was, however, vigorously opposed by Czechoslovakia and her friends, and the Anschluss was vetoed by the victors.

After the failure of the Anschluss plan, Austria again turned to the alternative solution of a Danubian union. By now it had begun to dawn upon a number of French and British statesmen that the unbridled nationalism which the Peace Treaties had unleashed in the area of former Austria-Hungary was a grave menace to peace and reconstruction. M. Allizé, the French Minister in Vienna, later expressed the view that France had made a blunder in not making the recognition of the new States dependent on conditions for securing the maintenance of the Danubian economic unity. M. Briand and other prominent French statesmen would have liked the formation of a new community among the former member nations of Austria-Hungary. But Austria's neighbours, in particular Czechoslovakia, rejected this idea with even greater intransigence than the plan of Austria's union with Germany. Dr. Benesh, then Czechoslovak Foreign Minister, in 1920 declared in various speeches and other statements—for instance, on September 1st and 2nd in Parliament—that the former economic union was "a system of exploitation" directed against the Czechs, who could not bear it, and who must therefore beware of any revival of it in the form of a confederation. He also declared in an interview:—

"The Czechs had fought not for political freedom—for this they had enjoyed to a certain extent even before the war—but for their economic independence, and therefore the scheme for a confederation of the Danubian States, or even of a 'Customs Union', is out of the question for the Czechoslovak Republic. A political union with Austria and Hungary would mean that these countries would gain influence in our internal affairs: Austria by way of the Germans living in our State, Hungary through the Magyars in Slovakia. The unfavourable economic conditions of Austria and Hungary form an obstacle to an economic union, and the consequence of any such alliance would be that the wealth of Czechoslovakia would again pour into Austria and Hungary. It is true they must be helped, but by the whole of Europe. Besides, the Austrian problem resolves itself into the problem of Vienna. It is possible that the population of the city will be reduced to one million within ten years. A depopulation of Vienna planned economically would help to solve the Austrian problem. Hungary, being an agrarian State, will survive. We must indeed work with Austria and Hungary, but instead of political and economic alliances of long duration, the solution seems to lie in a system of short-term contracts for certain different kinds of deliveries, and arrangements by which the independence and special interests of each of the three States concerned would be maintained."

Dr. Benesh's declaration was endorsed by many influential organs of public opinion. The Czech Socialist paper *Delnicke Listy*, referring to his statement that the population of Vienna would be reduced by half, wrote:—

"There are still many people in Vienna, especially in commercial circles, who cannot forget the hope that Vienna will in the end regain her former economic position. Consequently they will make every possible effort to save from ruin this centre of profiteers, agents and wire-pullers, supporters of debauchery, pseudo-art and pseudo-literature. Dr. Benesh, with inexorable logic, has dispelled the artificial combinations of these people, and has even gone so far as to predict a still greater downfall for the Danubian metropolis. Vienna lives at other peoples' expense. The parasites of former Austria still reside there. For them the only possibility of salvation for Vienna is the hope that she may again become a centre of commerce. Their Vienna, however, is doomed to ruin, and no one can blame Czechoslovakia for being unwilling to contribute to her preservation. The upright and serious part of the population of Vienna are quite alive to the fact that only a productive and working city has a chance of future prosperity."

The leader of the Czechs in Vienna, Mr. Klimesch, wrote in the periodical *Lidove Listy* that the majority of the Czechs living in Vienna had now made up their minds to emigrate. By such an exodus the importance of Vienna would be wiped out. "But", he continued, "a thriving Vienna would also be more dangerous for Czechoslovakia than Berlin or Munich would be." The idea that Vienna was only a "huge parasite" was also expressed by Professor Jan Kolousek of the Prague Polytechnic in an article published in the London weekly *The New Europe* of May 13th, 1920. He comes to the conclusion that the greater part of the population of Vienna lived at the expense of the subject territories and nations, and that this had now naturally come to an end. Therefore the necessity would arise for the Viennese to migrate to the rural districts where there was adequate room for them. Professor Kolousek further says:—

"In spite of all this British statesmen who wish to dictate to us declare that we ought to open our frontiers to Austria completely. Is Austria at the prompting of the Allied Powers to exploit us as formerly? Czechoslovakia could never comply with such a proposal, for to do so would be a suicidal policy. Nor will Czechoslovakia ever submit again to the abominable

66

and slavish yoke of the former Austria-Hungary, even though this yoke were to assume the more peaceful form, and the more flattering title, of the Danubian Federation."

These and similar statements make it clear why the prospects of close economic co-operation with the other Succession States were regarded by Austrian public opinion with the greatest pessimism. They resulted, moreover, in spreading a very gloomy view of the immediate prospects of Austria's economic life. Many writers went so far as to assert that new Austria was entirely unable to maintain herself, as she lacked adequate productive resources. This view was entirely misleading; Vienna and other districts of Austria were the seats of highly developed industries, though these were for the moment largely paralysed by the lack of coal and raw materials and by the loss of markets in the other Succession States. Austria, furthermore, possessed other assets capable of revival and considerable development. It was pointed out that she had in some respects more natural resources than Switzerland had. This was true, but Switzerland had for many hundreds of years had the unique opportunity of developing her resources in almost undisturbed peace; she had thereby become an exceedingly wealthy country and had built up an extremely efficient agriculture and highly specialised industries. Though Switzerland also suffered losses through post-war conditions, she was never faced with Austria's fate of economic strangulation and destruction of capital.

The intransigent attitude of her neighbour States discouraged the Austrian advocates of a Danubian Confederation and was as wind into the sails of the movement for union with Germany—the so-called Anschluss. The history of this movement need not be surveyed here.[1] It is sufficient to say that France and her allies were absolutely opposed to this idea. In 1931 the Austrian and German Governments made arrangements for the conclusion of a Customs Union between the two States which any other States should also be free to join. This plan, too, however, aroused the strongest opposition from France and Czechoslovakia, and had to be dropped. These two Powers then put forward another scheme

[1] Cf. Margaret Ball, *Post-War German–Austrian Relations. The Anschluss Movement, 1918–1936.*

—the so-called Tardieu Plan.[1] Its main feature was a preferential tariff between the Danubian States, consisting in a reduction of customs by 10%. It need hardly be said that the suggestion of reducing by 10% the excessive tariffs then in force was not a serious contribution to the solution of the economic difficulties. Whether a tariff is 50% or 45% makes no difference at all.

The discussion of the idea of preferential tariffs was continued, but led to no result. Among the Danubian countries the industrial States could offer no concession to the exporters of foodstuffs in the agricultural countries because the very powerful Agrarian parties vetoed this. On the other hand, the agricultural countries wanted to develop their own industries, and were therefore opposed to any concessions to the export industries of the industrialised States. But there was also opposition, or reluctance, on the part of certain States outside the Danubian area. Neither Germany, nor Italy, nor Russia liked the idea of a Danubian Confederation, and Britain and other Powers discouraged the idea of a preferential system.

The crux of the problem was that most of the great and small States regarded the formation of an economic union, or any other co-operation, far too much from the point of view of power politics, and not from that of economic interests. In the last years of the inter-war period Mussolini succeeded in securing the vassalage of Austria and Hungary by granting them some economic advantages. On the other hand, the Little Entente, which was primarily a military alliance for the maintenance of the new frontiers against Hungary, envisaged the intensification of trade relations between its members, Czechoslovakia, Yugoslavia and Roumania, and some progress was actually made. But all these and similar plans were inspired predominantly by political aspirations often incompatible with the requirements of a policy of improving economic conditions on a large scale.

[1] We need not enter into a detailed narrative of the various attempts at an economic *rapprochement* between Danubian States, since they all more or less failed, or led only to temporary alleviations. Cf. the excellent survey in A. Basch, *The Danube Basin and the German Economic Sphere*, 1944. The economic problem of the so-called "Little Entente" is treated in Walter Hildebrandt, *Die Kleine Wirtschaftsentente als agrarpolitisches Problem der Tschechoslovakei*, 1938.

8. The Commercial Policy of the Danubian States

A few years after the war nationalistic passions had sufficiently cooled down to render possible normal commercial relations between the Danubian States. The drastic restrictions on trade were loosened and numerous commercial treaties were concluded with a view to the encouragement of international trade. The history of this development cannot be surveyed here.[1] It was characterised by the striving for a compromise between Economic Nationalism and the needs of international trade. Yet soon nationalism regained the upper hand. Its progress was due to the fact that practically all governments, parties and influential groups regarded it as the easiest way to overcome difficulties. The military interests and the nationalists saw in it the main pillar of national security, power and prestige. The industrialists and farmers expected from it high prices and secure markets. The Labour parties often opposed high tariffs on food, but they were attracted by the prospect of increased employment and higher wages. The Treasuries hoped that tariffs would bring higher revenues, encourage the accumulation of capital and protect the currency.

The degree of protectionism in the individual States can to a certain extent be measured by comparing their tariff levels. The level of a tariff can be ascertained by calculating the average percentage relation between the Customs duties and the value of the corresponding commodities. The Economic Service of the League of Nations in the middle of the 'twenties investigated the problem and calculated various sets of tariff levels using different methods.[2] Besides the experts of the League of Nations, Mr. Layton and Prof. Rist made similar calculations, which were pub-

---

[1] Cf. *Commercial Policy in the Inter-War Period*, published by the League of Nations, 1942; *The Economic Situation of Austria*, Report presented to the League of Nations by W. T. Layton and C. Rist, 1925, p. 83, and other publications of the League of Nations; Leo Pasvolsky, *Economic Nationalism of the Danubian States*, 1923; H. Liepmann, *Tariff Levels and the Economic Unity of Europe*, 1938 (gives also surveys of commercial treaties); Ernst Haas, *Die Aussenhandels politik der ehemaligen Republik Oesterreich*, 1939; G. Gersdorff, *Die Entwicklung der polnischen Handelsvertragspolitik*, 1935; L. Pesic, *Die Handelspolitik Jugoslaviens*, 1935; K. Witt, *Wirtschaftskräfte und Wirtschaftspolitik der Tschechoslovakei*, 1938.
[2] The estimates are printed in the memoranda submitted to the International Economic Conference (1926).

lished in their report on Austria. The main results of these investigations are shown in the following table:—

	Estimates of Layton and Rist, 1925.	Estimates of League of Nations for International Economic Conference, 1925.	
		(a) General.	(b) Manufactured goods.
(New) Austria . .	16–21	12	16
Czechoslovakia . .	21½–30¾	19	27
Hungary . . .	28–40	23	27
Poland . . .	49–67	23	32
Yugoslavia . .	27–41	23	23
Roumania . .	19–26	—	—
Germany . . .	14–17¼	—	—
Italy . . .	16–21	—	—
U.S.A. . . .	—	37	—

Although the estimates refer to the same year they show considerable differences. Those of Mr. Layton and Prof. Rist arrive at higher levels than those of the League of Nations. It seems probable, however, that the higher figures are more correct than the lower ones.

Another investigation, based on a much wider range of data, and using a far more accurate method, was made by the Austrian Committee of the International Chamber of Commerce, and was also submitted to the International Economic Conference.[1] The Customs and values refer to the beginning of 1927. The tariff level was worked out for fifteen groups (e.g., textiles, metal goods, etc.); 402 typical commodities and fourteen States were investigated. The table on page 71 gives the tariff level for all commodities (excluding merely financial duties like those on tobacco, tea, etc.), and those for a few important groups. (Designations like "iron" include goods made of iron.)

The lowest tariffs were levied in the small States on the North Sea. The Netherlands had almost exclusively Customs of 8%, and in some cases of 5%. Belgium had a level of 11·4%, Denmark of 11·5%. Great Britain at that time belonged also to the countries

[1] Cf. *Zollhöhe und Warenwert, der Weltwirtschaftskonferenz überreicht vom Oesterreichischen Nationalkomite der Internationalen Handelskammer*, 1927.

with comparatively little protectionism, though she had some customs of $33\frac{1}{3}\%$ (McKenna tariff) and some of 50%.

Another group showed moderate Customs levels between 10% and 20%. To this group belonged: Switzerland, with 17·5%; Austria, with 18·6%; Sweden, with 18·9%, and Germany, with 19·8%.

France prepared at that time a tariff providing Customs not lower than 24·6% on the average for countries enjoying specially favoured treatment. But Austrian goods had to pay the general tariff of 54%. Italy's level was 27·4%.

AVERAGE TARIFF LEVELS IN PERCENTAGES OF THE VALUES OF THE GOODS

	Agricultural products.	Chemicals.	Textiles.	Leather.	Paper.	Glass.	Iron.	Metal.	Machines.	All goods.
Austria .	16·6	22·3	14·6	10·3	16·1	18·2	30·8	18·2	25·6	18·6
Czecho- slovakia .	34·1	42·9	28·6	20·9	31·9	31·5	53·3	27·9	46·2	35·8
Hungary .	32·1	19·1	29·8	27·5	26·5	38·6	49·2	28·3	33	30·7
Yugoslavia .	48·3	37·8	29·9	33·7	32·7	53·3	41·1	25	22·8	33·6
Roumania .	29·3	18	294·3	25·7	49·6	46·8	39·6	35·6	22·9	99·2
Poland .	27·5	29·3	49·6	34·5	63·1	70·2	56·3	28·8	41·6	43·4
Germany .	26·9	15·5	24	13·5	19·4	51·1	16·9	13·2	10·9	19·8
France [1] .	18·1	78·1	70·6	22·9	16·5	109·1	110	27·5	38·9	54
Italy . .	27·4	28·1	18·6	18·7	25·6	39·8	60·7	13	25·4	27·4

[1] French tariff valid for Austrian goods.

The levels of the Danubian States, except Austria, were much higher. Roumania, with 99·2%, topped the list; then came Poland, with 43·4%; Czechoslovakia, with 35·8%; Yugoslavia, with 33·6%, and Hungary, with 30·7%. A comparison of the levels of the groups shows that iron and iron goods enjoyed particularly high protection, obviously for military reasons. It is surprising, however, to find that some countries had very high customs even for products in which they were fully able to compete in the world's markets. This becomes still more clear if single commodities are envisaged. Czechoslovakia, for instance, raised a tariff of 118·3% on sugar, one of 41·3% on cotton fabrics, one of 59·1% on ceramics, one of 31·5% on glass, one of 20% on boots and so on.

Further careful investigations were made by H. Liepmann.[2]

[2] H. Liepmann, *Tariff Levels and the Economic Unity of Europe*, 1938.

He distinguishes two kinds of tariff levels—the actual and the potential. The potential refers to all goods scheduled in a tariff without regard to the fact whether certain goods were actually imported, while the actual takes account only of those commodities which formed part of the imports. Commodities barred out by a prohibitive tariff, therefore, would not be included in the calculations of the actual level, nor those which needed no protection because the country concerned was no market for imports of this kind.

The following table shows the movement of the general potential tariff level in the principal countries since the pre-war period :—

	1913.	1927.	1931.
	%	%	%
Austria	22·8	17·5	36·0
Czechoslovakia . . .	22·8	31·3	50·0
Hungary	22·8	30·0	45·0
Roumania	30·3	42·3	63·0
Yugoslavia	22·2	32·0	46·0
Poland	72·5	53·5	67·5
Bulgaria	22·8	67·5	96·5
Germany	16·7	20·4	40·7
France	23·6	23·0	38·0
Italy	24·8	27·8	48·3
Sweden	27·6	20·0	26·8
Switzerland . . .	10·5	16·8	26·4
Belgium	14·2	11·0	17·4
Spain	37·0	49·0	68·5

These figures show the continuous rise in the tariff levels, which became marked already before the outbreak of the world crisis and after it reached unprecedented heights. The U.S.A. played a big part in this movement, first by the tariff of 1922 and then in 1930 by the Hawley–Smoot tariff, which greatly aggravated the crisis. In Europe the Succession States constantly raised their customs levels. Austria had up to 1927 comparatively low tariffs, but later felt compelled to follow suit. In the great depression of the 'thirties trade barriers became higher than ever. But this was now effected less by raising tariffs than by import prohibitions, quotas, currency control, bilateral agreements, barter trade, depreciation of the currency and similar measures.

9. Export Subsidies and their Consequences

The advocates of protective tariffs represent them as necessary measures of economic defence against unfair competition, and in many cases this argument certainly holds good. But a system of high protection unavoidably encourages unfair competition and easily assumes an aggressive character. It leads to dumping—*i.e.*, exporting goods at abnormally low prices, even at a loss, and recovering the difference from the high profits in the home market. This way of aggression has often caused a great deterioration in international economic relations. Tariffs alone, however, are not enough to make large-scale dumping possible. There must also be an authority securing the full effect of the tariff on the home market by eliminating competition. This can either be a powerful cartel or the State, and the power of the State is naturally much stronger than that of any cartel. For this reason the worst acts of economic aggression have always been committed by States.

The Danubian States show numerous examples of a policy of State-subsidised dumping. Allowance must, however, be made for the fact that some of them did this under the pressure of acute financial need. They had to find certain amounts of foreign currency, and saw no other way than by exporting staple products at almost any price. In some cases a State possessing goods of which other countries were particularly short could even make a great profit. This was, for example, the case of Czechoslovakia immediately after the war.

Dr. Benesh, then Foreign Minister, in a statement to the International Labour Office on December 8th, 1920,[1] described this system in this way:—

> "We have taken account of the fact that the present economic policy of all States is characterised by an extreme nationalism—a protectionism, in fact, dictated by the nationalists. In practice this means that a country without raw materials keeps everything it can for itself, and tries to draw as much as possible from the others. Obviously we could not act otherwise than the whole world does. But we have elaborated a special system. We produce, for example, 800,000

[1] *Enquête sur la production, Rapport général,* 1925, Tome V, p. 543.

tons of sugar, and export, say, 400,000 tons. The State takes over all the sugar, determines the quantity for home consumption, and fixes a maximum price. The quantity not distributed in the home market is confiscated by the State, which reserves to itself the profit on its exportation. The Government pays to the owners the internal maximum price—for example, last year 1·3 K.—and sells the sugar to other countries at from 25 to 30 K. per kilo. Moreover, the State levies a tax for its budget on the sugar exported. The profit amounts to milliards! We did the same with paper, with hops, with oats. We bought the oats from the peasants at the maximum price of 80 K. and sold it to Switzerland for 1,000 K. The profit is enormous."

Dr. Benesh concludes by saying that this system had the result that Czechoslovakia was probably the only State in Europe with a balanced budget.

The enormous profits emphasised by Dr. Benesh were obviously due to the fact that at that time the Czechoslovak currency was depreciating and the goods were sold only to countries with a stable currency. While Czechoslovakia was selling sugar to America, Austria was forced to import sugar from Cuba and Java, though most sugar-factories in Czechoslovakia were then still owned by Austrians. Worse still, the lack of coal paralysed her industries and pushed her currency into the abyss. This experience later induced Austria to emancipate herself as far as possible from Czechoslovak exports, in particular to replace Czechoslovak coal by the water-power of her Alps, to produce her own sugar, and so on. In the last resort, therefore, the system praised by Dr. Benesh resulted in the permanent loss of important markets, and soon many of Czechoslovakia's greatest industries were in a most critical state.

The striving for increased exports at any price led to the system of State-subsidised dumping. It was not restricted to the financially distressed States of Eastern Europe. Even Powers with great economic resources resorted to dumping, mainly in favour of the agrarians who controlled a large number of representatives in Parliament.[1]

[1] Soon after the conclusion of the International Wheat Agreement of 1933, for example, the French Government, which had not received an export quota, sold wheat to British millers at 35 fr., for which it was paying 115 fr. to French wheat-growers. This regime cost the French exchequer 2,000 million fr. Cf. P. de Hevesy, *World Wheat Planning*, 1940.

In 1931 Yugoslavia introduced a Wheat Monopoly which was to purchase all wheat on the domestic market at 160 dinars per 100 kg., and to sell it to the flour-mills at 240–270 dinars. The profit thus realised was to provide the means of paying an export subsidy, enabling Yugoslav wheat to compete on foreign markets. The Liverpool price for wheat at that time was equivalent to about 60 dinars, taking the transport cost into consideration, or about a quarter of the official price which the Yugoslav customer was to pay. It was expected that Yugoslavia would in this way export no less than 5 million quintals; but the scheme was a failure. The framers of the scheme had overlooked the fact that only a small fraction of the wheat grown in the country is sold on the market, as the farmers consume most of it themselves.[1]

Sugar offers other examples of exaggerated economic nationalism. Java and Cuba could provide the whole world with excellent cheap sugar, but many other countries less favoured in climate and soil were determined to grow their own sugar, irrespective of cost.

At the beginning of September 1928, if not indicated otherwise, the internal prices of sugar, wholesale per 100 kg., expressed in Austrian schilling, were:—[2]

Cuba, c.i.f. New York	38·60[3]
Java, caf. Ind.	45·45[3]
Austria	76
Germany	87·36
England	90·09
United States	92·41
Poland	109·04
Czechoslovakia	120·0
France	135·98
Hungary	138·72
Roumania	141·27
Yugoslavia	152·40
Italy	240·18

The United States Government in 1938 embarked on a policy of export subsidies. In the fiscal year ending June 1939, 94 million bushels of wheat were sold abroad at an average price of 29 cents a bushel, as compared with a farm price of 55·3 cents. Cf. H. W. Arndt, *The Economic Lessons of the Nineteen-Thirties*, 1944, p. 88.

[1] Hevesy, p. 109, and Basch, p. 95, where a description of the further development of wheat policy in Yugoslavia can be found.

[2] Cf. H. Kallbrunner, *Die Landwirtschaft der mitteleuropäischen Staaten*, 1930, p. 42.   [3] Annual average.

This table shows that most European States paid double and treble the price which Cuba or Java received for their sugar, and the Danubian States, except Austria, paid particularly high prices. In Italy the price of sugar was altogether fantastic. It may cause surprise that even great sugar-exporting countries like Czechoslovakia had very high prices. But these prices were needed for paying export premiums. At a time when the Czechoslovak home-price for sugar was 120 Austrian schillings the same sugar was sold to Austria at 18 schillings.[1] Czechoslovakia therefore at that time dumped her sugar on foreign markets at one-sixth the inland price. In later years the Czechoslovak inland price was at least three times the export price.

After grievous losses eight States in 1931 signed the Chadbourne Agreement for restricting the production and export of sugar. Under this agreement Cuba by 1934 reduced her output from over 5 million to a little over 2 million tons, and Java hers from 3 million to 700,000. The total output of all restricting countries fell by nearly 7 million tons. But at the same time the rest of the world increased their production by about 4·5 million tons! One-third of this increase came from the United States and their colonies, and the other two-thirds from the British Empire. The agreement was thereby wrecked. In this way arose "a fantastic situation in which the most efficient sugar industries in the world, those in Cuba and Java, have been virtually ruined while consumers the world over are paying enormously more for their sugar than is necessary".[2] Also some of the Danubian States, among them Austria, increased their sugar production, while Czechoslovakia greatly restricted hers.

"The position in 1935 [writes a well-known economist[3]] has become almost incredible. The price of raw sugar at British ports is round about 4s. 6d. per cwt.: home-grown sugar in Great Britain receives a total assistance by the combined effect of the tariff and the subsidy of just under 12s. per cwt.: so that it costs British consumers nearly *three* times as much to grow their own sugar as they might buy it for. Colonial and Domin-

[1] Cf. *Österreichischer Volkswirt*, August 16th, 1930, and January 31st, 1931; cf. also Basch, p. 102, on Czechoslovak prices.
[2] Eugene Staley, *Raw Materials in Peace and War*, 1937, p. 303.
[3] J. W. F. Rowe, *Markets and Men*, 1936, p. 86.

76

ion sugar receive very broadly a preference of nearly 100 per cent., *i.e.*, it costs Great Britain twice as much as if bought in the world market."

Austria must import most of her coal from Poland and Czecho-slovakia, and these countries exploited this situation by charging higher prices to Austria than to other customers. Poland was in 1933 making great efforts to conquer markets which had hitherto bought mainly English coal—for example, in the Mediterranean. The high prices extorted from Austria were used to subsidise the competition with England. This led to the absurd situation that Vienna could sometimes buy Polish coal more cheaply in the port of Trieste than directly from the Polish mines in Upper Silesia, though Upper Silesia is only about 225 miles from Vienna by rail, while the distance Upper Silesia–Trieste–Vienna is about 700 miles by rail, plus about 4,000 miles by sea.

These few instances could easily be multiplied; but they will suffice as illustrations of the fruits of economic nationalism.

10. Economic Nationalism Creates the Mirage of Prosperity

In many countries the evils of Economic Nationalism were for a time obscured by an artificial prosperity which was, however, bound to lead to catastrophe. After the war there was everywhere a great and pressing demand for building. The building of residential houses had been stopped by the exigencies of the war, and this had now to be made good. Besides, numerous public buildings were urgently needed; the spread of motoring required better roads; the increasing use of electricity led to the construction of power-stations and grid systems; the railways and factories had to be repaired and re-equipped. To all this came now the stimulation of building and production by Economic Nationalism. Under the protection of high tariffs factories sprang up like mushrooms, new machinery was installed, and those countries which were able to export machinery and building materials got also large orders from abroad and made great profits. There was also in the new States a great demand for arms and military equipment, partly because of acute tension with their neighbours, partly

[1] Cf. *Österreichischer Volkswirt*, January 14th, 1933.

because of their national aspiration for the rank of a Great Power. This demand enabled Czechoslovakia, for example, to become one of the chief exporters of arms and machines to the other new States.

All these factors created an atmosphere of prosperity, unlimited optimism and over-speculation. It was too easily overlooked that a large part of this demand would soon have to come to an end. Tax-payers could not go on indefinitely financing large building programmes, regardless of economy. The exclusion of foreign goods by tariffs naturally provoked counter-measures against the industries of the excluding country. When a backward country had reached a certain level of industrialisation it could produce many machines and other goods itself and imports were much reduced. The countries which had equipped them with industrial plant were then doubly hit: they lost their export of machines and also that of the goods produced by the machines. The exports of armaments, too, could not be regarded as a permanent source of profit. Every country naturally laid stress on producing its armaments itself, in order to be independent in the event of war.

11. The Fruits of Economic Nationalism

The impact of the world crisis shattered the whole fabric of fictitious prosperity and revealed the true face of Economic Nationalism. But this system was now so deeply rooted in all nations that it was impossible to abandon it, and the Governments were even compelled to carry it to extremes. The collapse of trade, the withdrawal of foreign credits and the flight of capital threatened the stability of the currencies and forced all Danubian States to resort again to the stringent control of their currencies and to restriction of imports. At the Conference of Stresa (1932) it was stated that the Eastern and South-Eastern States owed to the Western States annual interests of 1,335 million S.fr. This amount could only have been paid out of a surplus of their trade with the States with a sound currency. But actually all those countries together showed no surplus, but a deficit of several hundred millions. The Danubian States were therefore forced to throttle imports to the utmost, and most of them had also to suspend the transfer of amounts owed to foreign creditors and to introduce blocked accounts. Soon the peak of Economic Nationalism was reached through the adoption of the principle of barter trade. Every country was to buy only as much from another country as that country bought from it, so that the claims of both sides could be compensated without any need for payment in money. A milder form was that of fixing a relation between exports and imports so that only a small surplus had to be settled in money. This system of barter had a devastating influence on international trade. Under it a country could not buy what it wanted, or in the best market, but had to take what the other country was able, or willing, to sell, and often on unfavourable terms. The consequence of this system was an increasing disorganisation of trade relations and a grave deterioration of the whole financial structure.[1]

No less fatal were the political consequences. The combination of jealousies between nations with bitter internal strife prepared the soil for the growth of Fascism. In the period between the two wars open or veiled dictatorships were established in almost all States of the Danubian area. The Balkanisation of Central Europe was to a large extent the consequence of economic ruin, mass unemployment and the proletarisation of the intellectual middle classes, who, in their exasperation, blamed all their misery upon democracy and became pioneers of Fascism. In Hungary it was a Communist dictatorship and nationalism which led to the establishment of Horthy's regime. The chronic economic malady of Austria paved the way for the triumph of Fascism, and soon afterwards of Hitler. In Czechoslovakia the consequences of Economic Nationalism hit the German population of the large industrial districts with special severity and greatly furthered the Nazi propaganda.

12. The Ruin of Inter-Danubian Trade

A comparison of the trade statistics of the Succession States over the whole period under review has to take account of various devaluations of the currencies and fluctuations in price levels.

---

[1] An excellent description and analysis of this system is given in A. Basch, *The Danube Basin*, etc., 1944.

TRADE BETWEEN THE SUCCESSION STATES

IMPORTS

(In million gold dollars (new))

	From Austria.	From Czecho-slovakia.	From Hun-gary.	From Yugo-slavia.	From Rou-mania.	From Poland.	Sum-mary.	Total imports for world.
Austria.								
1928	—	142	67	32	35	72	348	772
1935	—	29	21	15	16	14	95	227
Czechoslovakia.								
1928	71	—	43	23	27	63	227	960
1935	13	—	6	15	11	11	56	281
Hungary.								
1928	58	80	—	18	28	15	199	358
1935	22	6	—	7	16	1	52	118
Yugoslavia.								
1928	41	42	16	—	6	6	111	233
1935	10	12	2	—	2	1	27	83
Roumania.								
1928	38	48	15	3	—	14	118	331
1935	10	13	6	1	—	2	32	97
Poland.								
1928	42	40	8	2	7	—	99	638
1935	8	7	1	2	1	—	19	163
Summary.								
1928	250	352	149	78	103	170	1,002	3,292
1935	63	67	36	40	46	29	281	969

EXPORTS

	To Austria.	To Czecho-slovakia.	To Hun-gary.	To Yugo-slavia.	To Rou-mania.	To Poland.	Sum-mary.	Total exports to world.
Austria.								
1928	—	66	45	40	31	29	211	526
1935	—	12	18	10	11	7	58	169
Czechoslovakia.								
1928	156	—	74	47	44	44	365	1,061
1935	32	—	6	13	16	11	78	309
Hungary.								
1928	83	47	—	16	13	8	167	244
1935	25	6	—	3	7	1	42	133
Yugoslavia								
1928	35	17	17	—	2	3	74	192
1935	13	13	5	—	—	2	33	93
Roumania.								
1928	31	20	26	5	—	6	88	273
1935	19	9	12	2	—	1	43	146
Poland.								
1928	59	56	8	5	10	—	138	476
1935	11	10	1	2	2	—	26	175
Summary.								
1928	364	206	170	113	100	90	1,043	2,772
1935	100	50	42	30	36	22	280	1,025

The Statistical Bureau of the League of Nations has, however, calculated for certain years the value of imports and exports of all countries in new U.S.A. gold dollars (1 new dollar=0·59 old).[1] The table on p. 80 shows the trade of the Succession States for the years 1928 and 1935. The year 1928 formed, together with 1929, the peak of the boom period; and the year 1935 was in a large part of the world the first year after the great depression which showed approximately normal conditions. In this year in Great Britain, for example, the general level of employment was 99·2 and the index of industrial production 105·8 (on basis of 1929). Among the Succession States only Hungary and Roumania had in 1935 reached the level of 1929, while the other States were still far below it. The years following 1935, however, were too much under the influence of great armament production, stimulated by the menace of Hitlerism, to be comparable with normal years.

The figures for 1935 show the terrific destruction of trade wrought by the world crisis. Even when the crisis had passed in most countries of Europe, the Danubian States lagged far behind on the way to recovery. In 1935 their total imports amounted in money value to only 29% of the imports of 1928, and the exports to only 37% of 1928 exports. The decrease in weight was less, as prices had fallen. If we assume an average fall in prices of 20%, the reduction in imports would be about 64% and that in exports about 54%. Total trade (imports plus exports) fell in money value to about 33% and in volume to about 41%.

Trade between the six countries decreased even more quickly than total trade. This resulted in a constant reduction in the share of the trade between the Succession States in total trade. (Cf. table on page 82.)

The tables show all trade between two States from two sides. The export of one State to the other appears also as import in the statistics of the latter, but the two figures are usually not the same, since different countries have different methods of ascertaining trade values, and also for other reasons. It is advisable therefore to take account of the estimates of both sides.

The figures of the first two tables for 1928 throw some light also upon the disharmonies in the commercial relations between the Succession States. Austria, in particular, shows a very high trade

[1] Cf. *The Network of World Trade*, published by the League of Nations, 1942.

deficit which has been much discussed. The invisible assets in her Balance of Payments were certainly not sufficient to cover this deficit. On the other hand, Czechoslovakia had a great trade surplus, especially in her trade with the Succession States. To Austria she exported more than double the amount which she bought from that country, which was largely due to the difference in the levels of tariffs.

THE TRADE BETWEEN THE SIX SUCCESSION STATES AMOUNTED TO PER CENT. OF TOTAL TRADE [1]

	1922.	1928.	1935.
Austria.	%	%	%
Imports	44·9	45·1	41·8
Exports	51·3	40·1	34·3
Czechoslovakia.			
Imports	21·1	23·6	19·9
Exports	41·3	34·4	25·2
Hungary.			
Imports	67·5	55·6	44·1
Exports	76·9	68·4	31·6
Yugoslavia.			
Imports	—	47·6	32·5
Exports	—	38·5	35·5
Roumania.			
Imports	44·4 [2]	35·6	33·0
Exports	35·4	32·2	29·4
Poland.			
Imports	—	15·5	11·7
Exports	—	28·9	14·9
Total.			
Imports	—	30·4	29·0
Exports	—	37·6	27·3

[1] The figures for 1922 are taken from the League of Nations publication, *Memorandum on the Balance of Payments and Foreign Trade Balances, 1926–1927*, II (1927). [2] Without trade with Yugoslavia.

The degree of protectionism can be traced if the national income per head is compared with imports per head. The following table gives some significant data.[3] All data refer to 1928–1929, and are expressed in new gold dollars, and are per head of the population.

The table on p. 83 shows that Czechoslovakia was the richest of the three countries, but bought much less from abroad, and in

[3] The National Income figures are taken from a publication of the League of Nations.

particular from the other Succession States, than did the poorer countries. As regards wholly manufactured goods, Czechoslovakia imported less than one-half of what Austria imported, and as regards goods of other Succession States less than one-third.

1928–29 (in million gold dollars (new))

	National income.	Total imports.	Imports from Danubian countries.	Imports of manufactures.
Austria . .	267	117	52·7	46·3
Czechoslovakia	309	66	15·5	19·9
Hungary .	202	41·6	23·1	—

13. INTER-DANUBIAN TRADE FALLS TO ONE-SIXTH OF PRE-WAR AMOUNT

The shrinkage in trade between the Succession States is particularly striking if the amount of trade before and after the war is compared. In 1925 the experts of the League of Nations, Mr. Layton and Prof. Rist, estimated that seven years after the end of the war the exports of Austria and Czechoslovakia to Hungary were reduced to 40%. In the following years the destruction of trade between the Danubian States increased yet further.

The statistics available make it possible to compare at least the trade between two groups of countries: Austria, Czechoslovakia and Poland (called here Group A), and Hungary, Roumania and Yugoslavia (called here Group B). The bulk of Group A was formerly the Austrian half of the Empire, and that of Group B the Hungarian half. After the war certain territories were added to, and taken from, each group. The pre-war trade of old Roumania, old Servia and Russian-Poland must, therefore, be added to the Inter-State trade between former Austria and Hungary.[1] Furthermore, certain territories were, through the Peace Treaties, transferred from one group to the other and to Italy. But these alterations were of very little importance for our purpose, because these territories were all small and backward and had little

[1] The so-called Inter-State trade (*Zwischenverkehr*) showed the trade between the two halves of the Empire, though there was no customs barrier between them.

external trade, and because the additions and losses almost completely cancelled out.[1]

Taking the average of the years 1911, 1912 and 1913, the territories which after the war formed Austria, Czechoslovakia and Poland imported from the territories of the later Hungary, Roumania and Yugoslavia goods to the value of 1,478 million gold Crowns, or, expressed in new dollars, 508 million dollars. They exported to the same group goods to the value of 1,671 million gold Crowns or 574 million new dollars. In 1935 the imports had shrunk to 88 million new dollars and the exports to 79 million dollars. *The total trade decreased from 1,082 million dollars to 167 million dollars, or to 15·5% of its former amount.*

The decrease would appear still greater if it were possible to isolate the trade of the two great industrial territories of Czechoslovakia and Austria, since Poland naturally had little trade with the agrarian countries of the south-east. It must further be considered that in the years 1911–1913 the Balkan wars, the grave tension between Russia and Austria-Hungary, the mobilisation of large parts of their armies and a commercial depression reduced trade between the West and the East. *Nevertheless, the exchange of products between the two great areas was more than six times that of 1935.* In this year, moreover, the Austrian wholesale price index was still 10% above the pre-war level, and the trade of 1935 would have to be reduced by 10% to make it strictly comparable with pre-war figures.

14. Restriction of Migrations

Economic Nationalism restricts not merely the exchange of goods between countries, but also that of labour and capital. Before the war both emigration to overseas countries and internal migrations played a great rôle. After the war both movements were much restricted, and there cannot be any doubt that this had

[1] The economic weight of each of those territories can be expressed in percentages of the national income of former Austria or Hungary, according to the calculations of Fellner and Waizner. Group A received 10·1% and lost 10·6%, expressed in percentages of the Austrian income. Group B received 10% and lost 18·69% in percentages of the Hungarian income, which amounted to about half of the Austrian. This difference was, however, more than counterbalanced by certain other territorial gains of Roumania and Servia (Bessarabia, Macedonia, etc.), which are allowed for in post-war trade statistics.

a substantial share in aggravating the world crisis and unemployment. The United States led in cutting down immigration, and most other States followed with manifold restrictions on the entry of foreigners seeking admission for permanent settlement, excluding aliens from the labour market, or at least from remunerative occupations. Before the war, moreover, there was also a considerable movement of seasonal workers within Austria-Hungary and between parts of the Empire and neighbouring States.

These migrations were a great help to the rural workers and poor peasants of backward and over-populated territories. They obtained work at much higher wages than they could ever have got in their native land, and could save considerable amounts, which were partly remitted to their families at home. In former Austria-Hungary the annual remittances of emigrants who had settled in America amounted to several hundred million K.[1] Moreover, the new environment had a great influence in raising the standard of life, technical efficiency and cultural outlook of the immigrants. Hundreds of thousands of them returned to their homelands, and spent their savings on buying a farm or setting up a business, where they often introduced improved methods which they had learned in America. In many cases these people became pioneers of technical and cultural progress in their homelands.

In the ideology of nationalism, however, the benefit of individuals is considered less important than an increase in the number of the nation. A numerous population is regarded as the symbol of national greatness. The German nationalists, for instance, bitterly complained that the Germans who had found a new home overseas abandoned their German nationality and became loyal citizens of their new country. Italian and Slav nationalists shared this feeling in regard to their emigrants. Dr. Hubert Ripka, at that time Minister of State in the Czechoslovak Foreign Office, published in 1944 a pamphlet in which he declared that after the war the Czechoslovak Government would expel several millions of Sudeten Germans and Hungarians from their homelands which had been incorporated in Czechoslovakia. In defence of this policy he said :—

[1] Cf. the figures in Fellner, *Volkseinkommen Oesterreichs und Ungarns* in *Statistische Monatsschrift*, 1916, pp. 581, 591.

"I cannot refrain from indignation when I recall that no indignant protests were to be heard when, not so very long ago, hundreds of thousands of Polish, Czech, Slovak, Magyar or Yugoslav land-workers who were eking out a miserable existence in their own countries were compelled every year to leave their native countries and to emigrate overseas and there, in foreign lands, to struggle to found a new existence at the price of the loss of their nationality."

The severe restriction of immigration in the overseas countries, which was largely caused by the growth of nationalism there, did not therefore displease the nationalists in the emigrant countries. But it certainly contributed greatly to the increase of unemployment, misery and discontent in certain European countries.

15. NATIONALISM AND FOREIGN CAPITAL

The economic difficulties of the Danubian countries were to a very great extent due to their lack of sufficient capital. The industrialised countries, especially Austria, suffered from widespread unemployment and the agricultural countries from over-population and the technical backwardness of agricultural production. The improvement of these conditions would have required the investment of vast amounts of capital at a rate of interest which the countries could afford. But the internal capital had largely been destroyed as a direct or indirect result of the war. Enormous amounts of capital had been invested in war loans, which after the war became completely worthless. In the first post-war years all the Danubian countries experienced long periods of inflation which reduced the value of their currencies to almost nothing. Czechoslovakia alone succeeded in stopping this process, thereby salvaging at least a sixth of the monetary value, and attracting large amounts of capital from Austria. Inflation everywhere destroyed most of the liquid capital, though it also wiped out debts. The rise of Economic Nationalism aggravated the shortage of capital in various ways. On the one hand, it created a big additional demand for capital through the foundation of many new industries owing to stimulation by high tariffs. On the other hand, it entirely destroyed, or greatly reduced, the value of existing industries, which were cut off from their markets or had to face increased competition. Before the war the Vienna banks were the most efficient organ in providing all parts of Austria-Hungary with capital on advantageous conditions. They formed a sort of financial pool backed by all the resources of the Danubian States and enjoying the highest credit abroad. In this way even backward regions could obtain comparatively cheap credit. In the post-war period this whole banking system gradually broke down, inflicting on Austria a loss of about 3,500 million schillings.

In addition, after the war came many legislative and administrative measures and tendencies which made the creation of new capital increasingly difficult. In Austria before the war total public expenditure amounted to about 13% of the taxable national income. In 1927 the share of public revenues in the national income was in Austria about 31% or more, in Czechoslovakia between 20% and 26%, according to different estimates of the national income.[1] In the post-war period, moreover, the greater incomes, and capital income in particular, had in various ways to bear a considerably larger share than before in total taxation. The rent-restricting policy, which in Austria was especially rigorous, for a long time practically expropriated the house-owners, or at least considerably reduced their income. In several countries large estates were expropriated for very small compensation. The cost of industrial production rose through the increase in wages, social burdens and the rate of interest. All these and other factors contributed to the slackening of the formation of capital.

In the course of the great depression all the Danubian States had to face grave financial and economic difficulties which led to a new depreciation of their money. At that time, moreover, a deficit in the budget and the devaluation of the currency had come to be regarded in wide and powerful circles as a justifiable measure of "controlled economy". This laxity in the attitude to financial stability had already for a long time been feared by the owners of capital. It had rendered them averse from tying up their capital in long-term investments. Foreign capitalists in particular were

[1] The calculation was made by me, and formed the subject of my address to the Society of Austrian Economists on January 18th, 1927.

in most cases willing to give only short-term credits, and they also charged considerable premiums for the risk involved in investing money in the Danubian countries. Credit in foreign currency was cheaper than that in the Danubian currencies, which involved the risk of depreciation. The large amount of short-term foreign credits rendered the financial structure of economic activities extremely labile. When the great slump came the credits were hastily withdrawn, and this led to a terrible catastrophe.

The whole situation was mainly the outcome of the war and the post-war instability of political and economic conditions—both of them the consequences of Nationalism. The mentality of nationalism in regard to economic life and to international obligations contributed to the general lack of stability and confidence. The ideology of nationalism subordinates economic interests to national power and prestige, and puts one's own nation high above others. The attitude of nationalists towards foreign capitalists combines, therefore, contempt for the mean, unheroic way of making money by business (instead of by conquest), and contempt for the foreigner. Economically backward countries, or such as were impoverished by war, would naturally profit greatly through the influx of foreign capital, and through the co-operation of foreign experts in building up, or rebuilding, the economic structure. But nationalism is characterised by a very irrational mentality, and it is not always the case that nationalists welcome and encourage the participation of foreign capital and foreign entrepreneurs, technicians or financial experts in the economic life of their country. The most active elements in nationalism are mainly certain badly paid sections of the intellectuals, the officials and the military, who are naturally jealous of the commercial classes, but they are joined by elements from all classes seeking to exploit the powerful appeal of nationalism for their own purposes, especially by industrialists hoping to profit by high tariffs.

Roumania is a striking example of nationalistic hostility towards foreign capital. The country is rich in natural resources, and could be very prosperous but for her lack of capital and for her most unfortunate political conditions. The curse of Roumania has been the unparalleled corruption of her politicians and administrators, coupled with national megalomania. When, after the last war, the victors worked out the peace settlement, Roumania was very generously endowed at the expense of the vanquished nations, so that more than a quarter of her population was composed of minorities. Nevertheless she was not satisfied; her representative, Mr. Bratianu, trenchantly attacked the Great Powers, and left Paris as a demonstration against them. His Government refused to sign the Peace Treaty and the treaty relative to the protection of minorities, and behaved in such a recalcitrant way that relations with the Allies became exceedingly strained, and these finally addressed a sort of ultimatum to Roumania ordering her to withdraw her troops to the frontiers fixed by them. The three brothers Bratianu and their so-called Liberal Party were in power for the greater part of the post-war period, and exhibited in their policy a nationalist animosity towards foreigners and foreign capital which had a disastrous effect on Roumania's economic and political development.[1] They aimed at the complete exclusion of foreign capital so necessary for Roumania, and proclaimed the slogan: "By ourselves alone!" The country was to become self-sufficient, its industries were to be rapidly developed by the introduction of the highest tariffs in Europe, the mineral wealth was declared national property, and the activity of foreigners was restricted in various ways. The introduction of foreign capital was admitted only in the case of the oilfields, and even then under the most exacting conditions which discouraged new drillings and led to a decrease of output.[2]

This policy sprang partly from genuine nationalism, partly from the wish of the Bratianu Party to secure complete control of Roumania's economic resources for their own profit. Public and private interests are closely interwoven in every ideology, and often cannot be separated. At all events, this policy was ruinous to the wealth, the public morality and the reputation of Roumania, and in particular to the farming population. In the elections of 1928 the Liberals were completely defeated by the National Peasant Party, which opposed their Economic Nationalism, the hostility

[1] Cf. George Clenton Logio, *Roumania, its History, Politics and Economics*, 1932. This book, by an English expert, gives abundant proofs of the hostility to foreign capital and of the appalling corruption prevalent in politics and administration.

[2] Cf. the two reports by the Royal Institute of Foreign Affairs: *South-Eastern Europe*, 2nd ed., 1939, p. 68, and *South-Eastern Europe, A Brief Survey*, 1940, p. 95.

to foreign capital, the excessive tariffs and the appalling corruption connected with the Bratianu system. The new Government concluded two foreign loans and tried to introduce a policy of reforms and the strengthening of democracy. But it also allowed the former Crown Prince Carol to ascend the throne, and soon lost power through the rising tide of extreme nationalism and Fascism. In 1932 Roumania was in a state of complete financial ruin, and was compelled to appeal to France for help. A mission of financial experts, under the distinguished economist Prof. Rist, was sent there to investigate the situation and to devise means of rehabilitation. The work of this mission, though of the greatest value to the country, provoked an outburst of xenophobia. The Press, with a few exceptions, protested against this interference in the internal affairs of the State as an affront to the national dignity, and demanded that Roumania should stop paying interest on her external debt. When later two delegates of the League of Nations arrived for further investigations the most widely read paper published a leading article entitled "The Day of Shame".

The problem of foreign capital played a great part also in the politics of Poland. A considerable amount of foreign capital was invested in Polish industries before the country became independent, and later some further capital flowed in, though much too little. The public finances and the development of the natural resources urgently needed foreign capital, and the Government would have welcomed large credits under adequate guarantees. The foreign creditors, however, were for a long time deterred by the internal conditions of the country. Poland after the war was suffering from terrible financial disorganisation and chaotic currency conditions which paralysed economic reconstruction. She could have stabilised the budget and the monetary value by foreign credits, which, however, were obtainable only under the condition that the League of Nations should control the financial and economic policy, as it was doing in various other countries. But this very reasonable condition aroused the fierce opposition of Polish nationalism. The nationalists considered financial control by the League of Nations an intolerable infringement of national sovereignty. They proclaimed that Poland would overcome her difficulties without foreign help. But this experiment failed. The second inflation and the helplessness of the democratic forces led to the rise of Fascism, and, in 1926, to the establishment of Pilsudski's dictatorship. The new regime then carried out the stabilisation of the currency with the help of foreign loans.[1]

[1] Cf. Ferdynand Zweig, *Poland between Two Wars*, 1944, pp. 39–53, 120, 150.

IV. THE BALANCE-SHEET OF ECONOMIC NATIONALISM

A. CHANGES IN THE STRUCTURE OF THE POPULATION

1. Distribution according to Economic Branches

THE ECONOMIC structure of a country is primarily expressed in the distribution of the productive forces according to the main branches of economic activities. For this purpose the statistics of most countries distinguish the active and the passive population, understanding by "active" those engaged in occupations. The development of the active population is assumed to be the safest index of that of the productive forces. Unfortunately, however, a comparative study like ours is confronted here with peculiar difficulties. The statistics of different countries define the term "active population" in such different ways that any comparison is beset with pitfalls.[1] Even the same country, moreover, has frequently changed its definition, so that it is not always safe to compare its various censuses. The attempt has sometimes been made to make comparable the data of different countries, or of different censuses of the same country, by adjusting the figures to the same definition. But this, too, has often been misleading.[2]

For many purposes the best way is to compare the total number

---

[1] Cf. *Studies and Reports on Statistical Methods*, published by the League of Nations, Part I, 1938 ("Statistics of the Gainfully-Occupied Population, Definitions and Classifications Recommended by the Committee of Statistical Experts").

[2] The German Statistical Office, for example, has re-calculated the statistics of active populations for all countries according to the German classification, and published the result in its Yearbooks. But even this very useful compilation is not free from errors. It shows, for instance, that in Austria from 1923 to 1934 the population active in agriculture fell from 39·9% to 31·7%. This great decline would seem surprising. But closer examination of the Austrian statistics makes it clear that the Census of 1923 classed the housewives of peasants as family members aiding the head of the family in his work, while the Census of 1934 introduced a separate category "housewives". The whole difference is due to this change in classification.

of people connected with an occupation, whether active or passive, at least as long as the relation between these two categories does not change considerably.

TOTAL POPULATION ACCORDING TO OCCUPATIONS

	Agriculture, forestry, etc.	Industries, mining, handicrafts.	Commerce, transport, banking, catering.	Public service, liberal professions, Army.	Domestics.	Others.[1]
Austria.	%	%	%	%	%	%
1923	29·9	33·5	16·1	6·0	3·3	11·1
1934	27·2	31·1	15·1	6·7	2·8	17·0
Czecho-slovakia.						
1921	39·6	33·4	10·6	5·6	—	10·8
1931	34·6	34·9	13·0	6·2	—	11·3
Hungary.						
1920	55·7	20·6	9·5	6·3	2·2	5·7
1930	51·8	23·0	9·3	5·8	2·3	7·8
Poland.						
1921	63·8	15·4	9·5	—	—	—
1931	61·3	19·3	9·7	—	—	—
Roumania (active).						
1930	78·2	10·0	—	—	—	—
Yugoslavia (active).						
1921	78·9	9·9	4·3	3·8	—	3·1
1931	76·6	11·0	4·8	4·1	—	3·5

[1] The category "others" includes a certain percentage of non-classified, or casual, labourers. The bulk, however, consists of people forming a separate household but without occupation, such as retired people, rentiers, those living on assistance, students, inmates of institutions, etc.

These data show everywhere a decline in the numbers engaged in agriculture, and an increase (except in Austria) in those engaged in industries. There was also a widespread increase in commerce, transport, public service and the liberal professions.

2. THE SOCIAL STRATIFICATION OF THE ACTIVE POPULATION

The distribution according to the main branches of economic activities must be considered in conjunction with the distribution according to social classes. The following tables show the social stratification in Austria, Czechoslovakia and Hungary.

(In '000's)

	Inde-pendent.	Family members helping.	Salaried Employees.	Workers.	Total.
Agriculture, Fores-try . . .	291	354	11	348	1,004
Industries, Mining	166	8	104	702	1,060
Commerce, Trans-port . .	150	17	177	223	568
Liberal professions	28	—	92	25	146
Public Administra-tion, Churches .	—	—	19	63	82
Army . . .	—	—	37	—	—
Domestic service .	14	—	7	158	179
Others . .	1	—	11	81	95

Czechoslovakia, 1930. Active Population [1]

(In '000's)

	Inde-pendent.	Family members helping.	Salaried Employees.	Workers.	Total.
Agriculture . .	887	1,002	13	773	2,675
Industries, Mining .	312	22	118	2,071	2,523
Commerce, Trans-port . . .	225	44	142	438	849
Liberal professions	29	—	119	47	195
Public Administra-tion . . .	—	—	75	66	141
Army . . .	—	—	10	154	164
Domestic service .	14	—	—	321	335
Unspecified . .	—	—	—	100	100

[1] The data had to be re-arranged to make them to a certain extent comparable. The category "Other professions" was omitted (except the unspecified workers) because the Czechoslovak statistics include in it large numbers of people who cannot be said to have any profession, such as people living on the interest of capital or on assistance, students, etc. On the other hand, family members helping the head—for example, the wives of peasants—and domestics are excluded in the Czechoslovak statistics from the "active population", and domestic servants are shown as belonging to the same branch as their employers —for example, the cook of a banker as belonging to the occupation "banking", though not as an active member. In the above table we have included in the active population family members helping the father and domestics, and have shown all domestics under "domestic services", together with certain categories doing personal services without being servants.

	Independents.	Family members helping.	Salaried Employees.	Workers.	Total.
Agriculture . .	700	537	6	788	2,031
Industries, Mining .	247	8	44	653	952
Commerce, Banking, Transport .	93	11	79	157	340
Public service, Liberal professions .	20	—	118	58	196
Army . . .	—	—	6	36	42
Labourers, not specified . .	—	—	—	61	61
Domestics . .	—	—	—	177	177

If the family members helping on the farm or in the business are added to the independents, the social structure looks like this:—

	Independents.	Salaried Employees.	Workers.
	%	%	%
Austria . . .	33	14	52
Czechoslovakia . .	36	7	56
Hungary . . .	42	7	51

The large proportion of clerks in Austria is due to some extent to the part played by commerce, though it must be borne in mind that in 1934 the traditional preponderance of Vienna as a centre of banking and international trade had already disappeared through the breakdown of all the large banks and the decline of international trade in the great crisis. The percentage of employees in commerce may therefore perhaps be a sign of maldistribution. The number of salaried employees, however, may have been partly due to the fact that in Austria the labour organisations succeeded in securing for certain categories of manual workers the fixed position of a salaried employee.

It must further not be overlooked that in many cases there were no hard-and-fast demarcations between the classes. Many small peasants were also working part of their time on large estates or in forests or factories, or exercised some handicraft in their cottages.

Numerous small independents voted for the Left, and numerous workers for the Right. In Austria, where the Socialist Party was especially well organised, they polled at the last elections in 1930 43% of all the votes cast. In Czechoslovakia in 1935 the declared Left parties together polled about 36%.

The vast majority of the independents were peasants and adult members of peasant families. The peasant problem will be discussed later. The existence of a large number of small independent farmers, artisans and traders is particularly significant in regard to the question of the formation of capital. It is obvious that the division of the land among numerous small-holders, and an excess of small traders, do not encourage the accumulation of capital for large-scale undertakings. These classes will on the whole save less than large entrepreneurs of the same productive capacity, and their savings will be largely frittered away in investments of little value for the general economic development, or may even be hoarded by being "put away in a stocking", or in similar ways.

3. THE ECONOMIC DEVELOPMENT IN AUSTRIA

The changes in the economic and social structure of Austria require some further remarks. The Austrian Censuses of 1923 and 1934 are in some respects not strictly comparable, and for certain purposes a comparison of the Censuses of 1910 and 1934 is preferable (see tables on p. 97).

This comparison indicates significant tendencies in Austria's post-war development. In the twenty-four years from 1910 to 1934 the population remained almost stationary. The numbers employed in agriculture and industries decreased, but those engaged in commerce, transport and the liberal professions increased. This latter fact is surprising, since Vienna's position as the centre of banking and commerce for all the Danubian countries was destroyed after the war, and internal trade showed little increase. The rise in the numbers engaged in non-producing occupations must therefore be interpreted as a sign that agriculture and industries were unable to provide sufficient employment, so that ever more people were compelled to become small traders or to enter some liberal profession or public service. The decrease in domestics was largely due to the impoverishment of Austria, but also to smaller families and a greater desire for independence.

	1910.	1934.	The section of the population.	
			Increased.	Decreased.
	%	%	%	%
Agriculture . . .	35·2	32·9	—	11·3
Industries, Mining, Handicrafts . .	36·4	37·4	—	2·2
Commerce, Transport .	16·1	18·2	6·9	—
Public service, Liberal professions . .	7·2	8·1	4·3	—
Domestic services . .	4·9	3·4	—	32·8
Economic occupations together . . .	100	100	—	5·0
Total absolute figures .	5,902,000	5,608,000	—	294,000

[1] From the official publication *Die Ergebnisse der österreichischen Volkszählung von 1934* (1935), Part I.

Others (Absolute Figures)
(In '000's)

	1910.	1934.	Increased.	Decreased.
			%	%
Occupied without specification . . .	64	156	145·6	—
Preparing for an occupation		80		
Without occupation .	680	909 } 996	46·4	—
Without designation of occupation . .		7		
Total population .	6,646	6,760	1·7	—

A further symptom of the general deterioration of economic conditions is the big increase in workers without designation of a specific employment—probably largely unemployed or casually employed—and in the number of people without an occupation or preparing for an occupation. Many parents left their sons or

97

daughters at school or in some training because they could not find employment for them.

Roughly speaking, one may say that the population belonging to the great sections of economic and cultural activities decreased in twenty-four years by about 300,000, and that the adult population without an occupation or with an uncertain occupation increased by about 400,000.

This decrease in economic forces was, however, to some extent counterbalanced by a change in the age-structure. The high birth rate before the war, and the low birth rate during the war and after, had the effect that in the post-war period the percentage of children in the population was smaller and the percentage of middle-aged and old people higher than before. The age-group from 20 to 59, which is most suited for productive work, and the old people over 60, relatively increased.

TERRITORY OF POST-WAR AUSTRIA

Age-groups.	1910.	1923.	1934.
	%	%	%
From 0 to 19 . . .	39·1	34·7	29·5
From 20 to 59 . . .	51·5	55·1	58·2
60 and over . . .	9·4	10·1	12·2

These figures are of great significance for the problem of unemployment, and will be discussed later in connection with that question.

4. AUSTRIA—A PARASITE OR A WORKER?

In the first years after the First World War the view was very widespread that Austria's particular distress was due to her lack of productive workers. Some of her neighbours spread the propaganda story that Vienna had been but a big parasite battening on the fruits of the toil of subject nations. It was contended that new Austria had inherited an enormous number of officials and other unproductive elements, while the number of productive workers was too small. The idea of the preponderance of unproductive elements was, however, also put forward, though in a different form, by propagandists for the union of Austria with Germany. They pointed out that Vienna had hitherto mainly lived not on her production but on international trade and commerce and on her position as an administrative, financial and cultural centre, and that the new national States around her were out to destroy all these assets, thereby rendering her incapable of surviving. Austria was frequently compared to a head cut off from its limbs.

These views fostered an atmosphere of paralysing pessimism. They were for the first time closely examined in some of my writings, and I proved by statistical data that the territory of the Austrian Republic had before the war by no means a particularly high percentage of economically unproductive population.[1] The numbers of officials and of the members of the liberal professions were not very different from those in other comparable countries, and, moreover, a large proportion of the officials were employed in productive enterprises, like the State railways, the State tobacco factories, etc., or in schools and other cultural institutions. Statistics show that in the period immediately after the 1914–1918 War the percentage of productive population was greater in Austria than in almost any other European country. Only the Soviet Union and four small Baltic and Balkan States showed a still higher proportion. The reason for this high percentage of working population was that the proportion of women engaged in occupations was much greater in Austria than in most other countries, and that Austria had a particularly high percentage of persons employed in commerce and transport which was surpassed only by the two foremost commercial countries, Britain and Holland. But Austria also possessed large industrial resources. The territory had before the First World War more industrial workers than Bohemia, though that country had then 400,000 more inhabitants than later Austria. True, Bohemia was much richer in large-scale industries, while the workshops of Austria were mainly of small or medium size.

The statement that Austria's plight was due to her large proportion of unproductive population was therefore merely a slogan of anti-Austrian propaganda not founded on facts. But it must

[1] Cf. Friedrich Hertz, *Ist Oesterreich lebensfähig?*, 1921, and *Zahlungsbilanz und Lebensfähigkeit Oesterreichs*, 1925. The second book gives many statistics and other information referring to the questions treated above, which have not been inserted here, because they can easily be looked up in that book. It forms volume 167, part II, of the *Schriften des Vereins für Socialpolitik*.

not be overlooked that the percentage of the working population in the total subsequently decreased. My own calculation shows for the period 1923–1934 a decline in the active population from 53·6% to 48·7%. Moreover, in the post-war period a large proportion of the active population was not actually employed. Persistent unemployment was the cause of the fact that many juveniles could not find a post, and were even refused an apprenticeship. This obviously contributed to the decrease of the active population.

5. Tendencies towards Over-Population and Depopulation

The development of the productive force of a country depends largely on the increase or decrease of its population, which to a great extent determines its working and purchasing capacity. The following table shows the movement of the birth and death rates in the Danubian countries:—[1]

	1911–1913.	1921–1923.	1926–1930.	1931–1935.	1936.	1937.	1938.
Austria.							
Birth rate	24·9	22·2	17·6	14·4	13·1	12·8	13·9
Death rate	18·8	15·8	14·4	13·5	13·2	13·4	14·0
Difference	6·1	6·4	3·2	0·9	−0·1	−0·6	−0·1
Czecho-slovakia.							
Birth rate	29·6	27·1	23·2	19·6	17·4	17·2	17·6
Death rate	20·4	16·1	15·3	13·8	13·3	13·3	13·5
Difference	9·2	9·0	7·9	5·8	4·1	3·9	4·1
Hungary.							
Birth rate	34·3	29·4	26·0	22·4	20·4	20·2	19·5
Death rate	22·9	19·9	17·0	15·8	14·3	14·2	14·3
Difference	11·4	9·5	9·0	6·6	6·1	6·0	5·2
Poland.							
Birth rate	37·8	34·7	32·2	27·6	26·2	24·9	24·4
Death rate	21·7	18·5	16·8	14·6	14·2	14·0	13·8
Difference	16·2	16·2	15·4	13·0	12·0	10·9	10·6
Yugoslavia.							
Birth rate	—	35·0	34·2	31·8	28·9	27·7	—
Death rate	—	20·2	20·0	17·9	16·0	15·8	—
Difference	—	14·8	14·2	13·9	12·9	11·9	—
Roumania.							
Birth rate	42·6	37·9	35·2	32·8	31·5	30·8	29·6
Death rate	24·7	23·0	21·2	20·6	19·8	19·3	19·2
Difference	17·9	14·9	14·0	12·2	11·7	11·5	10·4

[1] *Statistical Yearbook of the League of Nations.*

These figures confirm the general observation that agricultural, backward and poor countries have a high birth rate, which decreases with the progress of industries, town life and wealth. The first-named countries have also a higher death rate, but in this regard differences between the countries are not so marked as in regard to the birth rates, and the backward countries therefore show also a much greater natural increase in their population. After the war both birth and death rates decreased everywhere, but at different paces.

The greatest change took place in Austria. The birth rate fell in the period between the two wars almost to half, and below the death rate. In the last years of that period the population of Austria was decreasing. The natural decrease shown in the table was enhanced by the surplus of emigration over immigration. In Czechoslovakia and Hungary too the birth rates fell considerably, but these countries still had an increasing population, though the rate of increase was reduced to less than half the former rate. The predominantly agricultural countries—Roumania, Yugoslavia and Poland—show still high birth rates, and their populations are increasing. This tendency constitutes a difficult problem, since large parts of these countries are regarded as already over-populated. Before the dismemberment of Austria-Hungary the pressure of population was alleviated by the migration of large numbers to other parts of the Empire where workers were wanted, or by emigration overseas. But both outlets have since then been practically closed, and it has now become the fashion among economists to recommend the rapid industrialisation of those countries as a remedy against over-population. This suggestion will be considered later.

B. STRUCTURAL CHANGES IN THE AGRARIAN CONDITIONS

1. THE QUESTION OF RURAL OVER-POPULATION IN EASTERN EUROPE

The great crisis which began in the late 'twenties and lasted for years hit the farmers of the Danubian countries with particular severity. The whole of Eastern Europe was afflicted by a devastating slump in the prices of its principal products, causing widespread and persistent distress among the populations and grave disturbances in trade, public finance and currencies. Prominent experts who investigated the problem came to the conclusion that considerable parts of Roumania, Yugoslavia, Bulgaria and Poland were over-populated, at least in the prevailing conditions of primitive farming, lack of capital and credit, and export difficulties. The remedies recommended were rationalisation, a freer commercial policy, emigration and industrialisation.

As this study is focused on three countries not primarily affected by the problem of over-population, we need not enter here into a discussion of its details.[1] It will be sufficient to say that the area and the fertility of arable land could have been greatly increased if the necessary capital for improvements had been obtainable. In Poland, Roumania, Yugoslavia and Hungary large parts of the enormous marshes could have been made into fertile soil by drainage. Other parts of the three latter countries, moreover, could have borne a much higher and more stable yield if the frequent droughts had been counteracted by irrigation. Many other improvements in agricultural efficiency could also have been made, and from a technical point of view it would not have been difficult to increase yields by 100% or more. But the crux of the situation was the extraordinary shortage of capital and credit. Roumania and other States had largely squandered their means on projects of speedy industrialisation and on a policy of economic nationalism in general. The result was that an excessive financial burden was laid upon the farming population, that their opportunities for export to the industrial countries were greatly diminished, and that insufficient means were left for increasing the productivity of agriculture. The political nationalism of those States, moreover, compelled them to devote huge expenditure to armaments and the building up of a big armaments industry. The problem of over-population is therefore to a large extent due to nationalism, partly that of the Succession States, partly that of

[1] Cf. the excellent treatment in Doreen Warriner, *Economics of Peasant Farming*, 1939. Very useful surveys of the agrarian conditions in the Danubian countries are given in O. S. Morgan, *Agricultural Systems of Middle Europe, a Symposium*, 1939, in *South-Eastern Europe, a Political and Economic Survey*, by the Royal Institute of International Affairs, 2nd edition, 1939, and in W. E. Moore, *Economic Demography of Eastern and Southern Europe*, publ. by the L. of N., 1945.

others, in particular the great overseas countries, which by their excessive restriction of immigration deprived the really over-populated parts of South-Eastern Europe of outlets for their surplus population.

Of the remedies mentioned above the need for technical and commercial rationalisation and of a revival of international trade require no further comments here. Industrialisation, too, is most important, but the bitter lessons of the inter-war period should be heeded, and the attempt at enforcing the growth of industries by measures crippling agriculture should not be repeated. It must not be ignored that in large parts of the south-eastern countries the natural and social conditions are not favourable to large-scale industrialisation. They lack coal, iron ore, the pre-conditions of cheap transport, and also certain moral factors, such as a secure reign of law, political and commercial integrity and the mentality indispensable for modern enterprise. The Balkan mentality of economic inertia, violence and corruption is still wide-spread, though there are also promising counter-forces. D. War-riner is certainly right in stressing that the main remedies must be the restoration of a freer exchange of goods between Western and Eastern Europe which precludes any policy of hothouse industrialisation of the East as well as excessive agrarian protectionism in the West. A further need is a return to a policy of freer migration and the encouragement of capital formation.

2. The Rural Exodus in the Western Danubian Countries

Conditions in the western parts of the Danubian area, in particular in Austria and Czechoslovakia, but also in parts of Hungary and certain territories of Yugoslavia and Roumania which formerly belonged to Austria-Hungary, are very different from those in Eastern Europe proper. The Bohemian countries and Austria are highly industrialised and agriculture is on the whole technically advanced and progressive. In these parts there is scarcely any rural over-population. If nevertheless there is a constant migration from the rural to the urban districts, this is not due to a marked pressure of population, but to the attractions of a higher standard of living, of certain advantages enjoyed by the industrial workers, and of the amenities of town life. A rural exodus has for a long time been in operation in many highly developed countries of the world. It is really a world phenomenon connected with fundamental tendencies of modern life. The war of 1914–1918 stimulated this movement, partly by recruiting large numbers of new workers for the war industries and accustoming them to factory work and town life, partly by uprooting many people from their rural soil and habits. After the war the migration from the countryside to the towns often aroused anxiety from the point of view of industrial unemployment. There is no doubt that one of the causes of industrial unemployment was the increase in the number of people seeking work due to the influx of non-industrial elements, among whom were many former agricultural labourers or sons of peasants. It has often been suggested that industrial unemployment should be reduced by checking the rural exodus, and even by inducing urban workers to settle on the land, or at least to produce part of their food on allotments.

In Austria's post-war territory the agricultural population between 1910 and 1934 decreased by 235,778, or by 11·3%. From 1923 to 1934 the decrease was 115,000. Vienna and the other towns showed a considerable surplus of immigrants over emigrants. It was only this influx of migrants from the rural districts which enabled Vienna to maintain her population, since her birth rate was very low, and was outweighed by the death rate.[1]

In the territories now belonging to Czechoslovakia the total agricultural population decreased from 1910 to 1930 by 605,000 or by 10·6%.[2] As in Austria, nearly half of this decrease, or 284,000, occurred in the post-war period (1921–1930). If, however, we regard the three provinces which formerly belonged to the Austrian Empire—namely, Bohemia, Moravia and Silesia—we find that from 1910 to 1930 the agricultural population decreased even more—namely, by 759,000 or by 21·8%, of which 429,000 was the decrease between 1921 and 1930. The backward Eastern provinces therefore had a growing agricultural population, whilst that of the advanced Western ones was rapidly

[1] Cf. the papers by Hecke and Winkler in the *Proceedings of the International Congress on Population*, Paris, 1937.
[2] Cf. on this problem H. Boeker and F. von Bülow, *The Rural Exodus in Czechoslovakia*, published by the International Labour Office and the International Institute of Agriculture, 1935.

declining. The peasants and workers decreased in the three Western provinces in twenty-four years by as much as 30%, but if the family members helping in the farm work are included the decrease in the active population was only 24·2%.

In Hungary the agricultural population did not decrease after the war, and from 1920 to 1930 even showed a slight increase of 1%, while the total population rose by 8·7%. Its proportional share therefore decreased. But in Hungary also there was a considerable migration from the rural to the urban districts. The agricultural population had in this period a surplus of births over deaths amounting to 473,300. Yet less than a tenth—namely, 45,152—remained in agriculture; all the others took up other occupations. The population active in agriculture decreased by about 5%. But the exact number of the active agricultural population is in all countries open to doubt. The large number of wives, sons and daughters assisting the peasant on his farm causes great difficulties of classification, and their registration as "active" has often changed from census to census.

3. THE PEASANT AND THE SOIL

In the Danubian countries the peasants form a very important element of the population. We may roughly call farms up to 10 ha. of cultivated land small peasant holdings, those from 10 to 50 ha. medium-sized farms, and those over 100 ha. estates.[1] The cultivated land comprises arable, vineyards, gardens, meadows and pastures, but no woods. The distribution of the cultivated land in 1930 (after the agrarian reforms) was as follows:—

	Farms up to 10 ha.	10–50 ha.	100 ha. and over.
	%	%	%
Austria . . .	20	46	26
Czechoslovakia . .	43	38	16
Roumania . .	60	25	15
Yugoslavia . .	58	35	4

[1] It would, of course, be more correct to define small, medium and large farms according to the quality of the soil. In a mountainous country like Austria with little good soil a much larger acreage is needed to make a living than in a fertile plain. In Austria "large estate" usually means one over 200 ha. (about 500 acres), while in more fertile countries 100 ha. would be adequate.

In Hungary the farms not exceeding 58 ha. constituted 59% of the cultivated land, and the farms over 115 ha., 43% of all land (including woods). Almost a quarter of the total land was formed by large estates over 1,151 ha.

In Austria the large holdings of more than 100 ha. comprised only 8·8% of the arable and meadows. The rest consisted of alpine pastures, mostly of little fertility. A considerable part of these large blocks of pasture, moreover, was communal property of peasant villages or associations. In comparing the Austrian figures with those for Czechoslovakia, Roumania and Yugoslavia, it must also be remembered that the Austrian farms comprise a much larger proportion of meadows and pastures. On the other hand, in Czechoslovakia the owners of small-holdings are frequently also workers in a factory or engaged in some domestic industry.

A large part of the forests everywhere belongs to big estates owned partly by the State, the Church and similar bodies, and partly by private owners. In most countries a fair share also of the woods belongs to peasants, though as a rule the management in large blocks is much better than in small units. The Austrian conditions may serve as an example. In Austria in 1930 the small peasants (up to 10 ha.) owned 5%, and the medium-sized (10–50 ha.) 24% of the woods. The large estates of over 200 ha. comprised only 6% of the cultivated land, but 57% of the woods, 54% of the uncultivated land (mountain pastures) and 93% of the unproductive land, such as rocks and swamps. Of the total area of forests one-third belonged to the State and other public bodies, as also a large proportion of the mountain pastures. The peasants have, moreover, considerable rights to the use of the land held by big estates (called servitudes), entitling them to an annual quantum of timber, or to grazing for a certain number of cattle, and so on.

These statistics make it clear that in Austria, Czechoslovakia and Roumania the peasants hold most of the cultivated land, while the large estates are important only in regard to the forests. The same holds good of Yugoslavia. Only in Hungary and Poland did the large estates after the war still comprise a considerable part of the cultivated land, though in these countries, too, their share was reduced by the agrarian reforms.

The question whether large, small or medium-sized farms are more advantageous has formed the subject of endless controversies. Each type has its good and bad points, and the question cannot be solved by means of sweeping generalisations, but only with due regard to the natural and social conditions of a specific country or part of a country. The answer depends on soil and climate, on the social structure, financial equipment and political organisation of the territory in question. Moreover, the mentality of the agricultural population is also an important factor of considerable persistence.

4. THE PEASANT MENTALITY

The rural populations of Central and Eastern Europe comprise very different types, which are usually lumped together under the designation of peasants. But this rather obscures the problem why there are such differences in the attitude of the farmers of various countries, though they are all called peasants. In the western parts of the Danubian countries large sections of the peasantry are very progressive and efficient, while others are not; again, other sections are less farmers than industrial workers cultivating some land as a sideline. In the east large masses are mainly labourers on big estates, and show on their own land neither the fitness nor the wish for modern methods of farming. The historical background plays a very great part. The German peasants of Transylvania and the Banat who immigrated centuries ago were always on a much higher level of productivity and civilisation than the Roumanians. There is still a great difference between peasants whose fathers or grandfathers were serfs, or in a serf-like position, and the peasants of Tyrol, who were always freemen, and sent their representatives to the Diet of Tyrol even in the Middle Ages. In certain Slavonic countries the peasants formerly lived in large house communities, each comprising several families of the same descent and inspired by a semi-communistic spirit. Remnants of this system are still extant. It was probably a major factor in preventing the growth of urban centres and of industries.

The word "peasant" does not mean merely a small or medium-sized farmer, but primarily an historical type. The peasant looks upon his farm not as capital designed to yield rent and interest, but as the homestead and the basis of subsistence for himself, his family and his domestics. Up to our time many peasants have maintained the tradition that it is wrong to sell products of the farm, except what is not wanted for the nourishment or clothing of the members of their households. A peasant selling milk or butter would often have found it difficult to get good domestics. Leather, too, boots, cloth, dresses, stockings, etc., were made on the homestead, frequently by itinerant craftsmen. All this has greatly changed in recent times. More and more peasants have assumed a more commercial outlook, they have organised their farms for market production, rationalised their technique and some have even begun to keep books. Nevertheless the old traditions still linger on, and hamper the full development of the striving for the greatest possible money income. It frequently happens that some product comes on the market only when the yield has been especially abundant, and then it appears in many different varieties and qualities, because every peasant sticks to his own way or his local tradition, and produces the quality which he likes, not that which the market wants. Peasants, for example, may prefer fat pork, while the urban consumer wants lean pork; or the peasants grow apples good only for making the cider which they like, but not for the refined taste of townspeople. The old-fashioned peasant will always produce according to his own taste, and often only as much as he and his family can consume. Now an organised trade in some commodity presupposes that there is a regular supply of large homogeneous saleable qualities. If this cannot be secured the trader is bound to lose his money. This is the reason why there is often no organised trade for certain home products and consequently no incentive to regular production for sale.

The attachment of the peasant to the soil often forms an obstacle to industrialisation. In the south-eastern countries the mines and factories were frequently unable to find sufficient workers willing to stay permanently and thereby acquire real skill. Most of the workers stayed for only a short time, and then went back to their farms, in spite of rural over-population. In those countries, moreover, feudal traditions have a strong hold on the minds of the upper and middle classes, making them despise both manual work and commercial gain. The consequence was that industries and trade were mainly run by foreigners or Jews, who were free from that aversion, and also often had better qualifications.

5. The Returns and Financial Conditions of Peasant Farms

The financial conditions of agricultural production, in particular of peasant farming, have been investigated by the Farm Accountancy Institutes, which, following the example of Switzerland, have been formed in many countries. A great number of farmers have been instructed in book-keeping, and the results have been collected, checked and worked up in elaborate statistics illuminating all aspects of agricultural economy. The statistics available in various countries have been compiled in several publications of the International Agricultural Institute in Rome, and have been presented in a comparable form.[1] It must, of course,

Social Income on Peasant Farms in 1928–1929

Amounts in gold francs per hectare (1 gold franc = 9·5 old d.)

	Average size of the farms investigated in ha.	Average man-working days per ha.	Social income per ha.	Social income per working day.
Austria . .	29·67	69·69	223·02	3·20
Czechoslovakia .	17·37	98·26	389·30	3·96
Hungary [2] .	—	—	228·73	—
Roumania .	29·06	—	65·83	—
Poland . .	13·54	64·21	225·89	3·52
Switzerland .	14·66	73·0	778·60	10·66
Germany .	33·39	—	373·33	—
Denmark .	22·68	40·37	578·41	14·32
Sweden . .	11·42	—	314·65	—

[2] Small farms, Transdanubia, quoted in *International Review of Agriculture*, 1938.

not be overlooked that the data of different countries are not strictly comparable, owing partly to differences in natural and social conditions, partly to such in methods of accountancy. Nevertheless it is most instructive to study the figures for various countries in a comparative way. The following tables show data

[1] Cf. *Comptabilité agricole* (Farm Accountancy Statistics), published by the International Agricultural Institute, 1932. The Institute has also published later data, cf. *Farm Accountancy Statistics for 1934–1935* (1938) and *The Capital and Income of Farms in Europe, etc., 1927–1928 to 1934–1935* (1939).

referring to some Succession States and to a few other countries for the purpose of comparison.

The Social Income consists of all net income, in money or kind, going to the peasant, his family, his workers, his creditors and the State. It is equivalent to the gross returns less cost of materials worked up, and amortisation. (See table on p. 109.)

The natural conditions of Austria may be compared with those of Switzerland, and those of Czechoslovakia, Poland and Roumania with those of Germany. But capital equipment, technical efficiency and the social environment exercise a much stronger influence than climate and soil. Roumania, in spite of her wealth of fertile soil and her predominantly favourable climate, produces an amazingly low income per ha.—about a sixth of that of Czechoslovakia or Germany! If the Austrian peasant gets less than 60% of the Czechoslovak return out of his soil, this is, of course, mainly due to the fact that a large part of Austria is very mountainous and lacks good soil and climate. But mountainous Switzerland produces per ha. three and a half times the value reached by the Austrian peasant and double the Czechoslovak income! True, the Swiss climate is more advantageous than the Austrian.[1] Yet that enormous difference in productivity is due not mainly to Nature, but to technical efficiency and financial equipment.

The following figures indicate the level of technical efficiency:

	Yield in mq. per ha. (average 1925–1929).		Cattle per ha.	Pigs per ha.
	Wheat.	Potatoes.		
Netherlands .	30·0	189·30	102·54	87·45
Denmark .	28·50	142·60	102·20	162·85
Switzerland .	22·6	150·20	73·25	42·08
Germany .	19·80	135·40	62·74	79·53
Czechoslovakia .	17·10	119·40	54·32	36·95
Austria . .	15·10	123·0	49·62	33·81
Poland . .	12·30	106·40	36·88	23·73
Roumania .	9·20	98·70	24·52	13·65

[1] The climatic conditions of Switzerland are considerably more favourable than, for instance, those of Styria, and also of other parts of Austria. Cf. the data in Prof. R. A. Thallmayer, *Die dritte alpwirtschaftliche Studienreise steirischer Landwirte in die Schweiz*, 1907, p. 134.

The average milk production per cow was in Austria 2,100 l. and in Switzerland 3,030 l., or 45% more. The quality of the milk, its processing and marketing, moreover, were much better in Switzerland than in Austria. In Galicia, which has better natural conditions than the rest of Poland, the average yield of the cows in the best villages was 1,200 l., which was regarded as a good level.[1]

The decisive factor, however, is the financial equipment of the peasant farms.

CAPITAL ENGAGED IN PEASANT FARMS (1928–1929)
(Gold francs per ha.)

	Total assets.	Farm debts.	Own capital.
Austria . . .	1,646·34	88·78	1,557·56
Czechoslovakia . .	2,699·88	372·41	2,327·47
Hungary . .	2,224·8	—	—
Roumania . .	756·12	7·56	748·56
Poland . . .	2,253·43	164·55	2,088·88
Switzerland . .	7,748·97	3,883·01	3,865·96

The Swiss peasant employed, therefore, a capital per ha. ten times that of a Roumanian, more than four and a half times that of an Austrian, almost three times that of a Czechoslovak peasant. Only half of it was his own capital, the rest was borrowed. The Roumanian had almost no debts, which was not, however, a sign of his wealth, but a sign of his utter lack of credit.[2] The peasants of other countries, too, were not deeply in debt, mainly because their debts had been wiped out by inflation after the war, while the Swiss currency had retained its gold value. The assets included the value of the land, and it is instructive to see what were their component parts. (See table on p. 112.)

A comparison of the single items is most informative, and comments are scarcely needed.

The peasants of the advanced Danubian countries are certainly not lacking in industry and intelligence. But they cannot attain to

[1] Cf. also the indexes of agricultural production in W. Moore, *Economic Demography, etc.* p. 35.
[2] It is surprising that only three years later the peasants were regarded as being so overburdened with debts that a law was enacted in Roumania cancelling all agrarian debts. Its consequence was the ruin of almost all rural banks, the loss of large savings and the complete stoppage of all further credit.

the levels of the Swiss, Danish or Dutch peasant, because—apart from the inequalities of natural conditions—they have neither sufficient capital at their disposal nor markets of great purchasing power. Switzerland, for example, has throughout the course of her history been spared the devastation of great wars, she has early specialised her economic activities in branches especially suited to her conditions, and has thereby become a wealthy

COMPOSITION OF CAPITAL ENGAGED IN PEASANT FARMS IN 1928–1929
(Gold francs per ha.)

	Land.	Plants.	Improvements.	Buildings.	Livestock.	Deadstock.	Circulating capital.
Switzerland .	2,901·98	616·98	63·99	2,320·05	969·99	459	416·98
Austria .	454·39	249·07	4·12	441·96	218·55	111·08	167·17
Czechoslovakia	1,126·59	102·85	20·0	688·54	291·99	179·31	290·60
Roumania	293·78	264·62	—	115·26	56·88	13·67	11·91
Poland .	1,347·70	68·23	16·10	495·46	169·81	107·80	48·33

country. The Swiss peasants have not reached their present position in a short time. They, and the whole Swiss people, have for generations saved,[1] and have thereby been able slowly and tenaciously to build up their country's admirable economic fabric.

The greatest obstacle to economic progress in the Danubian area is the shortage of capital and credit. In the time of the Austro-Hungarian Empire economic co-operation, under the lead of the Vienna banks, secured comparatively cheap credit to all parts of the Empire. But after the disruption of the Empire the Balkanisation of a large part of its former territories and the general non-co-operation prevented the restoration of the capital destroyed or diminished through the war. Before the First World War the Austrian farmer had to pay for long-term credit on the average 4·5% and the Hungarian about 5%. After the war these charges rose to double and treble, and the great majority of the farmers had no chance of obtaining any credit at all. This was not

[1] It is significant that even many Swiss peasant songs contain admonitions to save money, not to gamble, to economise, etc. The National Anthem of Berne boasts of the economic assets of Berne, her excellent currency, her splendid cattle, her tourist traffic, etc., while the anthems of other nations boast of military or naval power, war-like heroism, and so on.

merely due to capitalistic exploitation. Where the State tried to help by providing credit the rates of interest charged were also very high and the supply of credit limited. In Yugoslavia, for example, the State founded a Privileged Agrarian Bank, which, according to an official source, granted credits to individual farmers at 10%, and to farmers' associations at 8%, while private banks charged double these rates. In Poland State and communal banking to a very large extent superseded private banking, and the share of private banks in the sum-total of credits granted by Polish credit institutions between 1928 and 1937 fell from about 50% to 25%.[1] But the supply and conditions of credit remained very unfavourable. An expert states that in the period 1927–1930 the agricultural discount rate on first-class promissory notes varied from 15% in Western Poland to 40% in Eastern Poland, the approximate average being 24%.[2]

The agriculture of the Danubian countries could be raised to a substantially higher level of productivity only by the investment of large amounts of capital. Some idea of the magnitude of this task can be formed by a comparison of the amounts invested in peasant farms of various countries (cf. p. 111). A Czechoslovak peasant, for example, in 1928–1929 had 2,700 gold francs invested per hectare, and a Roumanian only 756 gold francs. If the difference of 1944 gold francs is multiplied by the 17·5 million ha. of agricultural land which Roumania possessed, the result is the staggering amount of 34,020 million gold francs or 1,360 million old gold pounds.[3] What the equivalent amount under present Roumanian conditions would be it is impossible to estimate. For the Roumanian peasant, however, to attain the efficiency of the Swiss peasant the above amount would have to be trebled, as the Swiss peasant's investment per hectare was three times that of the Czechoslovak.

But even this would not be all. The advanced countries have also invested colossal amounts in railways, roads, public utilities, industries, towns and other things which are a prerequisite of

[1] Cf. F. Zweig, *Poland between Two Wars*, 1944, p. 118.
[2] Cf. Prof. Schmidt of the University of Cracow in *Proceedings of the Second International Conference of Agricultural Economists* held at New York, 1930, p. 127.
[3] It may be mentioned that in 1928 the total amount of all capital issues on the British money market was, according to the Bank of England statistics, £326·7 million, of which £63·3 million were loans to foreign countries.

intensive farming, and which are not included in the accounts of the peasant farms.

6. THE AGRARIAN REFORMS

Soon after the war of 1914–1918 almost all the new States began to carry out the distribution of large tracts of land among small peasants, agricultural labourers and others.[1] The land was mainly taken from the big estates. Their owners received compensation, which, however, was in most States extremely low. The people who received the land paid only very little for it. Large tracts, mainly forests and pastures, were transferred to State or communal ownership. The most trenchant redistribution of land took place in Roumania, where over 6 million ha. were expropriated, of which 3·6 million were given to 1,368,978 persons. Before the reform large estates had constituted 49% of the arable land, and afterwards amounted to less than 8%. In Czechoslovakia by the end of 1936 as much as 867,160 ha. of agricultural land had been transferred to 638,994 new owners—an average of 1·36 ha. per head. Moreover, 717,985 ha. of forest land were taken over by the State and communal bodies. The former owners received compensation amounting to about a sixth of the real value, but they were allowed to retain a considerable part of their estates. Poland up to 1938 divided up 2,654,000 ha., of which 1·4 million went to the creation of new farms, 1 million to increase the site of small farms, and the rest to model farms, etc. Here the estate owners managed to a great degree to safeguard their interests. If one remembers the existence of a rural proletariat of several millions, the results achieved in Poland appear rather poor. The same may be said of Hungary, where 600,000 ha. were acquired by the State, and used partly for the settlement of 410,000 new small-holders, partly for enlarging existing small farms. This reform reduced the share of the large estates (over

[1] Cf. on Roumania the admirable work by David Mitrany, *The Land and the Peasant in Roumania*, 1930 ; on Poland, F. Zweig, *Poland between Two Wars*, 1944 ; on Hungary, *The Hungarian Economic Yearbook*, ed. by G. Gratz, 1939 ; and on all Danubian States, the chapters by Franges and Kallbrunner in the collective work *Die Landwirtschaft der mitteleuropäischen Staaten*, 1930, and the chapters by various authors in *Agricultural Systems of Middle Europe*, ed. by O. S. Morgan, 1933, Doreen Warriner, *Economics of Peasant Farming*, 1939, and S. von Strakosch, *Das Agrarproblem im neuen Europa*, 1930.

1,421 acres) from 38% of the total soil to 33%, or from 29% of the arable soil to 24%. The area expropriated in Yugoslavia was 317,700 ha., and 191,987 persons received land. Moreover, numerous farmers profited from the abolition of the semi-feudal right of the landlord to a part of the crops in kind. Austria was the only country where no land distribution on a large scale was carried out, because the amount of agricultural land held by big estates was insignificant. But a law was passed providing for the resettlement of former peasant land which landowners had acquired for enlarging their shooting preserves.

The agrarian reforms aimed at the improvement of the conditions of the large masses of agricultural labourers and small peasants, who in certain parts of Eastern Europe lived in great poverty. The distribution of small lots of land among them seemed to be the quickest and most impressive way of helping them, though it may be doubted whether it was also the best way. But political reasons were probably still more powerful than humanitarian ones. In countries like Roumania, Poland and Hungary the rulers after the war had grave apprehensions that the rural masses might follow the example of Russia, where the Bolsheviks had encouraged the peasants to seize the land of the landlords. The laws passed under the impact of these events were very radical, and were later whittled down when the danger appeared to have passed. But even then the winning of the small peasants seemed to the governments in power a promising way of strengthening the conservative forces against the revolutionary tendencies which were in the air. Lastly, considerations of nationalism also played a great part. In Roumania land was taken from Hungarian, Bulgarian and Turkish owners and settled by Roumanians or Vlachs. In Yugoslavia extensive Serb colonies were planted in territories settled by Hungarians, Croats and Macedonians. The Czechoslovak reform took most of the land from German and Hungarian landowners, and the Polish reform gave priority to the partition of land belonging to Russians. Each of the new nations, flushed with nationalism, wished to take revenge on the national enemy and to strengthen its own nationals.

The effect of the reforms varied in different countries and in different parts of each country, but on the whole it disappointed the hopes entertained. The main reasons for the shortcomings were the inadequacy of the land available, the parcelling out of the land in too small lots, the settling of people unfitted for their task, and, above all, the lack of capital and experience for progressive farming. The aim of the politicians in power was to reward their followers, such as electoral agitators and members of nationalist organisations, and to win thereby their further support. This resulted in the settlement of many people who had no agricultural experience, or were at least not suited for the frugal life of a small colonist. On the other hand, too many applicants had to get something, and so each got only very little. The reform led mostly to the creation of new dwarf holdings, or to slight enlargements of existing ones. This type, however, was not suited for modern, intensive farming. The establishment in medium-sized holdings of peasants with a good technical training and sufficient financial resources would often have been greatly preferable from the point of view of encouraging productivity and creating employment.

Professor Otto de Franges, former Yugoslav Minister of Agriculture, has trenchantly criticised the agrarian reforms in the South-Eastern States. He ascribed their failure to the fact that they were mostly carried out more in accordance with political tendencies than with economic considerations. In Yugoslavia, he said, it would have been better to reclaim the more than 2 million ha. of unproductive land capable of improvement and to settle peasants on it.

In discussing the Polish reform Professor Zweig says:—

"Did the land reform substantially ease the position of the peasant? An answer in the affirmative cannot be given. . . . The pressure of the increasing land population was greater than the easement produced by land reform. . . . The problem of the land proletariat became really worse in those areas where the large estates were divided up."

Miss Doreen Warriner summarises the effects of the reform in the statements [1] that in the worst provinces it relieved the pressure of population to some slight extent, that in the Bohemian countries it was extremely limited in scope and a success, and that in Roumania, where the scope has been much wider, it was a failure,

[1] *Economics of Peasant Farming*, p. 154.

and has undoubtedly led to a degeneration in farming technique. She attributes the failure mainly to the fact that no collective organisation was introduced, but, on the other hand, shows that the south-eastern countries cannot follow the example of Soviet Russia because of the great difference in natural conditions. Moreover, she points out that a system of small peasant farming tends to maintain and increase the capital invested in the farms, thereby temporarily increasing employment, but that it does not necessarily provide for increased employment in the future, because it does not encourage capital formation for general purposes. The existence of many small farms leads to over-investment in land and to an exaggerated rise in its price. It drives savings into many small channels, and in consequence there are no reserves available for investment in large-scale capital construction which would cause an increase in productivity. The same volume of savings, if mobilised and invested in irrigation or electrical supply, might permit a great increase in agricultural productivity; but it cannot be mobilised. This criticism implies that societies with widely dispersed ownership and a fairly equally distributed income would have too little concentration of capital to industrialise. But Miss Warriner adds that it is the political situation, rather than peasant structure as such, which is the main check to capital investment in large-scale undertakings.

The agrarian reforms also made many attempts at easing the financial difficulties of the peasants and providing them with cheap credit. In all parts of Austria-Hungary agricultural credit had already been organised partly on a co-operative basis, partly by means of numerous public or semi-public banks. Many thousands of peasant co-operatives (*Raiffeisenkassen*) used the deposits of their members for granting loans to them. The savings banks, which had a public character and devoted their profits, if any, to public purposes, also provided the agriculturists with credit. Mortgages were granted by public banks mostly founded and controlled by the provincial authorities. The commercial banks dealt only with large farmers. After the war the credit situation of the peasants became everywhere most difficult, and the Succession States were compelled to adopt far-reaching measures. In Roumania, Yugoslavia and Hungary drastic cuts were made in the agricultural debts and the State took over part of the losses, or founded special banks for this purpose. These banks were also designed to provide the farmers with loans at moderate rates. In Roumania the National Bank was authorised to re-discount agricultural bills up to 40% of its total holdings, and in fact did so up to 60%. In Czechoslovakia, where the financial situation of the farmers was much better than in the south-eastern countries, the National Bank re-discounted their bills at 3%. In several States the rate of interest was fixed at a moderate level.[1] But all these measures could not supply sufficient capital, and a large part had still to be obtained from private money-lenders, often on exorbitant terms.

7. AUSTRIA'S AGRICULTURAL DEVELOPMENT

The Republic of Austria had, in comparison with former Austria, less than a quarter of the population, but only about a sixth of the arable soil, and this was mostly mountainous, and not very fertile. On the other hand, new Austria possessed about a third of the forests, meadows and mountain pastures, a fifth of the vineyards, and half of the unproductive soil. The climatic conditions were not so good as in the neighbouring countries. This explained why about two-thirds of the cereals produced consisted of rye and oats, and only a third of the more valuable crops of wheat and barley. The producers of livestock for meat and fat were faced with difficulties in procuring sufficient cheap fodder. For these reasons a large part of the food required was imported from the northern and eastern countries, and was paid for mainly by the export of industrial products. With the disruption of Austria-Hungary and the rise of economic nationalism, Austria got into great difficulties. She first tried to maintain free trade in food and a policy of low tariffs in general, but was more and more compelled to adopt, like her neighbours, a policy of marked protectionism, which became constantly more rigorous. As the protectionism of the neighbouring States made it impossible to export sufficient Austrian industrial goods in payment for food and raw materials, the aim was proclaimed that Austria should strive for a large measure of self-sufficiency in food and certain primary materials. Great efforts were made to raise agricultural produc-

[1] For details cf. the publication of the League of Nations by L. Tardy, *Report on Systems of Agricultural Credit and Insurance*, 1938.

tion, not merely by high tariffs, but even by various direct subsidies. From 1927 to 1934 34,300 ha. of unproductive land—about 10% of the total land capable of being reclaimed—were made productive by drainage.[1]

The use of fertilisers increased considerably:—

(Tons)

	Potash.	Phosphates.	Nitrates.
1923 . . .	17,365	58,847	7,411
1927 . . .	17,530	97,781	18,737
1937 . . .	20,947	117,682	38,095

Nevertheless the use of fertilisers is still much less in Austria than in the western countries and in Czechoslovakia, though it far exceeds that in the other Danubian countries.[2]

The production of cereals was, according to the League of Nations statistics, taking the average of 1933–1937, higher by 7·4% than before the war, while the yield per hectare increased by 22·1%. In fact, the increase in production was even greater, since those statistics assumed too high a pre-war average.[3]

The principal crops in the post-war territories of Austria showed this development:—

(1,000 mq.)

	Average 1910–1914.	Average 1922–1924.	Average 1925–1929.	Average 1930–1934.	Average 1935–1938.	Increase from 1910–1914 to 1935–1938.
						%
Five main cereals .	16,660	11,756	16,160	17,498	18,454	10·8
Potatoes .	16,361	14,902	22,648	26,281	29,024	77·4
Beetroot .	5,090	2,826	6,225	10,897	11,121 [4]	119·0

[4] Average 1934–1937.

[1] The difficulty impeding drainage, however, is that the marshy land is not in big blocks, but widely dispersed in small plots, which makes drainage expensive.
[2] An interesting table comparing the quantity of fertilisers used in different countries is given in the report *Economic Development in South-Eastern Europe*, published by P.E.P., 1945, p. 31.
[3] The statistics (*Agricultural Production in Continental Europe*, 1943) state that

The number of livestock was (in thousands) :—[1]

	Horses.	Cattle.	Pigs.	Sheep and goats.
1910 . .	298	2,219	1,840	530
1923 . .	283	2,162	1,473	980
1934 . .	261	2,349	2,823	590

The principal crops of green fodder (turnips, clover, vetch, hay, etc.) rose from 1911–1913 to 1927–1929 by 23%, which seems to indicate an increase in the weight of the livestock and in milk production. The production of milk, butter and cheese has, indeed, developed favourably, partly owing to financial assistance from the League of Nations loan of 1923. The sugar industry has made great progress, and now covers the total requirements of Austria, which were formerly supplied mainly from the Bohemian countries.[2] Other important improvements in agricultural efficiency and output have also been achieved, and yet others are still possible. It must also be remembered that the population of Austria has remained stationary since before the war. The agricultural population even decreased by 11·3%. The increased production was therefore achieved with less labour, and helped to save imports.

The increase in cereal production was, however, effected by high tariffs, which burdened the consumers, urban and rural, with a higher cost of living, and which, moreover, contributed to the decline of Austria's industrial exports to the grain-producing countries. The rising protectionism of these countries caused much unemployment among the Austrian workers. The average retail price of 1 kilogram of rye-bread was, in gold centimes :—[3]

1909–1913 was taken as the basis. But in fact the year 1913 alone was taken. This year, however, was an exceptionally good one. The pre-war yields in the post-war territory are given in the *Statistik der Ernte in der Republik Oesterreich im Jahre 1930*. It begins with 1910.

[1] It must, however, be remembered that before the war the Census of livestock was taken at the end of the year, when the numbers were particularly low, while after the war the Census was taken in spring, when the numbers were much greater.

[2] In the last years before the invasion of Austria by Hitler the proportion of some food supplies covered by Austrian agriculture was: wheat, about 60% ; rye, about 84% ; potatoes, 100% ; maize, about 28%.

[3] This comparison is taken from the excellent work by Paul de Hevesy, *World Wheat Planning and Economic Planning in General*, 1940, p. 839. Hevesy's comparison of the prices of wheat-bread, however, gives much too high a price

	1929.	1933.	1936.	1938.
Austria . . .	47	32	37	51
Hungary . . .	38	24	31	33
Czechoslovakia . .	39	33	30	25
Yugoslavia . . .	34	24	23	24
Poland . . .	29	18	18	17

The price of wheat per bushel (60 lb.) in U.S.A. cents was in 1937–1938:—[1]

Great Britain, 112; France (Paris), 164; Germany (Berlin), 224; Italy (Milan), 200; Hungary (Budapest), 117; Yugoslavia, 118; Roumania, 104.

The price of wheat in Vienna was in autumn 1937 37·40 S. per 100 kg., which was equivalent to 189 cents per bushel.

In 1937, therefore, the price of wheat was higher by 61·5% in Vienna than in Budapest, and in 1938 rye-bread was 54·4% dearer.

Many economists, and also prominent agricultural experts, have severely criticised the policy of fostering the increase of the cultivation of cereals in a country where natural conditions would rather suggest the encouragement of livestock production, in particular for breeding and for dairy-farming.[2] Austria's Alpine pastures produce a particularly hardy and healthy race of cattle, which is indispensable for cattle-farmers in the lowlands of Central and Eastern Europe to prevent degeneration in their stock.

The majority of the Austrian peasants have no interest in high prices of grain, but rather the opposite. The Accountancy statistics

---

for Austria. As white bread is mainly consumed in Austria in the form of rolls, he takes this price, and compares it with the prices of loaves in other countries, without realising that rolls cost much more, even if the price of wheat is the same.

[1] From *Wheat Studies of the Food Research Institute of Stanford University*, 1938–1939.

[2] Cf. Hermann Kallbrunner, *Der Wiederaufbau der Landwirtschaft Oesterreichs*, 1926, pp. 26, 81, on the natural conditions unfavourable to grain production. One of the foremost experts, S. Strakosch, who formerly was a strong defender of maintaining grain production by tariffs, has changed his views and has come to the conclusion that the peculiar post-war conditions of Austria render that policy disadvantageous. Cf. S. Strakosch, *Das Agrarproblem im neuen Europa*, 1930, pp. 323, 341.

show that in 1928 the principal products sold were valued at (million S.) : cereals, 145; milk, 412; pigs, 182; cattle, 332; wine, 99; fruit, 37; timber, 186. Total, 1,796.[1]

The cereals therefore amounted to only 8% of the total sales of the farmers. In 1930—a year of severe crisis—this proportion had even fallen to 5·3%, while cattle, pigs and milk brought in 58·3%, wine and fruit 7·7%, forestal products 6·4%.

It was mainly the larger farmers in the flatter regions who sold cereals, while the small peasants in the mountains had scarcely any left to sell, and often even had to buy cereals.

Before the First World War the net value of agricultural production in the territory of the later Republic of Austria was, according to Fellner-Waizner, 955 million K. For the post-war years the Farm Accountancy Institute has made careful investigations, which showed that in 1927–1928 the net value per hectare was 384·4 S., and in 1928–1929 305·0 S. The agricultural price index in these two years was 119 and 122, and it was assumed that the average value was 20% below the value produced by the farmers reporting to the Institute, who were certainly an élite. The total cultivated area was 7·5 million ha. The net value of agricultural production in the two years was therefore 1,346 million K. and 1,042 million K., or 41% and 9% above the pre-war value of 955 million K.[2] A comparison of the weight of the cereals, potatoes, sugar-beet and green fodder also shows considerable increases. If we take the average of 1928 and 1929 the net output was 2,068 million S. at the then prevailing price level, or 20% less at the pre-war price level.

According to the Accountancy statistics, 70% of the output was consumed by the producers, and 30% sold. The annual gross income, including products consumed in kind, was about 1,000 S. per head of the agricultural population, which at that time corresponded to about £30. The gross income varied according to districts between 603 and 1,650 S. It had also to provide for taxes, interest and investments.

The International Agricultural Institute has also compiled the

---

[1] Cf. Dr. L. Strobl in *Österreichischer Volkswirt*, December 1929, and the same paper of 2.5.1931 and 1.4.1933. These articles summarise the results given in full in L. Strobl and F. Grünseis, *Die Rentabilität der österreichischen Landwirtschaft*, 1929.

[2] The pre-war value, however, was perhaps an under-estimate.

Accountancy statistics from 1928 to 1935. They show a constant fall in the social income.[1] The highest social income was produced by the farmers growing wine and cereals, while the Alpine dairy-farms and those producing cattle, and forest holdings, had a very low income. Indebtedness greatly increased in the big depression, and in 1938 was estimated at 1,500 millions.

8. CZECHOSLOVAKIA'S AGRICULTURAL PRODUCTION REMAINS STATIONARY

The long connection of the Bohemian territories with the other parts of Austria-Hungary has resulted in a very high level of agricultural and industrial productivity, and in a rare co-operation and balance between the great branches of production. Agriculture, mining and industries were to a large extent complementary. Most of the great export industries worked up the agricultural and mineral products of the country, and had also a big share in financing the primary production and improving its technical and commercial organisation. A large section of the workers or their families combined industrial and agricultural work. It was a highly efficient division of labour, and re-integration in an economic whole.

After the war the preponderant influence of the agrarians led not only to high tariffs on agricultural products, but also to a wide measure of Government regulation in regard to the principal foodstuffs, exercised in the interest of the farmers. In 1934 the whole grain trade was handed over to a monopoly directed mainly by the agrarian interest and supervised by the State. The farmers further demanded a monopoly for the trade in livestock. The production of flour, timber, milk, flax, fat, sugar, alcohol, malt, etc., was also regulated by the Government.

The Government of Dr. Hodza, himself a Slovak, made great efforts to raise agricultural production in the backward territories of Slovakia and Carpatho-Russia.

[1] *The Capital and Income of Farms,* etc. (contribution by the International Institute of Agriculture to the European Conference on Rural Life, 1930), p. 85.

The main crops in the territory of Czechoslovakia showed this development:—[1]

(1,000 mq.)

	1909–1913.	1927–1929.	1930–1934.	1935–1938.
The five principal cereals . . .	59,034	61,911	61,168	58,960
Potatoes . . .	67,695	98,809	91,457	101,427
Beetroot . . .	72,019	67,981	45,555	47,996

A reliable index of the total crops is the production of the six main crops of wheat, rye, barley, oats, potatoes and sugar-beet. In Bohemia, Moravia and Silesia their weight formed 82% of the weight of all crops, not including hay and straw. If the six crops are valued by the prices for 1936 (the latest available), the result is that their value from 1911–1913 to 1935–1936 increased from 8,485·6 million Kc. to 8,803·1 million Kc.[2] The increase in twenty-four years was therefore only 3·7%.

A publication of the League of Nations (*Agricultural Production in Continental Europe*, 1943) states that the cereal crops of Czechoslovakia were, taking the average 1933–1937, 16% greater than the average for 1909–1913. But this calculation is obviously an error, probably caused by the assumption of too low a pre-war figure.

In Bohemia, Moravia and Silesia the production of wheat from 1911–1913 to 1935–1937 increased by over 50%. But this was more than outweighed by the decline in all the other cereals. The total weight of the four main cereals was therefore in 1937 less by 7% than twenty-four years before, while the population of the three provinces was by 10% greater.[3] The big rise in wheat pro-

[1] The figures for 1919–1926 are omitted because the crop statistics were estimated on a method later found to be inadequate. In 1928 it was improved. Cereals include wheat, rye, barley, oats, maize. The last figure for beetroot refers to 1935–1937, as the figure for 1938 was not available.
[2] Kc. means Czech Crowns; K. is used for the former Austrian Gold Crown.
[3] The agricultural population, however, and in particular its working section, decreased considerably. The figures have been given in a previous chapter. The same production was therefore achieved by a much smaller number of workers. But against this must be set the fact that before the war many labourers and small peasants used to find seasonal work, like harvesting or building, in other parts of the Empire, or were employed in domestic industries, and that these opportunities largely disappeared after the war.

duction was the result of the policy of making the country independent of Hungarian wheat. It contributed greatly to the trade war with Hungary, which inflicted deep wounds upon Czechoslovakia's industries. The production of barley and sugar-beet—once the basis of flourishing export industries—declined by about 40%. These changes were encouraged by the agrarian reform, since the small farmers, owing to lack of capital, abandoned the cultivation of sugar-beet and grew potatoes and wheat. Military reasons worked in the same direction. Wheat was stored for the event of war, and potatoes were used on a large scale by the State Alcohol Monopoly for making motor fuel.

The numbers of livestock in all territories of Czechoslovakia were (in thousands) :—

	Horses.	Cattle.	Pigs.	Sheep.	Goats.
1910–1911 .	692	4,596	2,516	1,322	711
1925 . .	740	4,691	2,539	861	1,245
1937 . .	704	4,596	3,242	592	1,072

Since 1931 the statistics of livestock are available for every year. The number of cattle was constantly below the figure for 1925, and reached the lowest point in 1936, with 4,283,000, but in 1937 it increased to the level of twenty-seven years before. The number of cows was, however, 7% greater than before the war. The number of pigs showed a considerable increase, while that of sheep declined. The Czechoslovak Statistical Office estimates every year the meat produced. From 1928 to 1936 it decreased from 475,000 to 379,000 tons.

The State Institute for Farm Accountancy and Agricultural Economics has published very detailed statistics of agricultural returns, both for the pre-war years 1909–1913, and for most post-war years.[1] Its director, Prof. Brdlik, estimated the pre-war agricultural income at 2,605 million K., and the forestal income at between 280 and 300 million K. For the end of the 'twenties he estimated the agricultural income at 22 milliard Kc., which was equivalent to 2,534 million K. at pre-war price level. If we assume, in accordance with the crop statistics, that the three

[1] Cf. *Publications de l'Institut de Comptabilité*, etc., especially No. 5, 1935, and several volumes of farm accountancy statistics compiled by the International Agricultural Institute in Rome in 1931, 1932, etc.

western provinces had about three-quarters of the total agricultural income, Brdlik's estimate would amount for these provinces to about 1,900 million K., and this seems to agree well with that made by Waizner according to Fellner's method, except for the forestal income, which Brdlik estimated much higher than did Waizner and Fellner.

I have calculated on the basis of the Accountancy statistics Czechoslovakia's agricultural net income for the average of the two years 1927–1928 and 1928–1929 at 22,073 million Kc., of which 7,174·57 million were wages of labourers.[1] Allowance must, however, be made for the fact that the book-keeping farmers were more progressive and efficient than the rest, and a certain deduction should accordingly be made, perhaps 10%. The net income may therefore be estimated at about 20 milliard Kc.

If, however, one calculates the pre-war income in the three western provinces from the data of the Accountancy statistics, and compares the result with all other data available, a considerable discrepancy is shown. The only explanation I should venture is that the data for 1909–1913 were perhaps too low because the method of compiling and checking was still in its infancy. If this should be so, allowance must be made for it in studying the following figures.

	Social income per ha. Whole State.	Western Provinces (Bohemia, Moravia, Silesia).	Slovakia.	Carpatho-Russia.
1909–1913	280·81 K.	307·48 K.	247·21 K.	169·58 K.
1926–1930	2,328 Kc.	2,746 Kc.	1,785 Kc.	1,391 Kc.
	268·20 K.	316·36 K.	205·64 K.	160·25 K.

1 pre-war K. = 8·68 post-war Kc.

The Accountancy statistics show the above net incomes for 1909–1913 and 1926–1930 per hectare. The post-war figures have been converted by us into K., pre-war price-level, by the weighted

---

[1] I have taken account in this calculation both of the returns of peasant farms, and of those of larger estates assuming, on the basis of data on the distribution of the land according to the size of farms, that the large estates covered 10% of the cultivated land.

food index of 868,[1] which was the average for the five years 1926–1930.

The agricultural net income per hectare slightly increased in the western provinces, but greatly decreased in the eastern ones. The Republic as a whole shows a decrease of 4·5%. The area cultivated in the Republic seems to have remained about the same.[2]

It has already been mentioned that Czechoslovakia's agrarian policy aimed primarily at protecting the interests of the farmers by means of an elaborate system of State regulation. This involved not an expansion of agricultural production, but its contraction, in order to raise the profits of the farmers. The results of this policy can best be judged by studying the development of net returns in comparison with the years before the war. The Czechoslovak Institute of Farm Accountancy and Agricultural Economics has for all the years from 1913 to 1937 published the net returns per hectare,[3] expressed in old Austrian gold crowns, and we have added the wholesale price index for each year, and have converted the net returns into their equivalents at the pre-war price-level. (See table on next page.)

This table shows that, allowing for the price level, the net returns after the war were nearly always far below the pre-war figure. In the war the net returns soared to great heights, and also remained high in the first years after the war. But this was due to extraordinary circumstances, and with the return of normal conditions the returns soon fell below the pre-war level, in spite of rigid protectionism and stringent State regulation.

The forestal income is not included in the data of the Farm Accountancy Institute. Now in 1929 the net return of the great State forests was 106,363,000 Kc. or 149·1 Kc. per hectare.[4] If

[1] The Accountancy Institute has also ascertained indices of agricultural prices according to different areas and branches of production. The average for the years 1927–1929 is 881. This index would therefore give the same result as that applied above.

[2] There was a slight increase in the west, but in the east the area seems to have decreased. The pre-war area cultivated in the eastern provinces cannot be ascertained from the official statistics, as the data published refer to the territorial boundaries under the former Hungarian rule.

[3] Cf. *Rapports de l'Institut de Comptabilité*, etc., 1938, IX, 50. The Institute has published the data for all parts of Czechoslovakia, but for reasons of space we give only those for Bohemia, Moravia, Silesia.

[4] The *Manuel Statistique*, IV, refers to the data of 1920 as regards the area of the State forests. But this figure did not yet include the forests taken over by the State in the course of the Agrarian reform.

	Net return in K. per ha.	Wholesale price index on pre-war basis.	Net returns in pre-war value in K. per ha.
1913 . .	130·33	100	130·33
1918 . .	380·97	—	—
1919 . .	264·64	—	—
1920 . .	182·79	—	—
1921 . .	160·39	—	—
1922 . .	loss — 28·70	145·2	loss — 19·77
1923 . .	153·15	139·6	109·71
1924 . .	232·38	141·5	164·22
1925 . .	139·02	145·0	95·86
1926 . .	130·01	137·5	94·55
1927 . .	193·77	141·5	136·93
1928 . .	158·03	141·6	111·60
1929 . .	96·23	133·5	72·08
1930 . .	55·45	118·6	46·75
1931 . .	53·02	107·5	49·32
1932 . .	27·05	99·5	27·18
1933 . .	42·87	96·3	44·51
1934 . .	40·96	84·8	48·30
1935 . .	81·50	85·9	94·87
1936 . .	99·65	82·4	120·93
1937 . .	89·84	—	—

this return per ha. is multiplied by the total area of the forests, the return would be 695·3 million Kc. The State forests were much better managed, from a scientific and social point of view, than many private forests, especially those in the hands of peasants. On the other hand, they did not primarily aim at the greatest possible profit. We may therefore assume that the returns of commercial enterprises were higher, and we guess that the total forestal income was approximately 1,000 million Kc.

9. THE DECLINE OF HUNGARY'S AGRICULTURE

Hungary owes its high level of agricultural development partly to its soil and climate, but to a great degree also to the efforts of governments and farmers. In the course of the nineteenth century more than 9 million acres of marshy, or often flooded, land were converted into fertile fields by means of great dams and drainage. After the First World War Hungary was deprived of nearly three-quarters of its territory, losing about 56%

of its production of grain and almost nine-tenths of its forests. Post-war Hungary depends mainly on the products of its arable soil. In 1930 51·8% of the population lived on agriculture, but if we add small-holders, agricultural labourers, etc., cultivating their plots as a side-line, the percentage of the population directly connected with agriculture rises to 57% or 58%.[1] From 1920 to 1930 the number of landowners rose by 47·8% and that of tenants by 63·4%. But most of them had very small holdings, scarcely sufficient for making a living. The characteristic feature of Hungarian agriculture is the existence of large estates covering a great part of the land, and of very numerous small-holders, while the medium-sized farms of between 10 and 50 ha. are rare.

The principal productions showed this development:—

CROPS ON POST-WAR TERRITORY
(million mq.)

	1911–1913.[2]	1927–1930.	1931–1934.	1935–1938.	Increase or decrease, 1911–13 to 1935–38.
Five cereals .	57·7	55·3	56·4	63·1	increase 9·3%
Potatoes .	19·5	18·7	17·4	21·3	increase 9·2%
Sugar-beet .	—	14·9	9·2	9·7	decrease 35%

[2] The figures for 1911–1913 are taken from an article in the *Revue Hongrois de Statistique*, III, 1925, 329.

LIVESTOCK ON POST-WAR TERRITORY [3]
(In '000's)

	Horses.	Cattle.	Pigs.	Sheep.	Goats.
1913 . .	896	2,150	3,322	2,406	21
1920 . .	635	1,971	2,524	1,284	—
1928 . .	918	1,812	2,662	1,566	30
1933 . .	820	1,697	1,899	1,056	23
1937 . .	798	1,756	2,624	1,484	—
1938 . .	814	1,882	3,110	1,629	—

[3] The pre-war figures refer to the end of the year, when livestock was at its lowest. The post-war figures refer to the spring, when the number of livestock was greater.

The five principal cereals together increased by 9·3%.

The population increased from 1910 to 1937 by 18·7%, so

[1] Cf. *Struktur und Verfassung der ungarischen Landwirtschaft*, 1937, p. 41, a very valuable collection of essays on Hungary's agriculture by various experts, printed for the International Conference of Agricultural Economists at St. Andrews, quoted in the following as *Struktur*.

that the supply per head fell. Among the cereals, wheat increased by 5% and maize by 57%. All the other cereals decreased. The rise in the production of maize would be a good symptom if it were concomitant with an increase in livestock. But, since livestock decreased, the larger output of maize was obviously mainly used for human consumption. This is not a favourable symptom.

The development of livestock was very unfavourable. In 1938 it had not yet reached the level of twenty-five years before, and the number of cattle not even that of the time immediately after the war, which had greatly reduced the number of livestock.

The net product of agriculture within the post-war frontiers was:—

Value in Pengö (P.)

	Post-war value.	Agricultural price index.	Pre-war value.
1911–1913 (estimate Fellner [1]) . .	2,052·4 million P.	100	2,052·4 million P.
1926–1928 (Fellner) .	2,143·5 million P.	124	1,728·6 million P.
1936–1937 (Matolcsy and Varga) [2] .	1,494·1 million P.	80	1,867·6 million P.

[1] Cf. Fellner in *Bulletin de l'Institut Internationale de Statistique*, XXV, 1931, 367.
[2] M. Matolcsy and S. Varga, *The National Income of Hungary*, 1938.

Agricultural production was therefore less after the war than before. To a great extent this was the consequence of the policy of speedy industrialisation and of economic nationalism in general.

After the war considerable efforts were made to improve methods of production, and good results were achieved, but in the late 'twenties there came a severe crisis, which had devastating effects. Though the acreage cultivated increased, the yields per hectare decreased, and the use of agricultural machines and fertilisers was reduced.[3] On the whole, therefore, agricultural production became more extensive and the technical level fell. There were also many complaints about the deterioration in the quality of wheat and other products. In 1931 the Government took energetic action to control and improve the quality of the

[3] Cf. the statistics in Dr. G. Gratz, *Hungarian Economic Yearbook*, 1939; Dr. Karl Geller, *Die Strukturveränderung der ungarischen Volkswirtschaft nach dem Kriege*, 1938, p. 32.

wheat produced, and especially to prevent the export of inferior wheat. According to Dr. Nagy, a prominent official expert, livestock also degenerated, and showed a great loss in weight and quality. He attributes this partly to the effects of the war and to the loss of most meadows and pastures through the dictated peace, partly to the discontinuance of regular cattle import from the Alpine countries because of the financial difficulties.[1]

The decline in production and quality was also partly caused by the fact that the agrarian reform of 1920 was not carried out with due regard to economic efficiency. The land distributed was not sufficient for the number of applicants, and the endeavour to give some land to as many people as possible, regardless of experience and capital, led to the creation of numerous holdings too small to be cultivated in an efficient way. The settlement law of 1936 therefore tried to avoid this mistake. The statistics show that in Hungary, as in other countries, the yields in cereals, potatoes and sugar-beet are much higher on large than on small farms.[2] On the other hand, the small farms have far more livestock. The decline in the numbers of livestock indicates, therefore, the plight of the small farmers. This fact is also confirmed by many other symptoms showing a progressive impoverishment of the small peasants and labourers. Their standard of life decreased after the war. From 1929–1933 to 1934 the capital invested per Yoke fell from 1,563·5 P. to 1,030·5 P., or by a third, without allowing for the depreciation of the currency. The Accountancy statistics show[3] that, taking the average for 1929–1933, 57% of the peasant farms investigated were in a catastrophic plight, earning less than their expenses; 37% had a surplus over expenses, but earned less than 5% on the capital invested, and only 6% earned more. In 1934 conditions improved. Only 35% of the peasants had a deficit, and 48% earned less than 5% on their capital. By 1933 the gross return had decreased to 30·5% of the average in 1925–1929, and the cost of production had decreased less, so that the financial result was still worse than the reduction in gross return. The inflation after the war wiped out the debts

[1] Cf. Dr. Nagy in O. S. Morgan, *Agricultural Systems of Middle Europe*, 1933, p. 215.
[2] Cf. *Struktur*, p. 99.
[3] Cf. Dr. Juhos in *Struktur*, p. 195, and for the question of indebtedness Dr. Koos in the same publication, p. 240.

of the farmers, but in 1928 the new debts had again reached about a quarter of the pre-war level, and in 1933 about half. Most of these debts burdened the small farmers, whose plight became so desperate that in 1933 the Government was compelled to introduce a law protecting small farmers against forced sales of their farms and granting them a reduction of the interest on their debts at the expense of the State. In 1928 the average price of land was 83% of the pre-war price, and by 1935 it had fallen to 52%.

The situation of the agricultural labourers also deteriorated. Their real wage was on the average only two-thirds of the pre-war amount. In 1928 the summer wage of male workers was 77% and in 1935 62% of the pre-war real wage. Moreover, employment greatly decreased. Before the war the agricultural labourer worked on the average 220 days and earned between 450 and 850 P. In 1937 he was lucky if he could work 150–180 days and could earn between 250 and 300 P.[1] The mortality from tuberculosis was greater among women in rural districts than among those working in factories.

10. Agricultural Decline in Roumania

The two pillars of Roumanian agriculture are cereals and cattle. The development of the production of cereals in the post-war territory is shown in these figures in percentages of the pre-war level, computed by the Statistical Office of the League of Nations:—

	1909–1913.	1920.	1922.	1924.	1925.	1926.	1933–1937.
Area . .	100	84·4	94·5	101·2	103·5	102·8	114·3
Yield .	100	86·7	77·5	60·0	71·7	99·2	81·7
Production .	100	72·9	73·6	60·6	74·6	101·6	93·1

While the area cultivated constantly increased, the yield showed a somewhat regular decline. It had, taking the average of the five years 1933–1937, not even reached the level of the time immediately after the war, and was much lower than before the war. Yield and production were lowest in 1924, which was

[1] Cf. M. Kerek in *Struktur*, p. 226. Many further data illustrating the misery of the labourers are quoted in this paper.

obviously due to the agrarian reform then in operation. The pre-war level of production was not yet reached in the period 1933–1937.

The development of livestock in the post-war territory was as follows (in thousands) :—[1]

	Horses and mules.	Cattle.	Sheep and goats.	Pigs.
Before the war (1916)	2,678	6,760	15,250	4,634
1926 . . .	1,890	4,992	14,059	3,168
1930 . . .	1,819	4,011	12,273	2,323
1932 . . .	2,034	4,189	12,715	2,964
1935 . . .	2,163	4,326	12,237	2,969

The decline in livestock was still greater than in cereals. It is particularly significant that even in 1926, after all the devastation of the war, the numbers of cattle, sheep and pigs were considerably greater than in 1935. This refutes the argument that it was only the war which reduced the livestock.

It must further be considered that at the time of this decline the population of Roumania (post-war area) increased considerably. Before the war it was 15·7 million and in 1937 19·5 million. The increase was 24%. A considerably smaller agricultural output had therefore to cover the needs of a much larger population. If one remembers that 78% of the active population were engaged in agriculture and that 70% of the total national income came from agriculture, the significance of that divergence between population and agricultural output is obvious.

In the territories acquired by Roumania from Austria-Hungary the pre-war output of cereals was 31·3 million mq. and the average for the four years 1933–1936 28·8 million. Here the decline was 8·1%. Actually it was greater, because the pre-war figures of some territories are averages including the first two war years, or years somewhat distant. This reduces the average below the level reached immediately before the war.

The livestock in the former Austro-Hungarian territories showed these changes :—

[1] Most statisticians quoting pre-war figures overlook that in Transylvania the last census was taken in 1911, and in Bukowina in 1910, while Roumania entered the war in 1916. The increase in the intervening five or six years is usually neglected.

(In '000,000's)

	Cattle.	Horses.	Pigs.	Sheep.
1910–1911 .	2·40	0·58	1·70	3·62
1935 . .	1·82	0·57	1·08	3·00

Even in these territories, where agriculture and civilisation had reached a much higher level than in Roumania proper, the decline was marked.

The causes of this decline, and the question whether and when it will be overcome, have been much discussed. Many economists attributed it mainly to the agrarian reform, which was much more radical in Roumania than in any other country except the Soviet Union. Through this reform the area in small-holdings of less than 10 ha. increased from 57% to 92% of the total. There is no doubt that the way in which the reform was carried through was detrimental to agricultural productivity.

An English investigator comes to the conclusion that in Roumania the reform has led to the degeneration of farming technique, to the decline in yield and quality, and ascribes this mainly to the fact that before the elimination of the landlords these controlled the selection of seeds and the date at which sowing should begin, while after it the peasants neglected these essential operations.[1]

But it was not the reform alone which was responsible, and it is probable that after a certain period of re-organisation the peasantry will to some extent have made good the decline. Many experts stress the adverse influence on agricultural production of the general economic and financial policy. This policy was characterised by the high degree of economic and political nationalism, extreme protectionism, financial recklessness and appalling corruption, which inflicted heavy losses on the foreign creditors of Roumania and induced them to shun any further investment in that country. An English expert in Roumanian affairs, in discussing the effect of rapid industrialisation in the south-eastern States, comes to the conclusion:—[2]

[1] Cf. D. Warriner, *Economics of Peasant Farming*, 1939, p. 153.
[2] Cf. George Clenton Logio, *Roumania, its History, Politics and Economics*, 1932, p. 181. This book gives ample proofs for this statement.

"This policy brought about the gradual pauperisation of the rural populations, and the dissipation of the exiguous liquid wealth which the agrarian States have sunk in these artificially created industries. Thus the capital so urgently needed for the development of their agriculture was frittered away through the prevalence of the irrational idea that concentration on agriculture necessarily implies an inferior economic status."

11. THE DEVELOPMENT OF AGRICULTURE IN YUGO-SLAVIA

The comparison of crops in Yugoslavia before and after the First World War is made difficult by the fact that in drawing the frontiers of this State the old territorial units were partly broken up, and that in 1929 a new division into provinces was enacted which went still farther in this direction.

The League of Nation's Statistical Office has, however, published data, according to which soon after the war production was considerably above the pre-war level. I have checked this statement by compiling the figures from the official statistics and comparing them with the figures for 1913 given by Prof. Franges, with the following results:—[1]

('000,000 mq.)

	1913.	1927–1929.	1930–1932.	1933–1935.	1936–1938.
Wheat .	21·0	23·1	21·1	21·6	27·7
Oats .	5·9	3·4	2·7	3·3	3·2
Maize .	36·6	26·9	38·2	39·2	50·9

According to these figures the three crops together showed up to 1933–1935 no increase, but the three crops of 1936–1938 were bumper harvests far surpassing all previous ones. It remains to be seen whether this was due to a permanent improvement in production or perhaps to an improvement in statistical methods.

[1] I should have preferred to have the average of several years rather than the data for 1913, but average figures are not available. It must also be considered that pre-war figures for the territories later incorporated in Yugoslavia comprised Macedonia and other parts where agriculture had suffered much through the Balkan wars and long years of internal strife, and where the crops were therefore abnormally low.

The development of livestock can be followed in these figures (thousands) :—[1]

	Horses.	Cattle.	Pigs.	Sheep.	Goats.
1914 .	1,556	6,277	5,234	11,570	2,445
1919 .	1,009	4,555	2,973	5,250	1,200
1929 .	1,140	3,728	2,675	7,736	1,804
1935 .	1,201	3,982	2,931	9,211	1,896
1938 .	1,264	4,267	3,451	10,137	1,890

In 1938 all kinds of livestock were considerably lower in numbers than twenty-four years before. Cattle had not even reached the level attained at the end of the war.

D. Warriner thinks that in Yugoslavia the effect of the reform has been on the whole good, especially in the parts where formerly the peasants had to pay rent to the landlord in the form of a share in the crops, while no rent had to be paid for livestock. Consequently they kept as much livestock as possible, and reduced the corn area to the minimum needed for their own subsistence, leaving about half the land fallow. No wonder that after the abolition of crop-sharing cereal production increased and livestock decreased.

12. AGRICULTURAL DECLINE IN THE FORMERLY AUSTRIAN PARTS OF POLAND

The greater part of Poland has no connection with the Danubian countries. Only the southern territories belonged before the end of the First World War to Austria, and were then called Galicia. Later they formed the districts of Cracow, Lwow, Stanislawow and Tarnopol, or together "Southern Poland". A glance at the development of this territory after the war is sufficient for our purpose.

The principal crops were as follows ('ooo mq.) :—

	Wheat.	Rye.	Oats.	Barley.	Potatoes.
1908–1912 .	6,289	17,928	7,415	3,804	56,683
1932–1936 .	5,699	8,061	6,356	3,207	63,963

[1] The pre-war figures are taken from R. Aranitovic, *Les ressources et l'activité économique de la Yougoslavie*, 1930, p. 33. The later figures are from the *Annuaire Statistique de la Yougoslavie*.

The livestock showed the following development ('ooo's) :—

	Horses.	Cattle.	Pigs.	Sheep.
1910 . .	910	2,523	1,840	366
1936 . .	820	2,523	933	409

The population of Southern Poland increased from the end of 1921 to the end of 1935 from 7·6 to 9·0 millions, or in fourteen years by 18·4%.

An English investigator comes to the conclusion :—[1]

> "Both in S. Poland and large parts of Yugoslavia the rural population has increased faster than agricultural output. In other words, output per man has fallen and with it earnings per man. Each year the people plunge deeper and deeper into poverty from which there is no apparent escape."

C. STRUCTURAL CHANGES IN INDUSTRIAL CONDITIONS

1. BASIC CONDITIONS OF INDUSTRIAL PRODUCTION IN THE AUSTRIAN REPUBLIC

The most important structural change in Austria's industrial position after the war was the narrowing of markets. The population of new Austria was only 22·9% of that of former Austria. The shrinkage of markets, however, was still greater than indicated by this figure. Old Austria had formed part of the Austro-Hungarian Customs union, and through its break-up lost seven-eighths of its internal market, measured by the number of population. Equally damaging were the losses in raw materials and other resources. The territory of small Austria produced only 12% of the value of the mineral production of old Austria. The output of coal, in particular, was quite inadequate, though new Austria possessed a great amount of water-power.

[1] Cf. P. Lamartine Yates and D. Warriner, *Food and Farming in Post-War Europe*, 1943, p. 49.

The territory of the Republic of Austria is mainly mountainous, and it has no easy access to the sea. The conditions of transport are therefore difficult, and its cost is high. For this reason Austria is not a country for heavy industries and cheap mass production requiring low cost of transport. She was compelled to develop industries which do not depend on cheap raw materials and coal, but are based on the special skill of the workers, on the good taste of the designer, or on commercial efficiency. In cheap mass production Austria cannot compete with Germany or Czechoslovakia, but she has to a great extent specialised in goods of quality and taste. This holds good for many branches of industry. All heavy iron products and heavy machines were more cheaply produced in the Bohemian territories, but in special steel alloys, electro-technical engineering and similar goods Austria was foremost. Czechoslovakia manufactured cheap strong boots, Austria lady's fashion shoes and fine leather-ware. Many natural and historical factors had led to a far-reaching division of labour between the various parts of Austria-Hungary, which after the war was soon greatly diminished by the rise of economic nationalism.[1]

2. New Austria's Industrial Capacity was a Third of that of Former Austria

In order to compare production before and after the war it is necessary to estimate what proportion of former Austria's [2] industrial production was left to the new Austria. This will here be called the industrial quota.

In 1913 the number of factories in the post-war territory of Austria was 33·3% of the total and that of the workers insured against accident—mainly factory operatives and builders—was 34·4%. The Austrian share in the wages of the insured workers was as high as 39·3%. But if mines and workshops without motor-power are included the share of new Austria in the number of workers falls to 30·3%. On the other hand, according to the

[1] Statistical data and other materials on the pre-war production of various industries are given in Karl Hudeczek, *Die Wirtschaftskräfte Österreichs*, 2nd ed., 1921; Otto Beck, *Die Wirtschaftsgebiete an der Mittel-Donau vor dem Kriege*, 1922; *Wirtschaftsstatistische Materialien über Deutschösterreich*, edited by the Vienna Chamber of Commerce, 1919.

[2] Viz., the part of the Empire unofficially called Austria.

138

industrial Census of 1902, 35·6% of the power used in industries was located in the territory which later became the Austrian Republic.[1]

Waizner has worked out the share in the value of factory production, making use of Fellner's figures. He arrived at 29·6% for new Austria. If industrial and commercial production are taken together, the share rises to 31·3%. His method, however, leads to an under-estimate. He distributed Fellner's estimates of factory output according to the total number of workers, including those in handicrafts, and made no allowance for regional differences in industrial productivity.

The share of new Austria in factories, factory workers, wages and motor-power was greater than her share in the total of workers in small and large workshops. The strength of Austria was in the great number of small specialised factories. Her share in the giant plants for mass production was smaller than that of the Bohemian territories. The average worker in the great industrial district of Vienna did more skilled work, and was better equipped with tools and experience, than a worker in the less-developed parts of old Austria, such as Galicia, and even in the advanced parts like Bohemia, which were mainly engaged in mass production. In 1912, for example, the average daily wage, according to the Accident Insurance Statistics, was in the Insurance District of Vienna 4·17 K., in Bohemia 3·14 K. and in Galicia 2·58 K. This difference in the wage level was due to the fact that the average worker did more skilled work in Vienna than in Prague or Lemberg, because Vienna possessed more refining industries. The industrial net product per worker, however, increases with the amount of skilled work done. The watchmaker produces a greater net value than the worker producing pig iron.

It may therefore be assumed that new Austria's share in the industrial net product of former Austria was about a third. If commerce, banking, etc., are added to industries, the net output was certainly at least a third, and probably more than that. Postwar statistics, however, include an additional territory—namely, Burgenland.

[1] In using pre-war statistics allowance must be made for the territories lopped off from the provinces. The total loss in workers was 8%. For certain purposes, however, the figures for Styria and Tyrol must be reduced separately. The above quotas do not include Burgenland.

In comparing pre- and post-war conditions account must also be taken of the increase in industrial capacity during the war and in the period of inflation after the war. Both the war and the depreciation of the currency stimulated the foundation of new industries and the expansion of existing ones. From 1913 to 1923 the number of factories in the territory of new Austria rose from 5,670 to 7,645, or by 35·7% It has been estimated that the industrial capacity increased by about 20%. But this increase was to a great extent a doubtful blessing. Numerous plants set up for war purposes could not be switched to profitable peace-time production, and much capital was lost in attempts at adaptation. In the period of inflation production was artificially stimulated at the expense of the standard of living. Moreover, the constant decline in the value of money induced many people to get rid of their money as quickly as possible by investing it in new industries or banks without close scrutiny of their prospects. Most of these new enterprises soon broke down, with a great loss of capital.

3. The Development of Industrial Activity in Austria

The easiest approach to an estimate of production before and after the war seems to be by comparing the active population, and especially the workers employed, according to pre- and post-war Censuses. It must not be overlooked, however, that most Censuses class as active workers all those normally engaged in an occupation whether at the moment employed or unemployed.

Available Working Population in Post-War Territory (in '000's)

	Active population.		Workers.	
	1910.	1934.	1910.	1934.
Industries, mining, handicraft .	1,104	1,100	900	914
Commerce, transport . .	474	527	333	372

These figures show that in twenty-four years the number of industrial workers, including the unemployed, remained almost the same. The population employed in commerce and transport, however, increased, though the commercial position of Vienna was greatly reduced through the destruction of the economic community of the Danubian nations.

The actually employed personnel is shown by the statistics of the Accident and Health Insurance. After the war the scope of insurance was extended. The pre-war figures referred to the end of the year, while the post-war figures shown are averages of the monthly figures. Owing to seasonal variations the average number of insured persons was, however, higher than the number at the end of the year. The post-war figures include Burgenland, which did not belong to Austria before the war. The post-war figures are strictly inter-comparable only since 1928.[1] The Accident Insurance figures refer to "full workers"—*i.e.* the hours actually worked divided by 300.

ACTUALLY EMPLOYED PERSONNEL, EXCLUSIVE OF MINES, AGRICULTURE, RAILWAYS AND PUBLIC SERVICE

(In '000's)

	Accident Insurance.	Health Insurance.	
	(*Mainly workers in factories, transport and building.*)	Salaried employees.	Wage-earners.
1912 . . .	*ca.* 648	*ca.* 1,314	
1922 . . .	700	1,207	
1923 . . .	619	1,146	
1924 . . .	691	1,249	
1925 . . .	668	1,227	
1926 . . .	669	1,308	
1927 . . .	616	—	
1928 . . .	637	229	1,069
1929 . . .	642	235	1,057
1930 . . .	600	231	999
1931 . . .	529	217	914
1932 . . .	442	195	798
1933 . . .	395	184	734
1934 . . .	417	181	738
1935 . . .	—	187	739
1936 . . .	—	187	729
1937 . . .	—	194	761

[1] Since 1928 the salaried employees have been insured separately from the wage-earners and shown separately in the statistics (number at end of the year).

The fictitious prosperity and full employment of the inflation period came to an end in 1923, after the stabilisation of the currency. Inflation had fostered reckless gambling, and a decline in commercial solidity and public morality ending in the disclosure of many scandals and in heavy losses. From 1924 to 1927 Austria was affected by a severe crisis.[1] In 1928 and 1929 she had a moderate share in the world boom, but then the great crisis hit Austria with particular force, and had devastating effects.

The variation in the number of workers did not exactly indicate the real economic situation. Immediately after the war, on April 26th, 1919, a law forbade employers to dismiss workers without a special permit and prescribed that they had even to increase the number of their workers by 20%, irrespective of whether they were wanted or not. Permission to dismiss workers was regularly refused. This law expired only in 1928. It must further be considered that before the war the usual working time was nine hours, or even more, while after the war the eight-hour day was made compulsory. A larger number of workers was therefore needed for the same work than before the war. All these factors increased the number of workers far beyond the number considered normal in pre-war times, and render any comparison futile. On the other hand, many employers soon made efforts to introduce labour-saving machinery in order to reduce the cost of production and to overcome the barriers erected by economic nationalism, which threatened their existence. The high level of employment in the ten years after the war was by no means a sign of genuine prosperity, but rather the opposite. The majority of manufacturers for a long time cherished the hope that they would be able to maintain their export to the markets severed from Austria. Many also tried to adapt factories founded in the war, or during inflation, to the new conditions, and for a certain time they seemed to succeed, owing to the premium of a depreciated currency, the influx of capital, etc. But eventually the fact that a large part of Austria's industries had lost any chance of survival could no longer be blinked, and there came a catastrophe. Enormous amounts of capital had been spent in the effort to keep industries going and maintain employment, and the investments

[1] On the heavy losses resulting from this crisis cf. my paper on capital formation in Austria, printed in *Schriften des Vereins für Sozialpolitik*, 1929, vol. 174, IV.

made for rationalising production often only made things worse and increased the losses.

Industrial activity is often measured by the amount of coal used by industries. The Austrian statistics provide very detailed monthly figures of coal consumption for each industry and for other groups of consumers such as electricity works, households, etc. The consumption of coal for industrial production, exclusive of electricity, gas and water works, was ('ooo tons) :—

Pre-war, 4,530; 1922, 3,740; 1923, 3,125; 1924, 3,266; 1925, 3,506; 1926, 3,353; 1927, 3,650; 1928, 3,905; 1929, 4,211; 1930, 3,343; 1931, 2,950; 1932, 2,516; 1933, 2,472; 1934, 2,579; 1935, 2,757; 1936, 2,722,

These figures are useful indices for short-term comparisons. But over a long term of years their reliability diminishes. On the one hand, Austria replaced high-grade foreign coal by low-grade Austrian lignite; on the other hand, the utilisation of fuel was improved and the use of water-power extended. The statistics show that from 1918 to 1935 the capacity of hydro-electric plants of larger size (over 500 Kw.) for industrial purposes increased considerably. On the other hand, however, in the same period the amount of electricity produced from coal and water by industrial enterprises for their own consumption showed a great decline. How far this was made good by electricity purchased from big power-stations is not indicated.[1]

It has been estimated that the industrial output of Austria in 1924–1926 was between 75% and 80% of the pre-war capacity, which would make it about two-thirds of the increased post-war capacity.[2] Now, from 1925–1929 the industrial coal supply, the import of raw materials and the export of finished goods all increased by about 20%, allowing for the change in prices. This seems to indicate that in 1929—the peak of the short period of prosperity—industrial production had reached about 95% of the pre-war level, and about 80% of the post-war capacity. There are, however, reasons for regarding this as an over-statement. The League of Nations Index of Industrial Production showed for Austria the following variations :—

[1] *Oesterr. Statist. Jahrbuch*, 1937, pp. 69, 70.
[2] Cf. W. T. Layton and Ch. Rist, *The Economic Situation of Austria*, 1925, p. 19; L. Pasvolsky, *Economic Nationalism of the Danubian States*, 1928, p. 160.

1927, 90; 1928, 99; 1929, 100; 1930, 81; 1931, 69; 1932, 60; 1933, 62; 1934, 68; 1935, 77; 1936, 81. The index of the Vienna Trade Cycle Institute (1929: 100) was for 1936: 86 and for 1937: 103.

4. THE DEVELOPMENT OF THE PRINCIPAL INDUSTRIES

Statistics of output are available only for certain industries and for some others the import of raw materials like cotton or rubber can be taken as a safe index of the level of production.

Production of:	1913.	1929.	1933.	1935.	1937.
Pig iron . . .	100	76	15	32	63
Steel	100	71	25	41	69
Bars, rails, plates, wire,					
etc.	100	111	44	64	104
Iron ore . . .	100	93	13	38	93
Lignite . . .	100	117	100	98	107
Magnesite . . .	100	91	49	74	99
Cement . . .	100	78	37	49	57
Salt	100	51	49	58	54
Engineering . . .	100	69	22	32	36
Motor cars (capacity					
1918) . . .	—	17	—	—	—
Paper	100	122	111	105	123
Cellulose . . .	100	187	185	212	253
Wood-pulp cardboard .	100	72	59	56	76
Sugar	100	197	279	351	253
Beer	100	75	33	33	31
Tobacco . . .	100	100	96	78	70
Alcohol . . .	100	208	—	139	159
Glass (sheet) . .	100	250	—	—	320
Industrial consumption of:					
Cotton . . .	100	72	61	84	100
Wool	100	73	103	108	98
Jute, flax, hemp . .	100	121	—	109	110
Rubber . . .	100	346	244	313	325
Copper . . .	100	—	35	76	—
Zinc	100	—	30	44	—
Tannics . . .	100	—	55	43	—
Pyrites	100	—	328	361	—

These figures show a very unfavourable development in iron, steel, engineering, building materials, beer, tobacco, salt, while the production of paper, cellulose, sugar, glass, alcohol and rubber increased considerably. The bulk of the textile industries was for a long time depressed, but later it picked up. The rise in paper and rubber had a sound basis. The other increasing industries were stimulated by high tariffs shutting out the former imports.

The particularly grave depression in engineering was due to the lack of capital and the high tariffs in those countries which were Austria's natural markets. The decline in tobacco and beer was a symptom of the deterioration in the living conditions of the people, though changes in the habits of consumption also contributed to it.

5. THE DIFFICULTIES OF INDUSTRIAL PRODUCTION

When the great world crisis began gravely to affect Austria's economic life the Government appointed a commission of prominent economists and other experts charged to inquire into the causes of the difficulties. The Commission published its Report in 1931.[1] It contains a wealth of statistical and other information supplied by the various branches of administration and by industrial and financial experts and covers mainly the period 1925–1929, which was a time of expanding production. In their final conclusions the experts point out that the unfavourable economic development was principally due to the fact that from 1925 to 1929 the cost of production increased much more than prices did. Taxation rose by 32% (Federal by 27%, Provincial and communal by 40%), social insurance by 50%, industrial wages by 24%, agricultural wages by 13%, cost of transport by 15%. The only decrease was that in the rate of interest, which, however, was still very high. The bank rate declined from 1925 to 1929 from 13% to $7\frac{1}{2}$%, and the interest paid by industrial debtors from 16·5 to 13%. The interest charged by the agricultural co-operatives (*Raiffeisenkassen*) to farmers fell from 12·3% to 8·7%; in 1913 it had been only 4·75%. The decline in the rates of interest, however, was far outweighed by the increase in all the other burdens of production. From 1925 to the beginning of 1930 the index of prices of manufactured goods rose by 4·74%, that of home-produced raw materials by 4·5%, while that of home-produced food fell by 15·4%. The rise in wages led to considerable increases

[1] Cf. *Bericht über die Ursachen der Wirtschaftsschwierigkeiten Oesterreichs, herausgegeben von der Wirtschaftskommission*, 1931.

in the consumption of various foods, tobacco, alcohol, textiles, shoes, etc., as proved by statistical data. But export of manufactures was faced with great difficulties owing to the high cost of production. A still greater obstacle to export was the increase of protection in many States.

The excessive rise in the cost of production, the experts concluded, had the consequence that the earnings of the industries were inadequate and that new investments were discouraged. Consequently there was a constant rise in unemployment. Of the total of workers insured for unemployment there were out of work (including those not receiving allowances): 1925, 14·1%; 1926, 15·5%; 1927, 15·5%; 1928, 15·8%; 1929, 17·0%; 1940, 22·7%.

In the years of depression after the publication of the Report unemployment attained still higher percentages.

The data compiled by the Economic Commission certainly show that production was in difficulties through the rise in taxes, social burdens, wages, etc., and agricultural production also through the fall in prices. But this argument requires certain qualifications. In 1927 in an address to the Association of Austrian Economists I drew attention to the fact that total taxation amounted to almost a third of Austria's national income, while in Czechoslovakia the burden was only between a fifth and a fourth.[1] But I also pointed out that a large proportion of public expenditure was of a productive nature. In the Austrian Republic, for example, up to 1930 no less than 868,300 h.p. were newly installed in great water-power works, effecting a very considerable saving in coal. A large part of the money invested came from the State, the Provinces and the cities. The State railways electrified some of their main lines. Another example was the great housing programme of the city of Vienna. The increase in taxes was therefore not exclusively a burden on production, but contributed also to the improvement of industrial equipment and of the living conditions of the workers.

The Report, furthermore, did not take adequate account of the decrease in cost of production through the extensive measures of industrial rationalisation carried out in the period under review.

[1] Cf. statistical proofs in the report of my address in the *Neue Freie Presse* of January 19th, 1927.

True, the Report quotes a few figures concerning rationalisation; but they are not impressive. The Vienna Chamber of Labour and other investigators, however, have collected many data showing that in many industries the output per head of the worker had considerably increased. [1]

6. UNEMPLOYMENT IN AUSTRIA CHRONIC AND DEVASTATING

The International Labour Office has calculated an index showing the general level of employment in reference to 1929. The following table shows the situation in Austria in comparison with that in Czechoslovakia, Germany and Great Britain.

			Austria.	Czechoslovakia.	Germany.	Great Britain.
1929	.	.	100	100	100	100
1930	.	.	95·1	97·6	93·3	95·8
1931	.	.	86·6	92·3	81·5	92·2
1932	.	.	76·4	82·6	71·7	91·4
1933	.	.	70·6	75·4	74·0	94·7
1934	.	.	69·8	75·0	85·5	99·2
1935	.	.	66·8	76·6	90·6	101·5
1936	.	.	64·6	82·4	97·2	106·7
1937	.	.	67·4	90·0	104·3	112·3

These figures show that in Austria the industrial depression was more acute and lasted longer than in the other countries.

The unemployment situation, moreover, was much graver than is shown by the relative drop in employment. Austria already had a high rate of unemployment in the years preceding the depression, and even in 1928 and 1929. The figure 100 on which the above table is based is not, therefore, identical with full employment. In 1929—the best year of the post-war period— between 10% and 20% of the workers were unemployed in Austria, compared with 7·6% and 9·2% in Britain.

The table on p. 148 shows yearly averages.

The peak of unemployment was reached in February 1933, when the number of assisted unemployed rose to 402,200 and the real figure, including the unassisted, the juveniles in labour camps, those assisted under the old age pensions scheme, etc.,

[1] Cf. the data in *Österr. Volkswirt* of August 4th, 1928, January 31st, 1931, and the article by B. Kautsky in that paper of May 1931, p. 839.

	Registered unemployed.	Assisted unemployed.
1923	—	110
1924	—	94
1925	—	149
1926	—	177
1927	200	172
1928	182	156
1929	192	164
1930	243	207
1931	300	253
1932	378	309
1933	406	329
1934	370	288
1935	349	262
1936	350	259
1937	321	231

amounted to 580,000, or more than two-thirds of the workers insured against unemployment.

The unemployment rate in Austria showed unusually great seasonal variations. The following table shows the maxima and minima for some years:—

REGISTERED UNEMPLOYED

(In '000's)

	1930.	1931.	1932.	1933.	1934.	1935.	1936.
Maxima .	341	396	450	480	440	424	416
Minima .	180	231	328	355	326	290	304

In summer, when agricultural work was in full swing, the number of unemployed was much lower than in winter. The variation in the summer figures is therefore probably a better index of industrial activity than that in the yearly averages. From 1926 to 1929 the summer figures declined by 31%, and from 1929 onwards rose steeply. The constant increase of rural elements seeking industrial employment was a major cause of unemployment. The insurance was sometimes misused by rural claimants, who for a short time worked as seasonal workers in some industry, and when the season was over claimed the unemployment allowance. Precautions were, however, taken to check any misuse. The fact that agricultural labourers were not entitled to unemployment
148

assistance naturally contributed to the migration from the rural areas to the towns.

Another factor swelling the unemployment figures was the impoverishment of the middle classes, which forced many new people, especially women, to look for manual work. Lastly, the age structure of the population, to which attention has already been drawn (p. 98), had a great share in the rise in unemployment.

Even the appalling figures quoted, however, do not show the whole extent of unemployment. Various definitions of unemployment are possible, and the statistical data vary with the underlying definition. In popular parlance, of course, everybody is regarded as unemployed who is out of work, though he would be willing to accept a post. But any definition for insurance purposes, and for statistical measurement, introduces restricting qualifications. Now, the Census of 1934 tried to count the unemployed by asking in its questionnaire simply whether a worker was employed or not. The result obviously depended on the views of the people interrogated. No investigation was made as to whether the unemployment was due to seasonal causes, the wish for a time of rest, ill health, aversion to a post offered or similar obstacles. The figures were:—

EMPLOYEES AND WORKERS, 1934
(In '000's)

	Employed.	Unemployed.
Agriculture, forestry . . .	331	27
Mining	16	7
Industries, commerce, transport, liberal professions . . .	455	365
Other services	556	127
Unspecified	27	66
Total	1,385	591
Exclusive of agriculture .	1,054	563

The Census arrives at a much higher figure of unemployment than the statistics quoted above. In industries 44·5% of all workers were counted as out of work, and in all non-agricultural occupations 34·8%.

We may refer here to a calculation made in an earlier place (p. 48) comparing the Census of 1910 with the statistics of

149

employed workers according to the Health Insurance. The result was that in pre-war days only 3·7% of the workers and employees counted by the Census were not registered as employed by the Health Insurance. This percentage included all those who for seasonal reasons, or of their own will, were temporarily out of work.

7. The Rise of the Wage Level

The development of wages in Austria can be followed in the statistics published by the Statistical Office and the Vienna Chamber of Labour. The official yearbook gives a list of industrial wage-rates fixed in collective agreements, and has also published the corresponding rates for 1914. This enables us to calculate an industrial wage index showing the development since the pre-war period. For this purpose, however, we must first select a number of representative wages corresponding in composition to the distribution of the main classes of industrial workers. The Trade Census of 1930 showed that of all workers in industries (exclusive of mining) 38% were skilled workers, 11% apprentices learning a skilled trade, 21% semi-skilled workers,[1] 28% unskilled workers, and 3% home workers. 25·3% of the workers were women.

In order to calculate a weighted index, I have therefore selected sixteen wage-rates, of which six were those of skilled workers and the rest unskilled, of various types. Five wages referred to female workers, among whom one was skilled and one half-skilled.

The nominal wages must further be compared with prices. This can be done under various aspects—namely, (1) to assess the standard of life of the worker the wage must be compared with the cost-of-living index; (2) to assess the significance of the wage factor for cost of production it must be compared with the index of industrial prices; (3) to assess the relation between the income of the industrial workers and the income of other classes the wage

[1] Actually many of the "semi-skilled", especially females, were highly skilled, but were considered inferior to the *Professionisten*—here called skilled—who enjoyed a special status. The reason obviously was that women were paid lower wages than men, however skilled they might be, and this was justified by calling them less skilled than men.

level must be compared with the general price index, the index of agricultural prices, etc.

INDUSTRIAL WAGE INDEX

	1914.	1923.	1926.	1929.	1933.	1935.
Weighted average of sixteen weekly wages (S.) . .	35·64	31·23	45·26	52·50	51·06	50·16
Index of nominal wages . .	100	87·5	127·0	147·3	143·3	140·7
Cost-of-living index .	100	80 [1]	103	110	108	105
Real wage level .	100	109	123	134	133	134
Wholesale prices .	100	124	123	130	108	110
Food prices . .	100	—	115	122	100	102
Industrial prices .	100	—	140	146	124	126

[1] The index for 1923 was officially stated as 76, and this would mean a real wage level of 115. But the labour organisations pointed out that the official index was understated owing to an inadequate method of calculation. The method was actually reformed, and the figure of 80 would probably be more correct.

The real wage level rose considerably after the war,[2] partly owing to the fact that the cost of living was kept down by the policy of restricting rents, partly because food prices lagged behind wages. In the first ten years after the war the unflinching resistance of the Social Democrats to any substantial rise in rents had the effect that a great section of the population paid only nominal rents. The working class, though by no means they alone, received in this way a subsidy at the expense of the house-owners.

The rise of nominal wages was further due to the increase in the power of the Labour movement which took place after the war in all countries. An international comparison seems to show that wages rose in Austria even more quickly than in many another comparable country. The lower wages rose more than the higher ones. Among the wages on which our calculation is based those of the skilled male workers rose only by 33·29%, while those of female unskilled workers increased by 53·7%. The salaries of higher Civil Servants, scientists, etc., could not follow the rise in industrial wages, and were for a considerable time inadequate. This fact led

[2] Cf. also the data in *International Labour Review*, 1928, II, 785, and in a previous publication of the International Labour Office, *Wage Changes in Various Countries*, 1926.

to acrimonious public controversies between the Socialists and their adversaries.[1]

Our findings can be confirmed and supplemented from other sources. Just before the war the Office of Labour Statistics in the Ministry for Social Welfare collected 119 budgets showing in great detail the consumption and expenses of working-class families in Vienna. After the war the Vienna Chamber of Labour organised similar inquiries.[2] In 1912–1914 the average income of a working-class family was 2,472·8 K. or 3,560·8 S., and each family comprised on the average 2·2 wage-earners. In 1929 the family income was 5,242 S., or 47·2% more. The increase was exactly the same as in the above table. The Chamber of Labour does not indicate the average number of wage-earners. It is known, however, that after the war the workers had fewer children, so that the wages had to provide for a smaller number of family members. Moreover, the city of Vienna bestowed great care upon children's health and welfare, thereby relieving the burdens of the parents.

Before the war the average wage assessed for contributions to the Worker's Accident Insurance was a good index of the industrial wage level. After the war this changed, since the limit up to which wages were taken into account was considerably lowered and several times altered. In 1929 it was 2,400 S., a year. If we consider that the average wage of skilled and unskilled workers was, according to the Vienna Chamber of Labour, 3,241 S., it is clear that the total of wages assessed for the Accident Insurance was considerably below the real amount of wages. It is possible, however, to estimate the amount in excess of the limit, and if this amount is added, and if then the average wage per full worker (exclusive of railwaymen) is calculated for the time before and after the war, we find that wages rose by 44%. This seems to confirm the previous calculations.

[1] In the time of inflation a well-known meteorologist of the University of Vienna actually died of hunger, and large sections of the intellectual classes were near starvation, especially as their income from capital was also wiped out by the depreciation of the currency. Cf. the data in S. Strakosch, *Der Selbstmord eines Volkes*, 1922, p. 50.

[2] Cf. *Wirtschaftsrechnungen und Lebensverhältnisse Wiener Arbeiterfamilien*, 1916. The investigations were organised by Professor Schiff. Cf. also *Statist. Monatsschrift*, 1916, p. 701. The post-war investigations are published in the *Wirtschaftsstatistisches Jahrbuch der Wiener Arbeiterkammer*.

The Vienna Chamber of Labour has compiled very extensive and instructive statistics of wages, but we cannot go into details here. It may, however, be mentioned that the actual weekly earnings of the main categories of workers were:—[1]

	1925.	1935.
Skilled craftsmen	59·28 S.	62·33 S.
Qualified assistants, male	51·93 S.	54·47 S.
Qualified assistants, female . . .	31·34 S.	33·08 S.
Unqualified assistants, male . . .	44·45 S.	46·70 S.
Unqualified assistants, female . . .	28·78 S.	31·12 S.

The cost-of-living index was in these two years about the same.

The Health Insurance Institutions have, furthermore, published the distribution for 1926 of the employees and workers insured according to ten wage classes.[2] Both the statistics of the Chamber of Labour and of the Health Insurance can, in combination with the data of the Census of 1930 and other figures, be used for calculating the average weekly wage of all workers. I have done this, and found that the average weekly wage in the Health Insurance was 43 S.,[3] and the average weekly wage according to the Chamber of Labour 46·11 S. The corresponding figure in the above table of average wages was 45·36 S. The two last-mentioned calculations are therefore in almost full agreement. The difference is less than 2%. The average calculated from the Health Insurance Statistics differed a little more from that in the table, being about 5% lower. But the table shows only the average of industrial wages, while the Health Insurance includes also all kinds of employees in commerce, transport, liberal professions and domestic services, besides those employed in industries. The only category not in the General Health Insurance was that of the miners, who had their separate one. It may therefore be concluded that in 1926 the average weekly wage for all employees under the Health Insurance was 43 S.

The International Labour Office has several times made

[1] Cf. *Wirtschaftsstatistisches Jahrbuch*, 1936, p. 42.
[2] Cf. *ibid.*, 1926, p. 465.
[3] I assumed for the calculation that the average wage in each class was the mean between the upper and lower limit. For the lowest and highest class adequate amounts were assumed according to the detailed statistics of wages.

investigations designed to compare the real wage level in various countries. For January 1930 the following data were given: London, 100; U.S.A., 197; Canada, 165; Australia, 148; Sweden, 113; Denmark, 112; Irish Free State, 97; Netherlands, 87; Germany, 77; Czechoslovakia, 74; Poland, 65; France, 58; Austria, 52; Spain, 45; Estonia, 45; Italy, 43. According to this table the purchasing power of an Austrian worker's average wage was little more than half that of the average British wages, and a little more than a fourth of the American wages. His real wage was considerably less than those in Poland and Czechoslovakia. One point, however, must be mentioned which modifies this picture to a certain extent. The International Labour Office has only taken account of the prices of food, fuel and soap, but has made no allowance for the cost of rent and clothing. The Austrian workers benefited from the very low level of rents, which were kept down by the State.

Besides wages social services must also be taken into account. In Austria, as in other countries, the range of social welfare policy was greatly extended after the war. The Vienna Chamber of Labour estimated in 1924 that the total contribution of the employers to social insurance was between 11% and 12% of the wages. A Czech economist, A. Basch, estimated at about the same time that these contributions amounted in Austria to 14% and in Czechoslovakia to 8%.[1] In 1928 it was calculated by a well-known economist, J. Jellinek, that the cost of all social services was 16·8% of the wages, but that only 9·5% were borne by the employers. In 1933 Trčka came to the conclusion that the social contributions amounted in Austria to 15·1% of wages and to 25·5% of salaries, and were higher than in Czechoslovakia and Germany.[2] The differences between these estimates may be partly due to differences in the range of services included.

---

[1] Cf. *International Labour Review*, 1930, p. 557. The further development of real wages can be seen from the tables published in the *Year Book of Labour Statistics*, edited by the I.L.O. In 1936, for instance, the real wages had in Great Britain risen by 11% over the level of 1929, while in Austria it had declined by 4%. The real wages, therefore, of an Austrian worker had in 1936 fallen to 45% of the British rate.

[2] Cf. *Wirtschaftsstatistisches Jahrbuch*, 1924, p. 95; 1926, p. 491; A. Basch and J. Dvoracek, *Austria and its Economic Existence*, 1925, p. 56; Jellinek in *Österr. Volkswirt* of March 3rd, 1928; B. Trčka, *Soziale Lasten als Kostenfaktor*, 1933; cf. a criticism of this study in *Österr. Volkswirt*, 1933, p. 1138.

8. The Decline in Industrial and Commercial Returns

In pre-war times Austrian industries were remunerative, and sufficient capital was formed to expand and improve existing industries and to found new ones, thereby preventing widespread unemployment. The industrial limited companies of the whole of former Austria earned, after deduction of losses, the following dividends: 1908, 8·53%; 1909, 8·63%; 1910, 8·85%; 1911, 8·95%; 1912, 9·51%. The majority of the Austrian industrialists were very skilled and experienced, both technically and commercially, and enjoyed a high reputation and great credit on the international markets.

The situation after the war is shown in the table on p. 156.

The figures there show that the industrial companies of new Austria earned over a period of twelve years only 1·2% on their capital (share capital plus all reserves). This average dividend was certainly not an adequate compensation for the efforts and risks involved in the management of Austrian industries after the war; it neither allowed the formation of sufficient capital for industrial rationalisation and expansion, nor could it induce foreign capitalists to invest money in Austrian industries.

It is also interesting to compare the net profit with the turnover of the companies. The Statistical Office has published these figures:—[1]

Net Profits (or Losses) in Per Cent. of Turnover (1925)

Mining, 1%; Stones and Ceramics, 2·4%; Building, loss 0·1%; Electricity Works, 12·5%; Iron and Metals, 1·3%; Wood Industries, loss 1·5%; Leather, loss 1·3%; Textiles, 1·8%; Clothing, 0·5%; Paper, 0·2%; Graphic Industries, 1·1%; Chemical Industries, 2·6%; Food Industries; 3·5%; Catering, Hotels, loss 4·1%; Commerce, 0·6%.

9. The Social Structure of Business Returns

The profits of firms other than companies are shown by the statistics of the trade tax (*Erwerbssteuer*).[2] This tax was paid by every firm in industries, commerce and all other occupations, except agriculture, even by enterprises which showed no profit or had closed down, but had not dissolved.

[1] Cf. *Statistische Nachrichten*, 1937, p. 111.
[2] *Ibid.*, 1936, p. 100.

PROFITS AND LOSSES OF INDUSTRIAL LIMITED COMPANIES [1]

('000,000 Schilling)

	Number of companies reporting.	Number of these showing a		Capital of all companies (including reserves).	Dividends paid.	Placed to reserves.	Directors' fees.	Total profits (dividends, reserves, directors' fees).	Losses.	Profits minus losses.	Profit or loss in percentage of capital.
		Profit.	Loss.								%
1925	414	313	98	1,365·6	43·7	3·8	3·2	50·7	11·0	39·7	2·9
1926	515	336	175	1,518·8	47·3	5·3	3·0	55·6	23·2	32·4	2·1
1927	522	353	166	1,548·2	50·6	6·7	3·8	61·1	15·3	45·8	2·9
1928	540	381	155	1,609·9	63·9	8·5	4·4	76·8	26·2	50·6	3·1
1929	525	340	180	1,621·1	59·0	7·2	4·0	70·2	63·8	6·4	0·4
1930	470	270	196	1,543·2	47·6	6·0	3·0	56·6	41·2	15·4	1·0
1931	452	223	220	1,517·0	31·7	3·5	1·6	36·8	47·4	10·6 [2]	0·7 [2]
1932	455	218	233	1,589·7	25·4	2·8	0·9	29·1	77·5	48·4 [2]	3·0 [2]
1933	629	326	303	1,995·5	28·5	17·2	1·5	47·2	62·4	15·2 [2]	0·96 [2]
1934	636	353	283	1,931·7	33·5	15·9	1·9	51·3	32·2	19·1	0·98
1935	265	200	65	1,768·4	37·8	18·2	2·2	58·2	12·8	45·4	2·58
1936	275	217	58	1,787·6	41·7	26·7	2·5	70·9	9·3	61·6	3·4
	—	—	—	19,796·7	—	—	—	—	—	242·2	1·2

[1] Many of the existing companies did not send in reports because they had closed down for good, or were for other reasons unable to draw up a balance-sheet. The statistics refer to industrial companies; but in the two years 1933 and 1934 banks, insurance companies, etc., were also included, and in 1935 and 1936 many small and unimportant companies were omitted. This explains the changes in the numbers of companies.

[2] Net loss.

NET RETURNS OF FIRMS OTHER THAN COMPANIES

	Returns ('000,000 S.).	Monthly return per tax-payer.
1925 . . .	1,377	312 S.
1926 . . .	1,374	309
1927 . . .	1,419	320
1928 . . .	1,467	321
1929 . . .	1,417	306
1930 . . .	1,370	296
1931 . . .	1,261	272
1932 . . .	1,138	244
1933 . . .	1,059	230
1934 . . .	1,049	225
1935 . . .	1,071	229

In 1928, the best year, the monthly average income of the firms paying trade tax was 321 S. or in English money £9 5s. 7d. In the depression this figure decreased considerably. The statistics of trade tax show also the distribution of the net returns according to forty-three classes ascending by small steps. This makes it possible to calculate the return for each class assuming that the average return was the mean between the lower and upper limits. (It was, for example, assumed that in the class "from 1,600 to 1,800 S." the average income was 1,700 S., and this was multiplied by the number of tax-payers in this class.) We have made this calculation for the two years 1928, the peak year of prosperity, and 1934, the first year of recovery after the slump. The results of several classes have been summed up in a wider class in order to facilitate a survey. Furthermore, the pound-sterling equivalents of the Schilling amounts were added according to the exchange rate in 1928. In 1934, however, the relation was changed. The Schilling had depreciated by 21% and the pound by 38·2%. (See table on p. 158.)

The table shows that the industrial income consisted mainly of the returns of small businesses. If we assume, for instance, that the enterprises with a return of 34,500 gold Schilling or 1,000 gold pounds were to be considered "large", we find that in 1928 the total income from 1,000 pounds upwards amounted to only 245·7 million S. or 7·1 million pounds. It formed only 16·8% of the total industrial and commercial income (exclusive of companies) and was the return of 3,111 enterprises. In 1934 the amount of 34,500 S. was equivalent to 1,245 depreciated pounds.

	1928.		1934.	
	Number of enterprises.	*Returns ('000,000 S.).*	*Number of enterprises.*	*Returns ('000,000 S.).*
No profit and up to 3,400 S. (£100) .	262,372	380·7	305,406	385·2
3,401–6,000 S. (£100–175) . .	69,191	315·7	53,648	243·1
6,001–12,000 S. (£175–350) . .	32,432	269·3	20,660	168·7
12,001–34,500 S. (£350–1,000) .	13,550	255·9	6,497	133·9
34,501–120,000 S. (£1,000–3,500) .	2,785	155·2	1,157	77·1
120,001–500,000 S. (£3,500–14,500) .	294	58·5	125	24·8
Over 500,000 S. (over £14,500) . .	32	32	16	16·1
Total . .	380,656	1,467·3	387,509	1,048·9

The income above this limit amounted to 118 million S. or 4·3 million pounds. It formed only 11·2% of the total, and was the return of 1,298 enterprises.

It must also be considered that these returns were by no means identical with "profits" in the sense of income due to the ownership of capital. Most of the more than 380,000 tax-payers concerned were engaged in managing their business, and a part of the return was therefore to be regarded as remuneration for work done. If an amount adequate to the size of the enterprises is allowed for remunerating the work of the owners, the result is that the share of mere capitalistic ownership in the returns of the enterprises was comparatively small. In any case the table is a further illustration of the conditions which caused the insufficiency of capital formation.

10. Comparison of Returns Before and After the War

We may also compare the net income of the industrial and commercial enterprises before and after the war. In 1913, according to the Income Tax statistics, the income of all Austrian enterprises other than companies was 1,931·8 million K. To this must be added the income of companies amounting to 461 million K. As one-third of the industrial and commercial capacity was situated on the territory of post-war Austria, the share of this territory can be estimated at 797·6 million K. To this must further be added the income of small traders and independent workers not shown in the Income Tax statistics because their income, being below 1,200 K., or approximately £50, was not liable to tax. The number of these was in the post-war territory about 298,600,[1] and their average income may be assumed as 1,000 K. The total industrial and commercial income of employers and independent workers in the post-war territory of Austria was therefore in 1913 about 1,096·2 million K. or 1,578·5 million S. In 1928—the best post-war year—the total income of companies and other traders was 1,517·6 million S., and reduced to the price level of 1913 (index 1928 : 130) the amount was 1,167 million S. In the best year of the post-war period the income therefore amounted to only 74% of that of 1913. In fact the percentage was still smaller, since the assessment of all taxes was much stricter after the war. This was the income produced in the post-war territory, not the total income inclusive of the dividends paid to Austrian capitalists from enterprises situated outside the post-war territory.

The total income which before the war was received by firms in the territory of later, smaller Austria was much greater than that produced in this territory. It has been shown that the income produced in the workshops and businesses of smaller Austria was about a third of the income in the whole of Greater Austria. But the income tax statistics show that in 1913 54% of all the industrial and commercial profits in Greater Austria were assessed in the small post-war territory [2] and 61% of all income from capital, in particular that from dividends of companies and interest on bonds. The income assessed, plus that of the small independent workers not liable to income tax, was 1,811 million K. The income produced was only 1,096 million K. The difference of 715 million K. consisted largely in dividends and interest drawn by

[1] This was the number of traders assessed in the lowest (IV) class of the trade tax. Cf. above, p. 34. After the war the statistics of trade tax comprised also these smallest traders. The number of those liable to trade tax was even greater than that of all employers and independent workers shown by the Census, because those who, besides their main business, had a second subsidiary one were assessed twice.

[2] Deductions made for the lost parts, excluding Burgenland.

industrialists and capitalists living in Vienna and other places of smaller Austria from sources outside this territory. To this were added amounts from agricultural income, house-rent, etc., flowing in from places outside the post-war territory. It would be quite wrong, however, to assume that this huge income was entirely consumed in the places where it was assessed. Most of it flowed into the banks of Vienna, and was largely used for financing the economic development of all provinces, particularly the backward ones. The position of London in Great Britain, in the British Commonwealth and Empire, and in the world is a close analogy.

11. The Ruin of the Banking System in Austria

After the war the position of Vienna as the capital market of the whole Danubian area was entirely destroyed, though it took some time before the financial ruin was completed and could no longer be concealed. Before the war Vienna was the seat of eleven great banks with a share capital plus disclosed reserves of 1,310 million K. or 1,886 million S. The real capital was, however, much larger, since the banks had great undisclosed reserves. When in 1925, after the stabilisation of the currency, the banks stated their balance-sheets in stable money again, the total capital had shrunk to 309 million S., or to less than a sixth of the former amount. Allowing for post-war increases of capital, about 1,850 million S. had been lost. In the ensuing years all the great banks of Vienna broke down except one, which had become French and had transferred its headquarters to Paris, doing only a very modest business in Austria. Up to 1934 the losses caused by the collapse of the Vienna banks amounted to about 3,500 million S. —a colossal amount for Austria. But after the collapse about 1,350 million were guaranteed by the State in order to safeguard the interests of foreign creditors and owners of deposits. In this way a great part of the losses was put on the shoulders of the tax-payers. To these losses were added further huge amounts by the breakdown of provincial banks, the bankruptcy or insolvency of many thousands of other firms, the currency depreciation in all the Danubian States, and the violent fluctuations on the Stock

Exchange.[1] All these, and other causes, led to an extraordinary shrinkage in the capital needed for financing Austria's industries and commerce. Many factors, moreover, impeded or slowed up the formation of new capital. The lack of capital was one of the principal causes of mass unemployment.

12. The Shortage of Capital and the Rate of its Formation

The amount and composition of the capital invested in industries can best be ascertained from the statistics of limited companies which show detailed balance sheets for every branch. If the share of limited companies in the total of industries can be estimated, it is easy to ascertain the whole industrial capital. I have used this method for estimating the capital invested in Austria's industries in 1913,[2] and as new Austria obtained about a third of the industries of greater Austria, her share in the capital must have also been a third. The result was that before the war the industries in the territory of post-war Austria (without mining) employed 2,269 million S. fixed capital (buildings, machines, tools, etc.) and 2,531 million S. operating capital (raw materials, stocks of goods, funds for wages, etc.). The total was 4,800 million S. If this amount is divided by the number of the industrial personnel, which, according to the Accident Insurance statistics, was about 650,000, the capital per head of the workers, etc., was 7,385 S., or £213.[3]

I further found that the companies' own capital (share capital plus reserves) was mainly invested in the fixed assets, which formed 86% of that capital. For the operating capital, therefore, the industries depended on credit, mainly furnished by the commercial banks. The total loans amounted to 1,508·9 million K. or 2,172·8 million S. About 98% were short-term loans.

[1] The losses have been compiled in an article in the *Österreichischer Volkswirt* of May 5th, 1934.
[2] Cf. F. Hertz, *Kapitalbedarf, Kapitalbildung und Volkseinkommen in Oesterreich* in *Schriften des Vereins für Socialpolitik*, 1929.
[3] The Hungarian Industrial Census for 1937 shows a capital invested in industries of 1,986·7 million P. and a total industrial personnel of 336,844. The investment per head was, therefore, 5,898 P., which was equivalent to 5,072 K., and on the pre-war price level (index for 1937: 94) 5,395 K. This was equivalent to £224 per head.

It is interesting to compare the structure of capital investment before and after the war:—

	1913.	1926.
The borrowed capital amounted to percentage of the capital owned	% 82·7	% 92·8
The operating capital amounted to percentage of the fixed capital	111·5	121·5

This table shows two important facts. First, the industrial companies after the war were still more dependent than before on loans from the banks. Almost their whole working capital was borrowed from the banks. Moreover, more working capital was needed in relation to the fixed capital than in pre-war times. Both facts were largely due to the great increase after the war in the prices of industrial materials and wages. Industrial materials cost 40% more in 1926 and wages had risen by 45%. Moreover, the working capital was circulating much more slowly. This decrease in the velocity of circulation was illustrated by the decline in the use of bills of exchange. In 1927, for example, the amount of the bills of exchange passing through the Vienna Clearing House was only about one-eighth of the pre-war amount! It must further be allowed for that the limited companies were financially much stronger than most of the other enterprises. Financial conditions in the industries owned by individual entrepreneurs were, therefore, still more unfavourable than is shown in the accounts of the companies.

The fact that the working capital of industries was mainly borrowed from the banks suggests a comparison of the loans made by the banks before and after the war in order to estimate how far requirements were covered. It is not possible, however, to single out the loans made to industries. The balance-sheets of the banks show only the total amounts lent to industrial and commercial enterprises and for other purposes.

I have compiled two sets of figures showing the short-term loans of banks [1] before and after the war. Series A refers to all

[1] The short-term credits included bills of exchange, loans on securities or commodities and debtors in current account. To this was added the amount invested in syndicates. The holdings of securities, mortgages and loans to the State or other public bodies were excluded as far as the balance sheets indicated

commercial banks, which were the main source of credit for industries and commerce. Series B includes, besides the commercial banks, the National Bank, the provincial mortgage banks and the savings banks. The three last-named kinds of banks did little direct business with industrial or commercial enterprises. The National Bank gave credit mainly to banks re-discounting their bills. The provincial mortgage banks and savings banks invested their money mainly in mortgages on urban or rural property, and only a small part in short-term loans. Nevertheless these figures, too, may be useful for estimating the changes in the volume of bank loans. The post-war figures must be reduced to the pre-war price level to render them comparable.

SHORT-TERM LOANS
(In '000,000 S.)

	1912.[1]	1913.	1925.	1928.	1929.	1933.	1935.
A. Commercial Banks	3,385	3,613	1,572	3,155	2,632	1,218	1,028
B. Commercial Banks, National, Mortgage and Savings Banks . .	5,743	5,719	2,274	3,580	3,190	1,734	1,461
Wholesale Index .	100	100	137	130	130	108	110
A. On pre-war price level . . .	3,385	3,613	1,148	2,427	2,025	1,128	935
B. On pre-war price level . . .	5,743	5,719	1,660	2,754	2,454	1,606	1,328
A. Percentages of 1913 . . .	94	100	31·7	67	56	31·2	25·9
B. Percentages of 1913 . . .	100	100	29	48·1	42·9	28·1	23·2

[1] The pre-war amounts shown are a third of the totals for former Greater Austria, since a third of the industrial and commercial capacity was located in the territory of post-war Austria.

These figures reveal the complete insufficiency of the credits available to industries and commerce after the war. It must be pointed out that the pre-war amounts were only those needed for financing the industries and other enterprises located in the territory of later small Austria. They did not include the capital bor-

them. For 1933 and 1935 the commercial banks did not disclose their investments in syndicates, obviously because a great part was lost. In order to avoid overstating the financial shrinkage, I have assumed, however, that 100 million S., or about two-thirds of the amount in 1929, were in 1933 and 1935 still an asset.

rowed by Vienna firms for their factories, etc., outside this territory. Even at the peak of the short-lived boom, in 1928 and 1929, the loans amounted to only about 60% of the pre-war level, and in the other years the proportion was much lower.

It must further be considered that the reduction in the capital available was even greater than shown in these figures. Before the war it was easier to get capital from other sources than from the big banks. There were many wealthy private bankers who discounted bills. After the war they almost completely disappeared. Many firms financed their purchases of raw materials by drawing bills on London Acceptance Houses. Moreover, many industrialists and merchants themselves had considerable liquid assets, and invested them in short-term loans. On the other hand, the capital required after the war was greater owing to slower circulation. The Vienna banks, moreover, did not at once lose their business with the territories separated from Austria. They and their Austrian clients still possessed great interests in the Succession States, such as large industries and other enterprises, and they continued to a certain degree to finance them from Vienna. The corresponding pre-war amounts were not included in the pre-war figures based on the capacity of one-third, while the post-war figures include loans of this sort.

Lastly, before the war the financing of industries was to a great extent done by the issue to investors of shares or bonds. The commercial banks provided their client firms with capital till the conditions of the financial market were favourable to the issue of shares. This method, however, was greatly restricted in the post-war years. The number of capitalists able to take up new issues, and their financial strength, had greatly decreased. Moreover, the confidence of the public was badly shaken by the consequences of inflation, the growth of over-speculation and frequent financial scandals, and by the tense political atmosphere.

In great pre-war Austria the share capital of limited companies from the end of 1903 to the end of 1913 increased by 2,209 million K. or 3,181 million S. According to the industrial quota of the post-war territory, an amount of 1,060 million S. would have been the share of small Austria. In post-war Austria from the end of 1922 to the end of 1932 the issues of new shares amounted to 564·8 million S. Most of these issues were made in the time of economic ascent and prosperity, when the price level was 130 and more. Reduced to the pre-war price level, the increase may be estimated at about 440 million S. The yearly increase was therefore before the war 106 million, and after only 44 million S.

The above table shows that only in the peak years 1928 and 1929 did the total loans of the commercial banks (pre-war value) reach the amount which we had estimated to form the requirement of industries alone, assuming full utilisation of the pre-war capacity, but with no allowance for its growth during and after the war. But the banks had also to provide credits to commerce and other branches of economic enterprise. Both in 1925 and in the years of depression the total of loans was far below the pre-war level. The difference was greater than that in industrial production. This indicates that the economic decline after the war hit commerce still more than the industries. Before the war a very large part of the bank loans was used for financing Vienna's international trade and the manifold other activities which formed her economic basis.

The shortage of capital led to abnormally high rates of interest and additional charges.[1] In 1925, for instance, the charges on credits to first-class firms were between 18·65% and 16·15%. The Bank Rate was for some time 13%. In the subsequent years the rates slowly decreased. But even in the time of acute depression, at the end of 1932, when the Bank Rate was only 6%, the charges were for first-class firms 13·5%. Interest on mortgages was also very high. The Central Savings Bank of the City of Vienna, for example, charged in 1932 between 8% and 9%. In the second half of 1936 the Bank Rate was only 3·5%, but the charges for first-class firms were 8·05% and the interest for mortgages between 5$\frac{3}{4}$% and 5$\frac{1}{4}$%.

In spite of these high rates, the banks were in a parlous condition, and suffered heavy losses, which in the end resulted in the collapse of the whole banking system. The high rates of interest were not merely the outcome of excessive greed for profits, but a symptom of most unsound general conditions.

[1] Cf. details in *Wirtschaftsstatistische Jahrbuch der Wiener Arbeiterkammer*, 1936, p. 398.

13. THE SHRINKAGE IN HIGHER INCOMES IN AUSTRIA

The development of the distribution of incomes is very significant. Before the war incomes were taxed exclusively by assessment, while after the war the tax incident on wages and salaries
was deducted by the employer on the principle "pay as you
earn".[1] The distribution of incomes can be ascertained only for
the assessed amounts.

PERSONS ASSESSED IN THE POST-WAR TERRITORY

	1912.	1925.	1929.	1932.	1935.
Up to 3,400 S. (£98) .	462,739	306,992	292,940	299,886	303,277
3,400 S. to 7,200 S. (£98 to £208) . .	166,367	145,833	149,581	135,149	123,362
7,200 S. to 14,400 S. (£208 to £416) . .	58,827	41,343	44,843	36,895	34,464
14,400 S. to 24,000 S. (£416 to £694) . .	16,401	12,084	12,885	9,634	8,667
24,000 S. to 60,000 S. (£694 to £1,734) .	10,306	6,545	7,254	4,422	3,828
60,000 S. to 150,000 S. (£1,734 to £4,335) .	3,335	1,097	1,132	585	495
Over 150,000 S. (£4,335)	1,306	209	224	119	93

The equivalents in British currency are in gold pounds. In 1932
and 1935, however, the Austrian Schilling was considerably depreciated in comparison with the gold pound (by 17·6% and
20·8% respectively). The persons in the classes of high incomes
would therefore have to be greatly reduced to correspond to the
gold-pound classes.

The highest class "over 150,000 S." showed in 1935 the following details: Between 150,000 and 500,000 S., or (in depreciated
pounds) between £5,660 and £18,868, there were ninety persons
assessed. Between 500,000 S. and 1 million S., or between
£18,868 and £37,736, there were 3. No incomes exceeded this
limit.

The extraordinary shrinkage in the higher classes of income had
a great influence on the formation of capital. This mainly takes
place in the upper classes, at least as far as capital for large-scale

[1] The adoption of this method had the consequence that a number of employees and workers who before the war were assessed disappeared from the
number of assessed tax-payers after the war.

enterprises is concerned. The urban and rural middle classes also form capital, but it is not available for industrial development, and is either invested in small improvements on farms, etc., or in mortgages on farms and houses.

The changes in the amount and distribution of income had the effect that only those institutions showed a steady progress in the formation of capital which administered the savings of the middle classes and the workers. The most important were the Savings Banks, which largely had the character of public institutions without the purpose of making profits. In 1913 the territory of post-war Austria possessed 210 Savings Banks with savings of 2·96 milliard K., corresponding to 4·26 milliard S. in gold, or to 5·45 milliard depreciated S.[1] At the end of 1936 their saving deposits amounted to 1,611 million, and they had also 122 million on cheque account. Practically the whole of this amount had been saved since the end of inflation, which had wiped out all former savings. In the course of fourteen years, from 1923 to 1936, about 30% of the pre-war level was reached. In the first years after the war the rates of interest were abnormally high, and though they were later reduced, their level remained high till the onset of the great depression. Then the rate fell to 3% and 2·5%. Two-thirds of the number of savings were below 500 S., or less than £20, and 96% were below 5,000 S. But the aggregate amount of the savings over 5,000 S. made about half the total amount saved. The average in this last class was 13,180 S. Expressed in British currency (paper pounds), it can be said that about half of the total amount saved consisted of deposits over £200, and the average amount in this class was about £500. These larger deposits, however, were to a great extent the funds of associations of small people. Thousands of societies, welfare funds, savings groups, etc., entrusted their liquid assets to the Savings Banks. The decline and gradual breakdown of the commercial banks made the Savings Banks the last refuge for all those wishing to avoid undue risks.

The commercial banks, the Post Office Savings Bank, mortgage banks, and numerous co-operatives, building societies, etc., also accepted savings deposits. These and the Savings Banks together showed at the end of 1936 savings of 2,826 million S. The savings

[1] Cf. the detailed data in *Statistische Nachrichten* of 24.12.1937.

were mainly invested in mortgages, but after the war the Savings Banks enlarged the circle of their transactions, and often assumed almost the character of commercial banks. The results were frequently not fortunate.

A form of saving was further provided by life insurance. The social changes after the war contributed much to the rapid increase in the numbers of persons insured and the amounts of insurance. At the end of 1935 there were within Austria 1·4 million persons insured against death or old age. The capital insured was 2 milliard S., and the yearly premiums were 93 million S. Yet even this promising development did not escape the ill fate overhanging the whole economic life of Austria. The greatest Life Insurance Company—the Phœnix—failed, and its fall illustrated again the danger implied in certain powerful post-war tendencies—namely, the undermining of sound financial management by political influences and the spirit of speculation. The company had been compelled by the Government, for political reasons, to enter into dangerous commitments, and had tried to recoup itself by transactions of a highly speculative nature.

14. Basic Conditions of Industrial Production in Czechoslovakia

When the Czechoslovak Republic was formed out of parts of Austria-Hungary it received those richest in industries and agriculture. The configuration of the soil and its fertility offered very favourable conditions. Three great navigable rivers—the Elbe, the Oder and the Danube—provided possibilities of cheap transport. The country was rich in coal and many raw materials. A great part of the population possessed an old tradition of technical skill, economic efficiency and progressiveness, and had under the Austrian regime attained to a high level of civilisation. The three Bohemian countries—Bohemia, Moravia and Silesia—were the workshop of the Empire, and had developed besides a flourishing export trade. On the world markets their glass and china, textile products, paper, bent wood furniture, enamel ware, sugar, beer, malt and many other products enjoyed the highest reputation. The main seats of the great industries were the German

168

parts of the country, but the German and German-Austrian element had also created most of the industries in the Czech parts, and had given employment to large masses of Czech workers. Later on, however, the Czechs acquired a very large share in the ownership and management of great industries, banks and commerce.

A special advantage enjoyed by the new State was the very favourable balance between mining, industries and agriculture. While new Austria was lacking in the production of food and coal, and Hungary in that of coal and manufactures, Czechoslovakia possessed great resources in all these fields of production. Her home market had therefore a high purchasing power, and her balance of payments was more secure from disturbance than that of the other States.

15. Czechoslovakia's Share in the Industries of Former Austria-Hungary

The comparison of pre-war and post-war developments requires a knowledge of the industrial quota of the country—namely, that of its share in the industrial production of the former Empire. After the foundation of the Republic this share was estimated by various writers at very high percentages. Numerous official and semi-official publications spoke of 90% and 80%, while critical economists arrived at estimates of 70% or 60%. Now, it is undeniable that in certain large-scale industries Czechoslovakia's share was very great.[1] But those estimates did not take account of numerous other industries where the proportion was much smaller. The estimates of Waizner, largely based on those of Fellner, arrive at the conclusion that the share of the factory output of Bohemia, Moravia and Silesia in that of former Austria was 56·4%. If, however, large industries, mining, handicrafts, building, catering, commerce and transport are regarded together, the share was only 47·6%, and if Waizner's estimate of factory output is replaced by the figures as calculated by Fellner, the share was 48·6%. The share in the gainfully employed persons of this latter group in 1910 was 47·9%, and that in the workers alone 51·8%. According to the statistics of the Accident Insurance,

[1] Cf. official estimates for a number of industries in *Manuel Statistique de la République Tchécoslovaque*, 1925, II, 111, 137.

comprising all workers in factories and building, the share in 1912 was 50·9% of the insured persons, and 47·8% of the sum of wages.

To this share in the former Austrian industries must be added that in the industries which formerly belonged to Hungary. Fellner has made an estimate of this share.[1]

16. THE DECLINE OF CZECHOSLOVAKIA'S INDUSTRIES

The Statistical Office has regularly published carefully calculated indices of industrial production for the single branches and for production as a whole. The principal data are these: 1927, total index 89·0; 1928, 95·8; 1929, 100; 1930, 89·2; 1931, 80·7; 1932, 63·5; 1933, 60·2; 1934, 66·5; 1935, 70·1; 1936, 80·2.

These figures compare the volume of production in each year with that of 1929, which was the peak year of prosperity. If we wish to compare the level of production before and after the war we must therefore find out the relation between production in 1929 and in the period immediately before the war.

The general trend of industrial development can to a certain extent be judged by the amount of power and heat used. This amount is indicated by the heat-producing surface of the steam-boilers. It was at the end of 1920 in the whole of Czechoslovakia 1,892,916 square metres. This was about the surface taken over from former Austria-Hungary, as the Czechoslovak Republic had been formed only two years before. After a further two years—on January 1st, 1923—the surface was 1,933,440 sq. m., and of this 1,478,000 sq. m. were used for producing power amounting to 1,785,100 h.p. To this was added about 300,000 h.p. harnessed water-power. In the subsequent years the total surface showed only small variations. At the end of 1928, the peak of the post-war boom, it was 1,933,180 sq. m., or only about 2% above the initial level. In 1930 the mechanical energy in industrial and agricultural enterprises produced by steam was 2,156,738 h.p. and the water-power 312,063 h.p. In comparison with 1923 the steam-power installed had increased by over 20%. But it is doubtful whether the figures are strictly comparable. The calorific surface was in 1936 1,815,000 sq. m., or about 4% below the figure for 1920. Allowance must, however, be made for the increase in technical efficiency. It must further be considered that

[1] Cf. Fellner in *Metron*, 1923–1924, III, 226.

these figures do not exclusively indicate the power used for industrial and agricultural production. They include also the installation of power-stations producing electricity for transport, lighting of the streets, domestic consumption, etc. The increase in these uses of electricity was very considerable. After the war, moreover, the iron and metal industry, armament works and heavy engineering which need much power increased while many industries using little power decreased. All these changes make it difficult to use the statistics of power for estimating the development of industrial production as a whole.

An index of actual production would be the quantity of coal used by industries, provided the structure and calorific efficiency of the industries remain the same. The pre-war figure, however, seems not to have been made public. On the whole, the industries used more than half of the total coal consumption, the power-stations and railways took almost a third, and about a fifth was used for domestic purposes. The coal consumption in 1913—a year of severe industrial depression—was estimated at 14,177,000 tons pit coal and 15,017,000 tons brown coal.[1] This level was reached again in 1927, and two years later, at the peak of the boom, the consumption was even higher by about a quarter. But then followed a steep fall, and the level of 1913 was never again reached. In 1936 it was 12,442,000 tons pit coal and 14,519,000 tons brown coal.

A better index is the amount of raw materials used for industries. The value of the raw materials imported before the war into the territories which later became Czechoslovakia was estimated by the Government experts at 1,012 million K., pre-war value.[2] This figure may be compared with the actual amount of raw materials and half-manufactured goods imported into Czechoslovakia, and these amounts must be converted into pre-war value by means of the official index of imported raw materials. The result is that only in 1929 was the pre-war level reached and even exceeded, though only by 5%. In all other years the imports of raw materials remained far below the pre-war level.

[1] The requirements of Slovakia were, however, not included in the figure for 1913, while the post-war figures are inclusive.

[2] Cf. J. Cisar and F. Pokorny, *The Czechoslovak Republic*, 1922, and O. Butter and B. Ruml, *Tschechoslovakische Republik*, 1921. These two books were published by the Czechoslovak Propaganda Service. They contain many useful data collected, or calculated, by the Government departments. Cf. also F. Weil, *Tschechoslovakei*, 1927.

Prof. Tibal, a French economist who used for his research many data provided by the Czechoslovak authorities, states that the consumption of raw materials in 1928 was 12% above the level of 1913, and the index of industrial production 9%. He gives the following figures based on 1913:[1] 1913, index 100; 1920–22, 60; 1923, 68; 1924, 93; 1926, 85; 1927, 102; 1928, 109; 1929, 112.

Another economist—Dr. K. Uhlig—however, arrived at the result that industrial production was in 1928 only 2% above 1913.[2]

The problem can also be approached by means of the study of the development of single branches of industry. For the principal branches statistics of output before and after the war are available, and for some other industries which use entirely or mainly foreign raw materials the import of these is a reliable index of production.

The *Statistical Yearbook* for 1938 (p. 169) has compiled the industrial consumption of a number of raw materials, and the above-mentioned official sources indicate also the pre-war consumption. From these sources and the trade statistics this table has been compiled:—

IMPORTS OF RAW MATERIALS
('000's of tons)

	Cotton.	Wool.	Jute.	Raw hides.	Non-ferrous metals.
Pre-war (official estimate)	192	36	36	45	85
1922	69	25	14	4	26
1923	73	30	19	7	29
1924	102	31	31	24	40
1925	135	28	33	26	48
1926	98	29	25	20	47
1927	145	38	35	24	57
1928	123	37	31	24	69
1929	120	39	36	34	64
1930	109	36	36	34	55
1931	90	35	28	33	48
1932	81	26	17	15	37
1933	71	28	25	29	37
1934	79	29	38	41	45
1935	79	30	34	31	—
1936	95	35	34	40	67

[1] Cf. André Tibal, *La Tchécoslovaquie, étude économique*, 1935, p. 124.
[2] Quoted in Walter Levit, *Die wirtschaftliche Lage der Tschechoslovakei seit dem Umsturz*, 1936, p. 10.

According to these data the consumption of raw materials remained after the war far below the pre-war figure. It may be, however, that the difference was not as great as indicated because the amounts of raw materials needed might have been overestimated by the Government when the Republic was founded. We can, for example, check the estimate of the cotton required. In 1912 238,700 tons of cotton were imported into Austria-Hungary, and as Czechoslovakia inherited 75% of the spindles, her share would have been 179,025 tons, while the Government estimate was 192,000 tons. The difference, however, is not great. The decline in the cotton industry—the greatest industry of Czechoslovakia—can also be illustrated by the decrease in machines. The number of cotton spindles fell between 1920 and 1937 from 3·9 million to 2·65 million, or by a third,[1] and the number of cotton looms decreased in the same time by almost half—from 136,891 to 75,000. There was, besides, a great idle capacity. In 1936 the average employment per week was in Czechoslovakia 31 hours, in Roumania 51, in Hungary 56, in Austria 58, in Yugoslavia 79 and in Bulgaria 96. The technical level also fell. In 1936 the proportion of automatic looms in the total of looms employed was in Czechoslovakia 3%, in Hungary 18%, in Austria 24% and in Yugoslavia 44%.

The situation in the heavy industries which—for military reasons—enjoyed the special favour of the Government, was as follows :—

(Output in '000 tons)

	Coal.	Lignite.	Iron ore.	Pig iron.	Steel.
1913	14,087	23,137	2,176	1,237	1,257
1929	16,521	22,561	1,808	1,645	2,193
1936	12,233	15,949	1,090	1,140	1,560
1937	16,951	18,042	—	1,675	2,315

Pit coal, iron and steel showed increases, but brown coal and iron ore decreased.

In Austria-Hungary the Bohemian countries were the main seat of the production of sugar, beer and alcohol, which formed, next

[1] From 1902 to 1914, under the Austrian regime, the cotton spindles increased in Bohemia by 79%.

to the cotton industry, their most valuable industrial assets. The output was in the whole of Czechoslovakia:—

(In 'ooo's)

	Sugar, q.	Beer, hl.	Alcohol, hl.
1912–1913 .	14,544	12,204	1,143
1929 . .	10,357	11,611	703
1936 . .	5,727	7,557	828
1937 . .	7,236	8,311	1,005

In all these industries the decline was very heavy. The alcohol industry, however, became a State monopoly producing motor fuel for the Army.

Bohemia's porcelain and glass industries were her special pride, and were on a very high level of technical efficiency and quality. Both suffered terribly in the post-war period. The china-ware industry reached even in 1928–1929 no more than 60% of the pre-war output, and from 1928 to 1935 it shrank by about two-thirds, mainly owing to the trade war with Hungary. The glass industry could even in 1938 produce only about a third of its normal output.

The situation was better in industries which were supported by the Government for military, or nationalistic, reasons. The production of armaments, chemicals, machines, motor-cars and rubber products increased. The boot-and-shoe industry also showed a great development owing to the organising ability of the industrialist Bata. But after 1930 exports fell rapidly, and the industry suffered grave losses. About a third of all shoe factories closed down for good.

On the whole the great industrial legacy inherited from Austria could not be maintained at its former level. The industries of the Bohemian countries had been built up for supplying the markets of a wide Empire, and they had, in addition, created a large export trade. After the dismemberment of Austria-Hungary most of these industries suffered heavy losses, and large parts of them had to close down for good. The industrial difficulties were, moreover, dangerously complicated by the fact that the industries had been built up predominantly by the German element, and were situated in the German parts of Czechoslovakia. When the consequences

174

of economic nationalism could no longer be palliated, and the world crisis hit Czechoslovakia with special severity, the German territories were much more devastated than the Czech, and became known as a "graveyard of industries". Unemployment was much greater among the German workers than among the Czechs. The Government encouraged the foundation of new industries, especially such as were of military importance, in the Czech parts rather than the German, which were too near the frontiers. The ruin of a considerable section of the once flourishing industries of Bohemia, Moravia and Silesia created great bitterness among the German population, and fostered the rise of a pro-Nazi movement. The industries of Slovakia, which had been built up for the Hungarian market, also suffered great losses. As in all the Danubian States, the economic distress caused by the dismemberment of Austria-Hungary, and economic nationalism, paved the way for Hitler.

17. EMPLOYMENT AND UNEMPLOYMENT IN CZECHOSLOVAKIA

The number of persons normally active in industries [1] increased in Czechoslovakia, according to the Censuses, in the twenty years 1910–1930 by 22·3%, and those engaged in commerce and transport by as much as 44·2%. In the three western provinces the number of persons in industries increased by 17%, and those in commerce and transport by 34%. The number of workers insured against accident rose in the western provinces from 1913 to 1928 by 42·2%. It must not be overlooked, however, that these figures do not indicate the numbers actually employed.

The level of employment can be ascertained from the statistics of the compulsory insurance against illness and accidents. A comparison with pre-war level is not feasible because the scope of the insurance has been changed in various ways. [2] It must further be noted that the Health Insurance is organised in a number of different societies, and that the figures usually quoted refer only

[1] Exclusive of family members helping the head of the family in his profession.
[2] The Health Insurance was after the war extended to agricultural labourers, home workers and domestics. The Accident Insurance took over the miners from their former separate insurance, but lost the railwaymen and workers in the State tobacco monopoly.

to a section of the total persons insured—namely, to workers in private industries, exclusive of miners. The movement in this section does, of course, indicate the trend of industrial development, but for other purposes we shall have to refer to the total of persons insured, including also miners, clerks and other employees, the personnel of State enterprises like the railways, post, tobacco monopoly, the Civil Servants proper and a few minor groups. We designate the first-mentioned section as "workers", the persons insured against accident as "industrial workers" (though they comprise also others), and all categories together as "total of persons employed".

The number of workers rose considerably in the 'twenties, and reached the peak in 1929, amounting to 2,506,000. If the salaried employees in enterprises are added, the number was 2,853,346. The world depression made itself felt in Czechoslovakia later than elsewhere, but it lasted much longer. The bottom was reached in 1934 with 1,879,000 workers, or a drop of 25% in comparison with 1929. In the following years a slow recovery took place, but in 1936 the number of workers was still almost 20% below 1929. The employment of industrial workers decreased even more.

The number of unemployed registered at the Labour Exchanges was very low in the 'twenties—amounting in 1929 to an average of 42,000. Then it rose rapidly, and reached the peak in 1933, with 920,182. In 1936 the average was 621,019.

The number of assisted unemployed was rather low, and both the relief paid by the Trade Unions and the additional payment by the State were very inadequate, though in the worst years some food also was distributed among the unemployed. The table on p. 177 shows the scope of unemployment relief in the years of crisis.[1]

This table shows that only about a third of the unemployed registered at the Labour Exchanges received assistance—a very low proportion. Even those who had the luck to receive assistance got very little. Taking the average for 1931–1933, the allowance amounted per year to 2,547 Kc. only, which in English money was at that time equivalent to £15 16s. per year or about 6s. per

[1] The figures of unemployed and of relief are taken from the official *Statistical Handbook*, 1940.

	1931.	1932.	1933.	1934.	1935.	1936.
Registered unemployed, yearly average ('000's) .	291	554	738	677	686	623
Assisted unemployed, yearly average ('000's) . .	102	185	248	246	236	209
Total relief ('000,000 Kc.) .	249	461	672	446	481	420
Of this amount was paid : By the trade unions ('000,000 Kc.)	47	95	137	136	133	116
By the State ('000,000 Kc.) .	202	366	535	310	349	304
Relief per assisted unemployed per year in Kc. .	2,441	2,492	2,710	1,813	2,039	2,009

week. Allowance must, of course, be made for differences in the price-level.

It may be recalled that the German districts were much more severely hit by unemployment than the Czech, because they were much more industrialised. The figures quoted reveal one of the most important causes of the political unrest in Czechoslovakia which led to the disastrous Munich Agreement, to the Second World War, and to the later mass expulsions of Sudeten Germans from Czechoslovakia.

As regards the extent of unemployment, it must also be considered that the unemployment statistics are dependent on the organisation of unemployment insurance. Now, in Czechoslovakia the unemployed were not insured in a State institution, but were assisted by the Trade Unions, which were subsidised by the Government. It is probable that this system led to understating the real volume of unemployment.

According to the Census of 1930, the total number of workers and employees, exclusive of soldiers, was 4,283,000. But if we sum up the persons shown as employed by their registration in a Health Insurance society, we find for 1929 only 3,421,000, or 862,000 less. In 1930—the year of the Census—the number of employed was down by 60,000, and that of the unemployed up by about the same figure. We may therefore say that about 920,000 workers and employees counted by the Census were not actually employed. This discrepancy seems to indicate widespread undisclosed unemployment. A part was obviously due to the great seasonal variations in some Czechoslovak industries, another to the frequency of occasional work, which does not render the

177

worker liable to insurance. Before the dismemberment of Austria-Hungary and the rise of nationalistic seclusion the seasonal variations in employment were to a great extent alleviated by the opportunity for seasonal migrations. Every year hundreds of thousands of Czech, Sudeten-German, Slovak and other workers from the territories later incorporated in Czechoslovakia used to migrate to other parts of Austria-Hungary, or to Germany, for some temporary employment when there was no work for them in their neighbourhood. They were employed in sugar-beet cultivation, harvesting, felling wood, building, factory work and many other activities. A great number also of these migrants were pedlars who sold products made by themselves or their neighbours. These opportunities, however, came to an end or were greatly restricted when the new frontiers were drawn and everywhere high barriers erected not only against foreign goods, but also against foreign workers. The wide extension of undisclosed unemployment in Czechoslovakia was a consequence of the new system of intense economic nationalism.

18. Czechoslovak Wages and Social Services

The official statistics record the average wages taken into account in calculating the contributions to the compulsory Workers' Insurance institutions. Of these series that referring to the Accident Insurance seems to us no reliable index. Before the war the average wage calculated on the data of this insurance could be used as an index. But after the war the limit up to which wages were taken into account was greatly reduced, and thereby a considerable part of the higher wages was ignored in calculating the average. The Health Insurance has also a limit, but it is not likely to curtail the average to any appreciable extent.[1] The development of wages according to the Health and Old Age Insurance was this:—

[1] Account was taken only of the amount not exceeding 36 Kc. a day, or 4·31 Kc. per hour. Now, the minimum tariffs of thirty-two industrial branches in Prague (where wages were higher than in the rest of the country) showed in 1929 an average hourly wage of 4·27 Kc. Moreover, only 14·26% of all workers insured were in the top class, and only a part of them had wages exceeding the limit. These facts make it probable that the average wages shown by the Health Insurance gave a reliable picture of the actual average wage level.

178

	Average daily wages in Kc.		Wages index. (Health Insurance). 1929 = 100.	Cost of Living. 1914 = 100.
	Health Insurance (yearly average).	Old Age Insurance (end of year).		
1928 .	18·61	—	—	109·4
1929 .	19·11	19·44	100	108·7
1930 .	19·13	19·08	100·1	109·0
1931 .	18·66	18·26	97·6	104·3
1932 .	17·72	17·26	92·7	102·4
1933 .	16·72	17·43	87·5	101·2
1934 .	16·30	17·07	85·3	86·0
1935 .	15·93	—	83·4	85·7
1936 .	16·18	—	84·6	82·3
1937, Oct.	17·70	—	92·6	—

According to Western standards the average wages were low. The highest rate—that for 1929—was then equivalent to 2s. 4d. in English money, and the lowest—that for 1935—to 2s. 8d. in (depreciated) English money. But it must not be ignored that the wages included also those of agricultural workers, which were very low, especially in the eastern provinces. The level of industrial wages, in comparison with pre-war rates, can be gathered from this table referring to minimum wage tariffs in thirty-two different branches of industry and trade in the capital city of Prague, where wages were, of course, higher than in the other parts of Czechoslovakia.

	Average weekly wage in Kc.	Compared with pre-war level, 1914 = 100.		
		Weekly wage in gold.	Weekly wage in real value.	
			(Wholesale index.)	(Cost-of-living index.)
1930 .	214·75	132	111	121
1932 .	215·48	132	133	129
1934 .	209·76	108	127	128
1936 .	207·84	—	—	123

In English money the wage of 1930 was equivalent to £1 6s. 2d., and that of 1936 to £1 13s. 2d. a week. The average was about 5s. a day. In comparison with Austria the nominal wages in Czechoslovakia were lower, and had also risen less since the pre-war period, but the real wages were higher, owing to differences in prices and rents.

The contributions to social insurance and similar expenses were also rather low in Czechoslovakia. Trčka found that the share of these expenses in the cost of manufactured goods was in Austria 10·5%, in Germany 7·44% and in Czechoslovakia 6·28%.[1] In relation to wages the social expenses amounted in Austria to 15·1%, in Germany to 10·25% and in Czechoslovakia to 8·53%, and in relation to salaries in Austria to 25·54%, in Germany to 17·34% and in Czechoslovakia to 16·28%. A careful study leads to the conclusion that among the Central European industrial States Czechoslovakia had the lowest wages and the lowest social burdens, and was therefore in a strong position as a competitor on the world markets.[2]

In fact Czechoslovakia experienced in the 'twenties a much greater rise in industrial production than most other countries, but the ensuing fall also was much more marked. This would seem to warrant the conclusion that the low wages stimulated production and exports in Czechoslovakia during the time of the world boom, when the purchasing capacity was great everywhere and wages were rapidly rising in the Western countries, but that when this stopped the low wages within the country became a drag on production because they kept down the internal purchasing power. Besides wages, however, many other factors influenced the development, such as the marked deflation in the first years of the Republic, the later depreciations, the commercial policy and numerous measures designed to regulate marketing.

19. DECLINE OF CONSUMPTION

The consumption figures given in the table on p. 181 are taken from the *Czechoslovak Statistical Yearbook* (per head).

These figures show that in the ten years 1926–1936 consumption considerably declined. But if it was in 1936 lower than in 1926, it must have been by a still larger amount lower than in 1913. This follows from the fact that consumption had in 1926

[1] Cf. Boris Trčka, *Sociale Lasten als Kostenfaktor,* 1933.
[2] Cf. Walter Levit, *Die wirtschaftliche Lage der Tschechoslovakei seit dem Umsturz,* 1936, p. 57.

	1926.	1929.	1933.	1936.
Meat (kg.) . . .	27·04	28·70	25·40	25·39
Fat (kg.) . . .	6·64	6·80	5·13	5·86
Wheat flour (kg.) . .	59·9	—	57·1	56·1 [1]
Sugar, refined (kg.) .	25·48	24·70	21·97	22·35
Beer (l.) . . .	66·4	77·8	52·6	49·2
Wine (l.) . . .	3·18	3·19	2·86	2·98
Matches (boxes) . .	—	47·3	30·2	28·8
Tobacco (kg.) [2] . .	1·42	1·52	1·29	1·21

[1] 1935.
[2] Raw tobacco worked up by the State Tobacco Monopoly per head of
population. Cf. *Annuaire Statistique*, 1938.

not reached the pre-war level. Many facts prove that by 1926 the
national income and agricultural and industrial production were
below the pre-war level, and this implies that consumption, too,
had failed to reach it. The Minister of Finance, Dr. English,
estimated the national income in 1927 at 60 milliard Kc., which
was equivalent to 6·12 milliard K. at the pre-war price level. The
income before the war has been estimated by Prof. Gini at 7·22
milliard K. The cereal crops had in 1926 not yet reached the pre-
war volume, though that of livestock was greater. The index of
industrial output was 77% of that for 1929, or probably 85% of
that for 1914. The Statistical Office has further calculated a wage
index by taking the average of wage rates of 374 different trades
in Prague. For 1926 it was 20% over that for 1914, while the
wholesale index was 37·5% above the pre-war level.

All these facts prove that consumption must in 1936 have been
considerably lower than before the war.

In a few cases data are available for the pre-war time. The
consumption of sugar in Bohemia was in 1911–1912 30·1 kg. raw
sugar value, which corresponds to 27·9 kg. in refined sugar.[3] In
1936–1937 the consumption of refined sugar in Bohemia was,
according to the *Statistical Yearbook*, 27·2 kg. In twenty-five years
therefore there had been no increase, but actually a slight decrease! In 1910–1911 the consumption of beer in the whole of
former Austria was 78 l. per head. In Czechoslovakia it was in
1936 only 49·2 l. In 1910 the consumption of tobacco in Bohemia,
Moravia and Silesia was 1·54 kg. per head. The Czechoslovak
figures given above are considerably lower, but they include

[3] Cf. *Compass*, 1914, II.

Slovakia and Carpatho-Russia, which had a low consumption. In the whole of former Austria, inclusive of many very poor parts like Galicia, the consumption of tobacco was in 1912 1·35 kg.

A report by the organisation for political and economic planning [1] gives these comparative figures of consumption of manufactured goods for 1937:—

	Czechoslovakia.	Austria.	Western Europe.
Cotton goods (kg.) . .	4·2	5·1	8·0
Paper (kg.) . . .	13·9	14·8	30·0
Soap (fat content) (kg.) .	2·5	—	6·0
Sugar	22·4	19·5	32·0
Wireless sets (licences per 1,000 persons) . .	69	92	120·0

It comes as a surprise to see that Czechoslovakia—a country so splendidly endowed with natural resources and possessing a first-class industrial equipment inherited from old Austria—should lag so far behind Western Europe in purchasing power, and in some respects even behind crippled and impoverished post-war Austria.

20. TOTAL WAGE INCOME

The total income from wages and salaries for 1929 can be estimated in this way. The General Health Insurance, which is compulsory for all employees (except categories with a separate insurance), comprised 2,853,346 persons. Of these 2,506,200 were wage-earners whose average annual wage was 5,733 Kc. The total of wages was therefore 14,368·0 million Kc. The remaining 347,146 were salaried employees, of whom 287,540 were considered non-manual workers. The salaries of this section amounted, according to the Old Age Pensions Institute, to 4,719 million Kc. Their average yearly salary was therefore 16,400 Kc. The remaining 59,606 belonged to the "manual" class, and it may be assumed that their salary was somewhere between the pay of a worker and that of a non-manual employee—perhaps about 10,000 Kc. Further must be added the wages and salaries of cer-

[1] Cf. *Economic Development in South-Eastern Europe*, with an introduction by Prof. Mitrany, published by P.E.P., 1945, p. 40.

tain categories with a separate Health Insurance. Their earnings are shown in the official statistics. These categories and their pay were: miners, 1,376·6 million Kc.; railwaymen, 2,640·9 million Kc.; Post Office, 639·8 million Kc.; tobacco monopoly, 111·1 million Kc. The total of all these items is 24,451·4 million Kc.

The salaries of officials in the service of the central Government and the autonomous bodies are not included. The salaries of State functionaries, exclusive of those employed in enterprises, were 3,772·2 million Kc. Those of functionaries in the autonomous administration of the provinces, the school boards, towns, etc., are only partly indicated in the statistics, and the data do not all refer to the same year. The data available show that the salaries in the provinces of Bohemia, Moravia, Silesia and Carpatho-Russia, and those of the elementary school teachers in the three first-named provinces, amounted to 1,164·8 million Kc. We may assume that the total salaries in the central and local administration were about 6,000 million Kc.

The calculation can be checked by the income-tax statistics. According to them, 2,097,000 employees paying tax, including the officials in the service of the State, provinces, etc., had wages and salaries amounting to 24,746 million Kc. There were, besides, 1,140,000 labourers, etc., who were not liable to income tax because their income was below the limit. Their income must have been lower than the average of 5,733 Kc. shown by the Health Insurance, since this average included the workers with higher wages who paid income tax. If we assume 5,000 Kc. as their average income, the total amount of their earnings was 5,700 million Kc. The total of wages and salaries including Civil Servants was therefore 30,446 million Kc., and if we deduct the amount of 24,451 million calculated on the basis of the insurance statistics, there remains the amount of 5,995 million Kc., which must have been the income of the public officials who paid income tax but were not included in the calculation based on the insurance statistics.[1] This figure appears to agree quite well with the above-mentioned data concerning the salaries of officials.

[1] We had to compare the income-tax statistics for 1928 with the Health Insurance figures for 1929 because the income-tax statistics for 1929 seem not to have been published. But the difference cannot have been great.

The returns of industry, commerce and the liberal professions were subject to trade tax, which was divided into the General Trade Tax for individual enterprises, and the Special Trade Tax for limited companies. Almost all enterprises had to pay the tax. The number of taxed enterprises was greater than the number of independent traders counted by the Census. The returns taxed may therefore be identified with the total income from any sort of business, except agriculture. In 1930 the total of profits was 10,189 million Kc., and the losses amounted to 615 million. The net return was therefore 9,574 million.[1]

Further data regarding the returns of companies have been published for certain years. These include the years of prosperity 1927–1930 and the years of depression 1931–1933. For the other years only inadequate data are given. The figures available are as follows:—

FINANCIAL RETURNS OF LIMITED COMPANIES (INDUSTRIAL AND COMMERCIAL, BUT EXCLUSIVE OF BANKING AND INSURANCE)

('000,000's of Kc.)

	1927.	1929.	1930.	1931.	1932.	1933.
Share capital . .	6,426	7,262	7,194	7,746	8,002	7,965
Reserves and other funds . . .	7,723	9,761	10,833	12,765	12,655	12,858
Total own means .	14,149	17,023	18,027	20,511	20,657	20,823
Number of companies with profit . .	751	781	689	616	553	577
Number of companies with loss . .	298	256	274	416	530	500
Total of profits .	667	806	696	446	326	343
Total of losses .	209	355	144	212	443	337
Difference . .	458	451	552	234	−117	6
Profit or loss on total own capital in percentage . .	3·2	2·6	3·0	1·1	−0·6	0

[1] Unfortunately these returns seem only to have been published for a few years. But cf. for the distribution according to groups *Manuel Statistique*, 1932, 419.

This table shows that even in the peak year of prosperity (1929) all companies together had a profit of only 2·6% to pay dividends and directors' fees and to set aside for reserves. The other years of prosperity showed equally poor returns.

The statistics give also the per cent. profits for the years 1931–1935. But they refer only to the share capital, and disregard the reserves, which far exceed the share capital. This method is obviously misleading, and gives too favourable a picture.

22. The Formation of Capital in Czechoslovakia

An expanding economy needs a constantly growing amount of capital. Where this growth is seriously handicapped it becomes impossible to maintain a satisfactory level of employment. The increase of capital invested in industries and commerce can to a certain extent be observed in the movement of the share capital of limited companies. In Czechoslovakia the share capital of industrial and commercial companies, both public and private, developed in this way:—

('000,000 Kc.)

	1926.	1930.	1936.
Share capital of industrial and commercial companies . .	7,987	9,095	10,499

The increase in ten years was 2,512 million Kc., or 251 million Kc. a year. It is difficult to express this amount in another currency, since the Czech Crown was twice depreciated in this period, and 100 pre-war Crowns were successively equivalent to 684, 821 and 977 Kc. If, however, we take the exchange of 684, the annual increase was equivalent to 36·6 million pre-war Crowns. In former Austria the share capital showed an annual increase of 221 million K. It has been shown above that Czechoslovakia inherited about half of the total industries of Austria, and a still greater share of large-scale industries, to which was added a share of Hungary's industries. It is clear, therefore, that the formation of capital for industrial purposes was in the whole of

185

Czechoslovakia only about a third of the amount formed in Bohemia, Moravia and Silesia under the Austrian regime.

The development in the capital of the banks was still more unfavourable. The following figures are significant:—

CAPITAL OF BANKS IN BOHEMIA, MORAVIA AND SILESIA (LIMITED COMPANIES)

('000,000 Kc.)

	1927.	1936.
Share capital	1,801	1,267
Reserves	1,161	1,138
Total assets	29,332	25,135

The capital of the commercial banks decreased considerably.

The commercial banks were already in former Austria the main source of the working capital employed in industrial production. After the war practically all the working capital was supplied by them. But the amount available was much lower than before. In former Austria the banks (limited and others) had in 1912 lent to their debtors [1] 7,282 million K. As Bohemia, Moravia and Silesia had a share of about a half in all the industries, commerce and traffic, it may be assumed that their share in the loans was also a half, or 3,641 million K. Now, in 1929—the best post-war year— the loans made by the banks in the same territory were 27,668 million Kc., or 3,030 million K. at the pre-war price level. The loans therefore were only 83.2% of the pre-war amount. In fact, however, a much larger amount of bank loans was needed after the war because of the great shrinkage in private capital and the lower velocity of circulation. This calculation also confirms our finding that even in 1929 industrial production cannot have considerably exceeded the pre-war level. If trade could be maintained at about the pre-war level, or a little above it, in spite of the insufficiency of working capital, this was probably made possible by the reduction in certain other activities—for instance, international trade.

The further development of loans by the banks in Bohemia, Moravia and Silesia was as follows (million Kc.):—

[1] Bills, loans on commodities and current accounts.

1929, 24,991; 1930, 25,021; 1931, 20,427; 1932, 17,425; 1933, 16,384; 1935, 16,638; 1936, 17,069.

It must be recalled, however, that the gold content of the Czechoslovak Crown was in 1936 30% lower than in 1929. The wholesale price level in gold fell in the same period by 38·3% and that in Kc. by 22·6%. The index of industrial production went down by 19·8%, and the bank loans by 31·7%. The amount of bank loans required depends both on the rate of production and on the price level.

Savings deposits, especially small savings, developed at a much quicker rate than other forms of capital. The data compiled by the League of Nations' statistical office give two series of deposits. The deposits with the commercial banks include current accounts, correspondents, savings, and cheque accounts, and a considerable part of them are not real savings but amounts kept in a liquid form for business purposes. But the deposits with savings banks, the Post Office Savings Bank, co-operatives, etc., are mostly real savings. The development was as follows:—

('000,000 Kc.)

	1922.	1930.	1931.	1936.
Commercial banks .	27,920	35,796	31,851	30,278
Savings banks, etc. .	20,358	45,012	48,031	47,646

The deposits with the commercial banks reached the peak in 1930, and those with the savings banks in 1931. From these points onward they declined. In the period of prosperity the commercial deposits increased by 985 million a year (£6 million) and the small savings by 3,075 million Kc. a year (almost £19 million). The national income was in 1927 officially estimated at 60 milliard Kc., and the annual increase in small savings alone would have amounted to over 5% of the total national income.

The small savings are mainly made by the masses, the peasants and workers and the traders who profit by their expenditure. The rapid increase in these deposits is therefore significant of the social change after the war. On the other hand, the slow increase in the commercial deposits indicates a rather slack development of trade. The small savings are not available for industrial investment, and

187

the insufficiency of capital for investment in industries has certainly contributed to the rise of unemployment. When the world crisis broke out, unemployment rapidly increased also in Czechoslovakia, the peasants were severely hit, and trade became unprofitable. This led also to the decline in the total of savings.

Savings before and after the war are not entirely comparable. Bank deposits were, in the Bohemian territories, to a great degree entrusted to branches of Vienna banks, and appeared in their balance sheets. After the war these branches became Czechoslovak enterprises. We can, however, compare the deposits placed in the savings banks in the three western provinces. In 1914 the total amount was 2,820 million K. and in 1929 16,403 million Kc., which was equivalent to 2,398 million K. If, however, account is taken of the change in the price level this amount was only 1,796 million Kc. at pre-war price level. This was 63·7% of the pre-war amount. It must, however, be remembered that a considerable part of the pre-war deposits had survived the depreciation of the currency after the war owing to the policy of deflation followed in Czechoslovakia. Moreover, the price level was in the first decade of the Republic extraordinarily high. In 1922 the index was 45·2% above the pre-war level, in 1928 41·6% and in 1929 33·5%. This naturally facilitated the putting aside of considerable savings. When in the depression the price level went down the total of savings decreased.

In comparing savings before and after the war allowance must also be made for changes in the significance of savings. After the war savings deposits were for various reasons preferred to other forms of investment—for example, to long-term loans because of the fear of inflation and from lack of trust in the commercial banks. Such changes in preference render comparisons precarious.

The difference described above in the formation of large and small capital explains itself by a study of the distribution of incomes. The total income for which in 1928 income tax was paid amounted to 46,276 million Kc. It was distributed in this way:—

	%
Up to 25,000 Kc. (£152)	72·9
25,000–50,000 Kc. (£305)	12·9
50,000–100,000 Kc. (£610)	5·9
100,000–500,000 Kc. (£3,048)	5·4
500,000–1,000,000 Kc. (£6,096)	1·0
Over 1,000,000 Kc.	1·9

This table shows that the higher classes of income comprised only a small proportion of the total income. The bulk was in small incomes, and their share becomes still greater if we include also the incomes too low to be liable to tax. We have above estimated this income at 5,700 million Kc. for the workers alone. But the greater part of the income of peasants also belonged to this class. Of the total income of farmers estimated on the basis of the Farm Accountancy statistics, 7,228 million Kc. were not liable to income tax. If these two amounts are added to the taxed income it rises to 59·2 milliard Kc., of which 78·8% was income below 25,000 Kc., or £152. All income over 100,000 Kc. or £610 amounted only to 6·4%.

The taxed income covers so large a section of the total national income that it may be used as an index of the development of the total. The amounts taxed were (millions Kc.) :—

	Directly (other than wages).	Indirectly (wages, gross).	Total.
1928 . .	22,328	24,466	46,794
1933 . .	16,306	12,007	28,313

The taxed wages and salaries decreased therefore in the time of depression by half, while other income fell by almost 30%. Later data than for 1933 have not been published in the *Statistical Yearbook*.

23. Basic Conditions of Industrial Production in Hungary

The dismemberment of Austria-Hungary destroyed also the well-balanced economic structure of Hungary and, in particular, had a devastating effect on her relations with the other Danubian States. The territory of the Hungarian Crown was reduced to 29% and the population to 36%, but if the loss of markets through the disruption of the Customs union is taken into account, the economic area open to Hungary shrank to less than 14% in territory and to less than 18% in population. The former industrial capacity and income of Hungary were reduced to about a half. It was not only the loss of markets, however, which seriously affected Hungary's industries. They were also faced with the situation that by far the greater part of the raw materials needed were produced in the territories separated from her. She lost 65% of her coal supply, 84% of the timber, 80% of the iron ore, and almost all her water-power and oil. The only mineral of which new Hungary had an abundant supply was bauxite, which is used for making aluminium. But the production of aluminium requires also large amounts of cheap power, which are lacking in Hungary. Only the agricultural industries were well provided with home-produced materials.

24. HUNGARY'S INDUSTRIAL DEVELOPMENT AFTER THE WAR

Hungary had already before the Great War made efforts to build up her own large-scale industries. The State encouraged by direct and indirect subsidies the foundation of factories. Moreover, Hungary then possessed great natural resources and other advantages for industrial production. The result was a considerable development of industries, mainly those which worked up the products of Hungary's agriculture and mining. But the Magyar nationalists were not content with this success; they constantly denounced the economic union with Austria as hindering Hungary's industrial progress, and clamoured for its dissolution and for protective tariffs around Hungary. Neither the Poles nor the Czechs within old Austria shared this striving for economic separatism. After the war Hungary obtained her full economic independence and joined in the general policy of protection.

The general rate of post-war progress is indicated by the index of industrial production showing the relation to the output of 1929. The latest figures are:—[1]

	1929.	1930.	1931.	1932.	1933.	1934.	1935.	1936.	1937.	1938.
Investment goods .	100	83·6	73·0	57·7	55·5	67·6	79·8	96·4	110·4	115·6
Consumption goods	100	99·8	94·5	93·6	104·1	114·6	119·9	129·1	138·8	137·3
General index .	100	94·6	87·4	81·9	88·2	99·2	106·8	118·4	129·5	126·5

[1] The figures are taken from the *League of Nation's Statistical Yearbook* for 1939–40. It may be noted that the Hungarian statistical yearbooks for 1936 and 1937 gave a series of figures considerably below the above general level.

The index is based on the net output of manufacturing industries. Hungary has most detailed and informative statistics of industrial production. The following table shows a few principal data. The gross output is first shown, according to its current value, and then in its volume, expressed in value of 1913.[1]

PRODUCTION OF FACTORIES (LARGE-SCALE INDUSTRIES)
('000,000 P.)

	1913.	1929.	1933.	1935.	1936.	1937.
Gross output .	1,909	2,867	1,763	2,201	2,582	2,952
Volume at price level 1913 .	1,909	2,241	1,674	2,024	2,272	2,404
Net output [2] .	—	1,275	837	976	915	1,236

[2] Gross less cost of all materials worked up, but without allowance for maintenance and replacement.

This table shows that the output surpassed the pre-war level at the peak of the industrial boom, 1928 and 1929, and thereafter only towards the end of the period, in particular in 1937. In that year production was about 26% above that of 1913. But this calculation is not free from doubts. Prof. von Fellner stated in a paper that the industrial income in 1928 was already greater than in 1913. But the statistician in charge of the industrial statistics showed that the increase was due to the improvement of statistical methods, and that the factory output of 1928 was at least 10% smaller than that of 1913.[3] Now, in 1928 the output was 0·9% above that of the basic year 1929. If we assume, therefore, that it was only 10% below the pre-war level, we must deduct about 10% from the figures indicating the level of production to shift it from basis 1929 to basis 1913. The index for 1937 was 129·5, and accordingly the increase since 1913 would be about 20%—not 26%, as estimated above.

<hr>

But as the *League of Nation's Yearbook* was published later we assume that it gives revised figures, and have put them into the text.
    [1] The value of 1913 was calculated by means of the two indices of industrial prices. The first refers to flour and sugar, the second to other industries. The usual conversion by means of the general wholesale index is obviously misleading, as this index is determined also by the agricultural prices. The figures from the industrial Census of 1913 are taken from *Magyar Statistikai Szemle*, 1923, I, 300, and from the article by Farkasfalvi in *Revue de la Société Hongroise de Statistique*, 1923, I, 162; II, 190.
    [3] Cf. Fellner in *Bulletin de l'Institut de Statistique*, tome XXV, 1931, and Farkasfalvi in *Revue Hongroise de Statistique*, VIII, 1930, I, 20.

Matolcsy and Varga have supplemented the Census data by calculations of their own, showing also the net value with allowance for maintenance and also estimating the output of handicrafts.[1] The principal figures are:—

	1928–1929.	1932–1933.	1935–1936.	1936–1937.
Factory output:				
Gross	2,894	1,805	2,398	2,777
Net	1,137	704	879	995
Handicrafts and domestic industry:				
Net	485	383	356	370
Total industries:				
Net	1,622	1,087	1,235	1,365
Mining and smelting:				
Gross	170	120	145	166
Net	90	64	75	83

The greatest increase took place in the textile industries, in particular the cotton branch.[2] From 1913 to 1936 the number of workers rose to fourfold, and the gross output to fivefold the prewar figure. The leather industry and chemical production could about double their output. Also the paper industry and electricity showed good progress. On the other hand, the iron and metal industries, engineering and the food industries were throughout almost the whole period in a very depressed condition, and only picked up in its last years, stimulated by a new increase in protection. The depressed industries had all a far too great capacity, which had been designed for the much larger pre-war market. The flour-mills formerly worked for all parts of Austria-Hungary. After the war the new States introduced high tariffs on flour, and the Hungarian mills could on the average work at a rate of only about 25% of their capacity, except in a few particularly good years. The sugar industry at first increased, and in 1924–1925 reached an output of over 2 million tons. But in 1935–1936 the output had dwindled almost to half. In 1913 the breweries produced on the territory of later small Hungary 2·2 million hl., but in 1934–1935 their output was down to less than a tenth, or to 185,107 hl.

[1] Cf. M. Matolcsy and St. Varga, *The National Income of Hungary*, 1938.
[2] Cf. for the single industries Karl Geller, *Die Strukturwandlung der ungarischen Volkswirtschaft nach dem Kriege*, 1938.

23. THE RATE OF DEVELOPMENT BEFORE AND AFTER THE WAR
COMPARED

Was the rate of industrial progress quicker before the war, when Hungary formed part of the Austro-Hungarian Customs union, or after the war, when the aim of full commercial independence and protective tariffs had been realised? The development of the total industrial population was :—

	Pre-war period 1900–1910.	Post-war period 1920–1930.
	%	%
Industries and mining . .	+33·0	+21·6
Industries, mining, commerce, transport . . .	+33·7	+16·6

The industrial population therefore developed at a much quicker pace when Hungary's industries were not protected by high tariffs but enjoyed the advantage of a wide market and of a natural division of labour.

The difference between the two periods is still more marked if we compare the output of manufacturing industries. In great pre-war Hungary the Censuses showed these figures :—

	Industrial output.	Number of workers.
	('000,000 K.)	('000's.)
1898	1,400	246
1906	2,407	371
1913	3,579	475

In the eight years 1898–1906 the output rose by 72%, or by 9% a year, and the workers increased by 51%, or over 6% a year. In the seven years 1906–1913 the increase in output was 49%, or 7% a year, and that in workers was 28%, or 4% a year. The relation between the increase in output and that in workers indicates the rate of technical progress.

From 1898 to 1913 the increase in the value of output was 155%. But a part of this rise was due to the increase in prices of industrial raw materials, which in the same period, according to the index of the *Statist*, rose on the world markets by 33%. But Hungary's industries at that time chiefly worked up materials provided by her

193

agriculture and mines. The internal rise may be estimated at 25%. On this assumption the increase in the real value of industrial output was 124%, or over 8% a year.

In the subsequent twenty-four years from 1913 to 1937 the gross output in the post-war territory rose in real value by about 25%, or a little over 1% a year. The pace of development was before the war about eight times that of the post-war period.

It must, of course, be taken into account that after 1913 four years were years of war, and three were a time of acute world crisis. The war, however, stimulated certain industries, and by 1917 there were 513 more factories in the post-war territory of Hungary than in 1913. In the long run, of course, the influence of the war was detrimental to the economic organism.

We may also refer to Fellner's estimates of industrial net output for the years 1901 and 1913. The rise in net output was 121%.[1]

26. The Price of Enforced Industrialisation

The advocates of industrialisation at any price stressed the argument that the policy of artificial stimulation of industrial production would also confer great benefits on agriculture. The market for agricultural products would be considerably expanded, prices and wages would rise, and the purchasing power of the farmers and their labourers would become much greater. But in fact the agricultural population, which still formed the bulk of the Hungarian people, was by that policy plunged into new depths of misery. The enforced industrialisation not only burdened it with heavy expenses, but also contributed to the narrowing of the markets for Hungary's agricultural products, since the States which saw their export of manufactured goods to Hungary reduced retaliated by increased tariffs on Hungarian wheat and cattle.

The variation of agricultural and industrial prices was (July figures) :—

	1913.	1925.	1929.	1933.	1936.	1937.
Agricultural .	100	125	114	57	71	80
Industrial .	100	138	133	107	117	125

[1] Cf. F. von Fellner in *Statistische Monatsschrift*, 1916, p. 604, and in *Bulletin de l'Institut International de Statistique*, XIII, 1903.

The comparison of agricultural and industrial prices reveals a wide discrepancy between them. After 1929, in particular, it became so great that sometimes producers of food had to give almost double the pre-war amount of grain and cattle for the manufactured products required by them. The purchasing power of the rural population sank to such a low level that many industries also were gravely affected. The production of agricultural machines was for a considerable time almost at a standstill. The use of artificial fertilisers decreased between 1926 and 1936 from 143,143 to 50,046 mq., or by nearly two-thirds. The policy of industrialisation led also to an increase in the capacity of shoe factories. But in 1935 the shoe industry could only work at half its capacity, and several plants had to be closed down. The Association of the Shoe Trade estimated that the consumption of shoes was in the United States 3 pairs per head, in England 2¼ pairs, in Germany 1 pair, and in Hungary only ½ pair. This was to a great extent due to the low purchasing power of the agricultural population.

The policy of rapid industrialisation aimed at the greatest possible increase in exports. To a certain extent this was justifiable, since Hungary must import most of her raw materials. But Hungary, like so many other States, adopted measures bound to depress internal purchasing power in order to enhance her exports. Direct and indirect subsidies were paid to exporters not only of many manufactured goods, but also of the most important foods, like wheat, sugar, fruit, milk. The prices on the home market were kept high in order to enable exporters to dump Hungarian products on foreign markets at abnormally low prices. This contributed to the decline in the standard of life of broad masses, and to the spread of under-nourishment in one of the most fertile agricultural countries of Europe.

27. The Development of Wages

In Hungary wages rose after the war less quickly than in the western neighbour countries.

A publication of the International Labour Office gives data for the years immediately following the war.[1] According to them the

[1] Cf. *Wage Changes in Various Countries, 1914–1925*, published by the International Labour Office, 1926.

average of forty-eight real wages in Hungary was at the end of 1924 only 86·7% of the level of 1914, while the average of twenty-seven Austrian wages was 117% and that of eleven Czechoslovak wages 90·4%. In July 1925 the workers in the Hungarian engineering industry had a real wage amounting to between 50% and 80% of the pre-war level. Skilled workers had 76%, semi-skilled 73% and unskilled 78%. At about the same time the engineering workers in Czechoslovakia had reached between 81% and 95%, and in Austria between 105% and 117% of the pre-war level. True, engineering was particularly depressed in Hungary. The highest wages were reached in printing and bookbinding, where they amounted to between 100% and 120% of the pre-war level.

It seems that by 1927 the rise in wages and the fall in the cost of living had about restored the pre-war level of real wages.[1] In 1913 the average wage of all kinds of employees on the Hungarian railways was 1,482 K., and in 1926–1927 2,019 P., or at pre-war price level, calculated by means of the cost-of-living index, excluding rent, 1,400 K., or 6% below the pre-war amount. If rent is included, the wage was 17% above the pre-war rate. But not all workers profited from the low rents, and those who did received a benefit at the expense of the house-owners which must not be confused with the change in price level. In any case, the conclusion seems warranted that the pre-war wage had about been reached by 1927.

I have checked this view further in this way. The Statistical Office of the City of Budapest has compiled for hundreds of categories of workers the wage rates for 1914 and for the separate post-war years.[2] From these data I have selected ninety representative rates, covering all great branches of industries and the various classes of workers, both men and women. The averages of these ninety wages show this movement:—

	1914.	1927.	1929.
Nominal wage . . .	100	112	111
Real wage:			
Including rent . . .	100	102	93
Excluding rent . .	100	90	85

[1] Cf. the data published by the Labour Exchanges on wages offered.
[2] Cf. *Statistical Year Book of Budapest* (in Hungarian and German).

This comparison confirms the previous finding that the real wage level had in 1927 come very near that for 1914. But in 1929 the rise in the cost of living lowered it again.

From 1929 onwards the movement of nominal and real wages can be followed in these figures, compiled by the International Labour Office:—[1]

	1929.	1930.	1931.	1932.	1933.	1934.	1935.	1936.	1937.	1938.
Nominal	100	91	96	89	84	81	77	79	81	86
Real .	100	101	112	107	108	106	99	96	92	98

The statistics of factory production contain numerous data about wages, from which a few have been compiled in this table:—[2]

	1927.	1929.	1932.	1934.	1936.	1937.
Average number of workers ('000's) . . .	226	235	171	196	246	277
Wages ('000,000 P.) . .	320	352	204	222	281	320
Hours worked ('000,000's) .	586	613	400	488	621	692
Average wage . . .	1,416	1,498	1,193	1,133	1,142	1,155
Real wage basis, 1913:						
Including rent . .	1,287	1,262	1,214	1,273	1,201	1,132
Excluding rent . .	1,133	1,161	1,169	—	1,168	1,079

As has been shown, the real wage level of 1927 was approximately the same as that before the war. Now, the above table shows that real wages, including rent, constantly declined from 1927 to 1937. Those exclusive of rent rose in the years of the great depression, owing to the heavy fall in food prices, but in 1937 they were again below the level of 1927, and therefore also below the pre-war level.

28. UNEMPLOYMENT

According to the statistics, industrial unemployment was much less severe in Hungary than in most other comparable countries.

[1] Cf. *Year Book of Labour Statistics*, 1943–1944.
[2] The data of the Census 1913 have not been added because those which have been published are not comparable with the post-war figures.

In the following table the first line gives the number of unemployed registered by the trade unions at the end of the year, and the second shows the difference between the applications for posts at the Labour Exchanges and the number of posts filled :—

1927.	1928.	1929.	1930.	1931.	1932.	1933.	1934.	1935.	1936.	1937.
14	15	20	22	33	32	27	22	19	16	17
60	62	65	68	70	66	54	52	56	56	57

These figures are surprisingly low. But closer study raises grave doubts in regard to their significance. Their movement agrees neither with the index of industrial production nor with the number of workers insured. According to the above-quoted statistics of the trade unions, the number of unemployed was in 1932 greater by only 17,000 than in 1928, and according to the data of the Labour Exchanges by only 4,000. But, as the Budapest Chamber of Commerce pointed out,[1] the number of workers insured, and therefore employed, decreased in the same period by no less than 248,600. The insurance statistics prove that the number of unemployed must in all years have been much greater than shown by the first-quoted statistics. It is obvious that these do not really express the scale of unemployment.

It must not be ignored that the factory workers whose number increased through the policy of high tariffs constituted in 1930 only one-fourth of the total of the population active in industries and mining. The majority were small artisans and their workers. The Census of 1930 showed 203,000 independent artisans, of whom 58% worked alone without employing hired labour. This class was particularly hard hit by the crisis, and their standard of life was incredibly low.[2]

Further, it has already been mentioned that there was considerable unemployment among the agricultural labourers, whose living conditions greatly declined after the war—miserable though they were before.

[1] Cf. *Report of the Budapest Chamber of Commerce for 1935* (German edition), p. 64.
[2] Cf. *Report of the Budapest Chamber of Commerce for 1934*, pp. 7, 40, and *Report for 1935*, p. 68.

29. The Decline in Consumption

In a largely agricultural country consumption varies with the crops, and it is therefore necessary to compare averages of at least three years. The pre-war consumption on the territory of the later small Hungary can be deduced by a simple calculation from the statistics of consumption for former large Hungary. As regards crops, we can ascertain the share of the small territory in the output of the large one. For the five great cereals, for instance, this share was 41% of the weight, and for potatoes 36%. We may assume that this was also the share in the consumption of these products, since the peasants consumed most of their grain themselves, and the labourers were largely paid by a share in the crops. As regards other articles, and the consumption of the non-agricultural classes, we may take the share in the net national income as the key figure.[1] According to Fellner this share was 40%, or almost the same as the share in cereals and in the total agricultural income.[2]

A comparison of the average cereal crops for 1910–1911 to 1912–1913 with those for 1935–1936 to 1937–1938 shows that the consumption per head remained almost exactly the same—namely, 546 kg. per head. This includes, of course, consumption by animals and by industries. The consumption of potatoes fell from 210 kg. to 184 kg., or by 12%, and that of beer from 16·4 l. to 2·77 l. per head, or by 83%. On the other hand, the consumption of sugar rose from 8·7 kg. to 10·6 kg., and that of wine from 14·8 l. to 36·4 l.

All these articles of consumption were products of the Hungarian soil. If the Hungarian farmer lost markets for his wheat, sugar and wine abroad, he consumed his products himself, and in some cases even increased his consumption. But he was not able

---

[1] The income of individuals is, of course, not proportionate to their consumption of specific articles, because the structure of demand alters with the height of income. But it is different with the national income. A share of 40% means a certain volume of income of a given average structure, and this average structure does not change quickly.

[2] In reality the share was greater because Fellner did not take account of the inflow of dividends, interests, tourist expenses, taxes, etc., from the outlying provinces into the central territory to which Hungary was later reduced while those provinces were lopped off. But this kind of income had little influence on the consumption of mass articles. Fellner's estimate, however, includes payments to and from foreign countries.

to maintain his consumption of meat and fats, as is shown by the reduction in livestock :—

DOMESTIC ANIMALS IN THE POST-WAR TERRITORY PER 1,000 INHABITANTS [1]

	Cattle.	Horses.	Pigs.	Sheep.
1911 . .	282·6	117·9	436·8	316·3
1929 . .	209·9	102·9	298·0	181·4
1936 . .	195·2	88·3	284·1	150·2

The decline in consumption is confirmed also by the statistics of the city of Budapest, where meat and alcoholic beverages are subject to the municipal excise. The development was as follows :—[2]

	1912–1913.	1927.	1928.	1929.	1930.	1933.
Meat consumption per head, kg. . .	50·6	36·1	36·7	32·2	41·3	40·5
Milk supply per head per day:						
Municipal dairies .	0·33	0·26	0·29	0·31	—	0·19
Rural dairies . .	—	0·07	0·06	0·06	—	0·05

The increase of meat consumption in the years of severe crisis was due to the great fall in agricultural prices, which from 1929 to 1933 decreased from 114 to 57, or to exactly half, while wages fell much less.

The consumption of beer, wine and other alcoholic beverages per head of the population over fifteen years fell in Budapest from 1910 to 1930 from 130·7 l. to 66·2 l., or to about half.

The consumption of foreign goods was particularly affected by the decrease in purchasing power.

	1910–1913.	1926–1928.	1935–1937.
Consumption per head of:			
Coffee, kg.· . . .	0·61	0·42	0·24
Tea, kg. . . .	0·02	0·04	0·03
Tobacco, kg. . . .	1·28	1·35	1·03

[1] Calculated by the Hungarian Statistical Office.
[2] Cf. the statistics of the City of Budapest.

The *Hungarian Statistical Year Book* gives data on the consumption of cotton which seem to show a considerable increase. But this is the consumption by the cotton industry, and as this was stimulated by high tariffs, it was natural that it consumed more cotton. But did the consumption of the population also rise? If we wish to find this out we must compare the imports of raw cotton, yarn and fabrics, less exports. If it is further assumed that of the pre-war consumption 40% was in the territory of later Hungary, the result is that in 1912 the consumption of cotton and cotton goods per head was 4·12 kg., and in 1937 3·00 kg.

In 1936 a calculation was published comparing the requirements of a modest middle-class household with the actual amounts consumed. There was a deficiency of 38% in calories, and of 33% in weight. Single items were (in kg. per head and year) :—

	Needed amount.	*Actual consumption.*
Cereals . . .	200	185
Meat, fat . . .	60	25
Sugar . . .	18	10
Fruit . . .	150	20

30. The Returns of Enterprises and the Formation of Capital in Hungary

Hungary has very detailed statistics of limited companies, from which the following data on the development of their capital, and on profits and losses, have been compiled. The net profit or loss has been expressed in percentages of the total capital :—

All Limited Companies
('000,000 P.)

	1925.	1926.	1927.	1928.	1929.	1930.	1931.	1932.	1933.	1934.	1935.	1936.	1937.
Share capital .	903	1,152	1,254	1,398	1,509	1,529	1,555	1,563	1,500	1,468	1,443	1,445	1,447
Reserves .	766	965	1,010	1,080	1,146	1,233	1,261	1,330	1,326	1,332	1,356	1,409	1,471
Own capital .	1,669	2,117	2,264	2,478	2,655	2,762	2,816	2,893	2,826	2,800	2,799	2,854	2,918
Profits .	98	136	208	222	224	181	124	94	89	99	112	140	161
Losses .	30	41	43	63	83	119	161	219	194	166	168	141	150
Surplus .	5·8%	4·5%	7·3%	6·4%	5·3%	2·2%	—	—	—	—	—	—	0·4%
Loss .	—	—	—	—	—	—	1·3%	4·3%	3·7%	2·4%	2·0%	—	—

If all profits are added and all losses deducted, the profitability of the total capital over thirteen years was 0·9%.

The above table shows also the rate of investment of capital in limited companies. The increase in share capital and reserves of all companies was from 1925 to 1937 1,249 million P., which corresponds to an annual increase of 100·5 million P., or about 3·6 million (old) pounds, if the Pengö is assumed at par. In the ten years before the war the annual increase was, in former great Hungary, for the industrial and banking companies alone 232 million K., or about 9·6 million pounds. Now post-war Hungary possessed, according to Fellner, 48·5% of the industrial and commercial income of former Hungary. On the other hand, the price level was, in the 'twenties, when most of the capital was raised, about a third above the pre-war level, which fact necessitated also most capital. The capital formed, therefore, amounted only to about half the annual increase before the war.

The development of savings deposits in banks and co-operatives of all types was as follows (million P.): 1925, 309; 1929, 1,022; 1937, 970.

In 1913 savings in the former territory were equivalent to 4,480 million P.

From 1925 to 1937 the annual increase was 66 million P., though it must be considered that the increase actually took place in the four years 1925–1929, and that in the following years savings decreased. In former Hungary (without Croatia) the savings deposits rose in this way: 1903, 2,051 million K.; 1913, 3,853 million K.

The annual increase was in former Hungary 180 million K., or 209 million P.

The formation of savings deposits was therefore also much slower than before the war.

31. INDUSTRIAL DEVELOPMENT IN YUGOSLAVIA

The statistical data available are not sufficient to form an opinion on Yugoslavia's development as a whole. Various Government publications give figures which are either inconsistent with one another or about which it is not clear to what exactly they refer. The number of industrial enterprises existing when the

State was formed in 1919 is in one publication given as 630, and in another as 1,891. One states that in 1929 there were 4,031 enterprises, another puts their number for 1935 at 5,000, and a third for 1936 at 2,833.[1] The *Statistical Year Book* for 1938–1939 shows 3,594 factories. This publication also gives on p. 192 a table on the size, motor power and workers of enterprises, but it obviously refers only to a section of the total industries.

The number of workers employed can be ascertained from the insurance statistics. The general insurance comprises all workers and employees, including domestics, but exclusive of miners and railwaymen, who have their separate insurance. Of the agricultural labourers only a small part are insured.

	Workers insured in General Insurance. (1,000's.)	Average daily wage in dinars.	Miners. (1,000's.)	Railwaymen. (1,000's.)
1927 .	511	25·04	—	—
1928 .	566	25·82	—	—
1929 .	605	26·32	—	—
1930 .	631	26·56	53	—
1931 .	609	26·19	45	—
1932 .	536	24·58	44	—
1933 .	521	23·22	44	—
1934 .	544	22·24	48	—
1935 .	564	21·65	52	76
1936 .	616	21·68	54	78
1937 .	680	22·71	62	77
1938 .	715	23·64	71	80

The consumption of coal by industries can serve as an index of industrial activity. It was:—[2]

INDUSTRIAL CONSUMPTION OF COAL AND LIGNITE

(In 1,000 tons)

1924.	1925.	1926.	1927.	1928.	1929.
2,093	1,685	1,486	1,636	1,760	1,919

[1] Cf. *The Kingdom of Yugoslavia*, 1930, p. xlii; *Yugoslavia, an Economic Survey*, 1936, p. 135; *La Yougoslavie d'aujourd'hui*, 1936, p. 417.
[2] Cf. F. Lakatos, *Mining in Yugoslavia*, 1931, p. 16.

The figures for the following years are not available. But the total output of coal and lignite was from 1930 to 1937 considerably below that of 1929. Only in 1938 was the level of 1929 reached again and slightly surpassed. Nevertheless many new industries were founded in this time. The exploitation of the great resources in water-power made little progress. The total installation in hydro-electric power-stations amounted in 1937 only to 160,245 Kw., and a further 96,013 Kw. were installed in plants using both water-power and coal, besides a number of purely calorific works.

The largest industries are those producing food and working up wood, but the metallurgical, textile and leather industries are also of importance.

Protective tariffs and exchange control have been used for fostering industrial development, and in many respects progress has been made. The textile industry is now able to cover almost the whole demand of the population. The country possesses also great mineral resources, which have not yet been sufficiently utilised owing to transport difficulties and lack of capital.

The peasant mentality of the people and its social structure are not propitious for rapid industrial progress. Mr. Kenneth S. Patton,[1] the American Consul in Belgrade, reported :—

"There is no well-defined labour element in the kingdom. Mines and industrial plants are usually worked by persons from the rural districts who regard such employment as temporary and, after short periods of service, drift back to the farms."

The policy of industrialisation of Yugoslavia was designed to improve the living conditions of the agricultural population, which suffered under the consequences of the high birth rate, technical backwardness and lack of capital. But the results were scarcely satisfactory.

A Croatian peasant said to an English investigator :—[2]

"Life is getting more and more difficult. The prices we can obtain are so very low. Look, before 1914 I could get two pairs

---

[1] Cf. *The Kingdom of Serbs, Croats and Slovenes, a Commercial and Industrial Handbook*, by K. S. Patton, 1928.
[2] Cf. P. Lamartine Yates and D. Warriner, *Food and Farming in Post-War Europe*, 1943.

of boots for a hundredweight of wheat. To-day I must give two hundredweight of wheat in exchange for one pair of boots. For one kilogram of nails I must give one kilogram of wool. When I sold a sheep before 1914 I could buy fifty metres of cottons in exchange. Now I cannot get fifty metres of cotton-stuff even for four sheep. Things are no better on the coast of Dalmatia either. Before 1914 they could get a suit of clothes for a hecto-litre of wine. To-day they must give three hectolitres of wine for a suit. Before 1914 they could get ten boxes of matches for a litre of wine, to-day they must give a litre of wine for every single box."

32. ROUMANIA'S INDUSTRIAL DEVELOPMENT

Already before the First World War Roumania followed a policy of industrialisation by means of tariffs and direct and in-direct subsidies. After the war her industries greatly increased through the incorporation of parts of Austria-Hungary, and, moreover, the Government intensified its efforts to enforce a rapid industrialisation by all possible means. This policy re-sulted in a considerable increase in industries, though it laid heavy burdens on the agricultural population. The Roumanian tariffs were among the highest in the world. The progress achieved in manufacturing production is shown in the following table:—[1]

FACTORY PRODUCTION IN POST-WAR TERRITORY

1913.		1919.	1929.		1937.	
Value of output. '000,000 lei (gold).		Person-nel. (1'000's.)	Value of output. '000,000 lei (paper).	Person-nel. (1'000's.)	Value of output. '000,000 lei.	Person-nel. (1'000's.)
Gross.	Net.		Gross.	Net.	Gross.	Net.	
1910	874	157	60,965	— 207	64,567	— 279

[1] Cf. *Roumanian Statistical Year Book.* The pre-war data were ascertained by the Ministry of Trade in 1920. Cf. C. O. Rommenhoeller, *La Grande Roumanie,* 1926.

The lei had before the war the same value as the gold franc. After the war it greatly depreciated, and in 1929 32·26 new lei were equivalent to 1 old lei. If the pre-war gross output is converted into new lei the amount is 61,617 million, and allowing for the rise of about 26% in the price level on a gold basis it is obvious that the output of 1929 was considerably smaller than that of 1913. In 1937 the nominal value of output was higher by 6% than in 1920, but the price level was lower by 21·8%, and the currency was at a discount of 38%. The index of industrial production was 37% above 1929, but receded in 1938 to 33%. Roumania has therefore succeeded in increasing her industries in comparison with the pre-war period. This result was, however, achieved at the expense of the peasants, who had much to suffer through the high industrial prices and many measures adopted to further the industries. In pre-war Roumania industrial production doubled in the period 1900–1916. It is very probable that after the war under a more liberal system greater progress would have been achieved.

D. THE NATIONAL INCOME BEFORE AND AFTER THE WAR

1. AUSTRIA'S NATIONAL INCOME

Estimates of Austria's national income have been made by me for various years, the last for 1927, amounting to 6,678 million S. In the meantime many new data have become available, and the following calculation makes use of them. It is, moreover, based on a wider concept of income, and employs a new method.

	1928.	1929.
(1) Agricultural income (farm accountancy) .	2,306·5	1,830·4
(2) Wages and salaries (except agriculture and public service):		
Workers in General Health Insurance (wages and distribution of 1926)	2,390·3	2,363·5
Increase in wages from 1926 to 1929 . .	382·4	378·2
Miners	62·5	60·8
Railwaymen	374·5	389·0
Post, telegraph, telephone	122·4	123·6
(3) Profits (except agriculture):		
Individual enterprises	1,467·0	1,417·0
Limited companies:		
(a) Industrial	50·6	6·4
(b) Banks	66·1	53·6
(c) Others	ca. 10·0	ca. 10·0
(4) State monopolies and enterprises . .	192·9	202·0
Enterprises of the provinces	74·5	54·7
Total	7,499·7	6,889·2
(5) Price-raising taxes (excise, turnover tax, railway ticket tax, customs) . . .	609·9	650·2
Total	8,109·6	7,539·4

For reasons already pointed out, this list includes neither the salaries of public officials nor interest on public loans, nor house rent. These amounts are:—

('000,000 S.)

	1928.	1929.
Salaries of officials in the central administration	501·7	526·6
Salaries in provincial administration [1] . .	ca. 308·0	ca. 316·0
Interest on public loans	225·9	182·7
House rent assessed for income tax . . .	21·4	31·6

[1] Salaries in the provincial administration have been estimated on the

The amount of house rent assessed for income tax increased between 1926 and 1932 from 12·6 million S. to 90·0 million S. owing to the relaxation of the Rent Restriction Act.

The income-tax statistics give also a figure of all taxed income which can be used as an index for the variation of the total national income, since only the lowest incomes are excluded and income from public enterprises. This figure, however, includes salaries of public officials, interest on public loans and house rent.

INCOME FOR WHICH INCOME TAX WAS PAID

1929.	1930.	1931.	1932.	1933.	1934.	1935.
6,036	6,173	5,871	5,036	4,293	4,337	4,382

It may be recalled that only a part of the agricultural income appeared in the income-tax statistics, mainly because most peasants had a very low income.

2. CZECHOSLOVAKIA'S NATIONAL INCOME

The share in former Austria's national income which fell to Czechoslovakia was, according to Waizner's calculations, 6,710 million K., and if his under-estimate of former Austria's industrial output is corrected, and replaced by Fellner's estimate, 7,316 million. To this must be added the share in Hungary's national income which went to Czechoslovakia. This has been estimated by Fellner at 1,131·6 million K., and to this 30·5%, or 345·1 million, must be added to adjust Fellner's figure to the wider concept of national income as used by Waizner. The total amount of the pre-war income produced in the later Czechoslovak territories without payments from or to other territories was therefore 8,793 million K. This was the wider national income, inclusive of non-economic services, such as public service, domestic services and house rent. If we omit these items, as Fellner did, then the national income in the narrower sense was 7,608 million K.

---

assumption that they formed the same percentage of the total expenditure as in the budget of the central administration. Whether this is so I am unable to say.

Another estimate was made by Professor Corrado Gini, who was requested by the League of Nations to calculate the national income of various States. He came to the conclusion that Czechoslovakia's pre-war income was 7·22 milliard K. His concept of the national income was obviously nearer to that of Fellner than to that of Waizner.

No detailed official calculation of the Czechoslovak national income has been published. But on various occasions widely divergent figures were quoted by Czechoslovak statesmen and economists. The Minister of Finance, Prof. English, in his speech on the budget for 1927, put the national income at 60 milliard Kc.[1] On another occasion the Minister of Commerce, Dr. Hotoveč, spoke of a national income of 70 or 76 milliard Kc.[2] In 1935 Mr. Nečas, Minister of Social Welfare, said in Parliament that the income had fallen since 1929 from 80 to 40 or 50 milliards.

All these figures were put forward without any definition of what elements were included in the national income and without stating the method employed in calculating it. We have therefore made an independent estimate in which all main elements have been based on official statistics.

The agricultural income for 1926–1930 has been calculated by means of the data provided by the Czechoslovak Farm Accountancy Institute. These statistics did not, however, include the return of the forests, which had to be estimated separately. The total of wages and salaries in industries, etc., was calculated on the basis of the social insurance statistics. The returns of industrial and commercial enterprises are shown by the statistics of trade tax (general and special), and all other items, such as returns of public enterprises, price-raising taxes, etc., can be taken from the State Accounts. If all these data are assembled, the result is as follows:—

---

[1] Cf. K. English, *The Budget for 1927*, 1926.
[2] The *Bulletin of the National Bank of Czechoslovakia*, No. 147, 1939, refers to the estimate by Hotoveč. According to the *Bulletin*, it was made for 1926–1927, and was exclusive of the incomes of public employees, the professions, personal and domestic servants and house rent. It amounted to between 76 and 83 milliards of Kc. If the items excluded are added, the national income in the last years prior to the great crisis was 90 milliards. The *Bulletin* further gives figures showing the development of this wider national income from 1929 to 1937. They are quoted at the end of this chapter, and have also been inserted into the statistics of the League of Nations.

	Milliards Kc.
Agricultural Income:	
Income from farming and labourers . . .	ca. 20,000 [1]
Income from forests	ca. 1,000
Industrial and Commercial Income:	
Returns of enterprises, less losses	9,574
Wages and salaries	24,451
State Income:	
State enterprises and monopolies	1,866
Price-raising taxes :	
Excise tax	1,686
Coal tax	252
Customs	1,430
Turnover and luxuries tax	2,346
Total	62,605

[1] Including 7,174·6 million Kc. wages of labourers.

A few additions ought to be made to this figure. Workers doing only occasional work were not included in the Health Insurances and their wages therefore escaped observation. Business returns may have been under-stated, though the tax inspectors were extremely vigilant and efficient. Many small traders, however, did not keep proper books, and others, too, often found ways of hiding part of their profits from the attention of the tax authorities. The unpaid work of housewives and children on peasant farms is taken into account by the Farm Accountancy, but the value of other housework done by wives or other unpaid relatives cannot be ascertained. The salaries of Civil Servants have not been included. They amounted to approximately 6,000 milliard Kc. Nor have we included house rent. The amount of rent assessed for income tax in 1928 was 521 milliard Kc. But this amount was considerably below the real value. In the three western provinces, for instance, the house rent assessed in 1913 was 175 million K., while in 1928 the amount, at pre-war price level, was only 40 million K.

In any case, the result of our estimate agrees quite well with English's figure for 1927, but it is considerably lower than all other statements.

If we assume an income of 64 milliard Kc., this would be equivalent to 9·357 milliard gold Kronen, and, reduced to the price level of 1913, 7·01 milliard K. The estimates quoted at the beginning of this chapter amounted for the time before the war to between 7·22 and 7·61 milliard K. All these estimates excluded non-economic services and house rent. They are therefore inter-comparable. The result is that the post-war income was even in the best year below the pre-war level. It must further be remembered that the income for 1929 was to a considerable extent inflated by a fictitious prosperity produced by high tariffs and over-speculation. If we accept the estimate of Dr. Hotoveč, the income before the crisis surpassed the pre-war income. But Hotoveč did not publish the details of his calculations, and the figures quoted by him were considerably smaller than those later attributed to him by the *Bulletin of the National Bank*.

The *Bulletin* has further published estimates of the national income in the wider sense (inclusive of salaries of Civil Servants, the income of the professions and domestic servants, and of house rent). These figures are quoted in the table below. We have converted them into figures at the pre-war price basis by dividing them by the wholesale price index, and have added also the index of industrial production and the average number of unemployed.

	1929.	1930.	1931.	1932.	1933.	1934.	1935.	1936.	1937.
Wider national income in milliard Kc.	90·0	79·2	68·4	58·1	53·6	56·2	58·4	59·6	66·7
Real income at pre-war price basis (1914)	67·4	66·8	63·6	58·3	55·6	66·2	68·0	72·3	—
Index of industrial production	100	89·2	80·7	63·5	60·2	66·5	70·1	80·2	—
Number of unemployed ('ooo's)	42	105	291	554	738	677	686	621	—

A comparison of these figures reveals glaring inconsistencies. How is it possible that the real national income on the 1914 price basis was in 1934 little below that of the peak year of 1929, and in the subsequent years even higher, though the index of industrial production was so far below that for 1929, and the number of unemployed was so high? Allowance must, of course, be made for the margin of error involved in the shifting of income figures to another price level. But it is obvious that the fault was also due to the concept of the wider national income. Its variations do not adequately express the variations in economic production, especially if the salaries of officials and the maintenance of the Army and similar posts are included.

It must also be remembered that from 1910 to 1936 the population increased by 12%. The income per head was certainly lower in 1936 than in 1913.

3. Hungary's National Income

We have already referred to the various studies of Prof. F. de Fellner on the Hungarian national income.

Among them is also a paper comparing the pre-war income with the average for 1926–1928.[1] If the income for these three years produced in the post-war territory is converted into pre-war value it amounts to 3,343 million P., while the figure for 1911–1913 was 3,431 million P. The income had not, therefore, reached its former level. The main item was the agricultural income, which decreased from 2,052 to 1,588 million P. On the other hand, the income from industries rose from 952 to 1,261 million P. Fellner himself, however, expressed doubts as regards the reliability of this figure. In fact the rise was mainly due to an improvement in statistical methods, and the production of 1928 was, according to an official statement, smaller by at least 10% than that of 1913. Besides, the population had increased by 12%, so that the income per head was considerably smaller than before the war.

If we wish to compare the income available for consumption we must deduct from the produced income payments to other countries, less receipts from abroad. Before the war Hungary owed 8,395 million K. to foreign investors, of which amount 4,704 million K. were owed to Austrians. This huge amount was wiped out by the depreciation of the currency, and the consumable income was thereby increased. Nevertheless it is doubtful whether the loss in productivity was in this way made good, especially if those revenues also could be taken into account which Hungary received from the territories separated from her after the war. Fellner gives no estimate of these amounts, but they were certainly very great.

After Fellner, two other Hungarian economists—M. Matolcsy and S. Varga—have made careful investigation concerning the

[1] Cf. Fellner in *Metron*, III, 1923–1924, pp. 226–307.

national income. Their book on this subject shows the income for every year from 1924–1925 to 1936–1937. It gives a detailed analysis of all issues involved, based on elaborate statistical materials. The book is indispensable to the student of the problem. But it does not touch the question forming the subject of this study—namely, the relation between the national income before and after the war.

Matolcsy and Varga use a much wider concept of the national income than Fellner does. They include house rent, unpaid and paid domestic services, certain indirect taxes increasing the price level, the income of theatres and cinemas, and even the cost of pleasure trips. All of these items are not counted by Fellner as part of the national income. They also give a much higher estimate of the amount added to the national income by transport and commerce. A minor difference is that they make their calculations for the fiscal year (1.7–30.6), which has the advantage of giving a truer picture of the influence of the harvest on income.[1] A danger implied in their wide concept is that superficial readers may have the impression that the national income has risen greatly in the post-war period.

The estimates of these two economists cannot therefore be compared with those of Fellner without a previous adjustment. This is not difficult to achieve, since to a considerable extent both studies follow the same methods, in particular as regards the computation of the agricultural and industrial income. We have therefore converted the net income from agriculture, mining and industries as calculated by the two authors into pre-war value by means of the respective indices. For mining the price index for coal was taken, since the output of the mines consisted mainly of coal. To the agricultural income the agricultural index was applied, to industries the industrial one, and to commerce and transport the general wholesale index.

A very great discrepancy exists between the two studies in regard to the income from commerce and transport. Matolcsy and Varga arrive at much higher amounts than does Fellner. Closer investigation shows that this is the weakest point in Fellner's estimates, and leaves no doubt that he greatly under-

[1] Cf. Matthias Matolcsy and Stephan Varga, *The National Income of Hungary 1924–1925 to 1936–1937*, London, 1938.

estimated the income from these sources. We may assume, however, that this income is in a fixed proportion to the income from production. Hungary's commerce and transport are quite predominantly engaged in distributing the products of her own agriculture, mining and industries. The country has no international trade or shipping independent of its own production, except some transit transport, which does not count. The income from commerce and transport must therefore vary with the volume of the output of the productive branches. If we make use of the estimates by Matolcsy and Varga we find that the income from commerce and transport amounted to 25·77%, or about 26% of the income from the three branches of production. It may be assumed that the proportion was about the same before the war as after.[1] On this assumption we have calculated the pre-war income from commerce and industries by taking 26% of the value of the net income of agriculture, mining and industries. This amount represents the increase in the value of the goods on their way from the producer to the consumer. A great part of the agricultural output is, of course, consumed by the producers themselves, which explains why the proportion is not higher.

We do not include in our estimate the items of house rent, domestic work of the housewives and international payments. The reasons have already been stated. Nor do we include income from theatres and other minor items. It would be difficult to estimate them for the pre-war years, and hardly worth while, as the amounts are negligible.

The amount of price-raising taxes and customs has been stated at the end of the list. The pre-war statistics showed them only for the whole of the territories under the Hungarian Crown. But as post-war Hungary's share in their national income was, according to Fellner, 40%, we have assumed that 40% of the excise duties on consumption also, and of the customs on imported goods, must be credited to the territory of later small Hungary.

The following table shows the result of these calculations. The pre-war figures are based on Fellner's estimates and official data,

---

[1] The number of people engaged in commerce and transport actually increased more quickly than the workers in the productive branches. But this was probably counterbalanced by the decrease in consumption. International trade, in particular, decreased considerably.

the post-war figures are those by Matolcsy and Varga, exclusive of certain items mentioned before.

NET INCOME AT PRE-WAR PRICE LEVEL
('000,000 P.)

	Average 1911, 1912, 1913.	Average 1934–1935, 1935–1936, 1936–1937.
Agriculture . . .	2,060·0	1,717·8
Mining . . .	79·3	59·1
Industries . . .	955·6	1,104·0
Commerce and transport (26% of the above amounts) . . .	804·7	773·8
Total . . .	3,899·6	3,654·7
Price-raising taxes .	193·3 [1]	321·9
Total . . .	4,092·9	3,976·6

[1] State Excise taxes, share in Austro-Hungarian customs, transport tax, road tolls, Budapest excise taxes.

The figures show that the post-war income was smaller than that before the war. In about twenty-five years it decreased by 3%. The population increased in this period by 17·4%, and the income per head was therefore smaller by 17·2% than before the war.

4. YUGOSLAVIA'S NATIONAL INCOME

The national income of Yugoslavia before the First World War was estimated by Prof. Gini in a report to the League of Nations at from 4 to 4·7 milliard of gold francs, or 310 to 370 fr. per head. This would correspond to an amount from 36·5 to 42·9 milliard of Dinar. After the war the national income was officially stated at :—[2]

(Milliard Dinars)

	1929.	1932.	1935.	1937.
National income . . .	69	32	37·5	44·2
Wholesale price index (basis 1913)	139·7	90·8	92·2	104·8

[2] Cf. La Yougoslavie en chiffres. Prof. Franges in Weltwirtschaftliches Archiv, 1938, p. 337.
The method employed by Yugoslav economists for estimating the national income is discussed by Alexander Wegner in Weltwirtschaftliches Archiv, 1927.

If we assume the Dinar at par (though it was actually depreciated), the national income for 1937 was equivalent to 3·8 milliard gold francs at pre-war price level, or 249 fr. per head. This was considerably below the estimate of Prof. Gini for the years before the First World War, amounting to from 310 to 370 fr. per head.

5. ROUMANIA'S NATIONAL INCOME

The statistical department of the Dresdener Bank has made an estimate of the national income of Roumania before and after the last war, expressed in Marks at pre-war price-level.[1] According to this computation the kingdom of Roumania had in 1913 an income of 2 milliard M., or 264 M. per head. The territories which later formed Great Roumania had before the war an income of 4 milliard M., or 247 M. per head. In 1928 this income had increased to 5 milliard M., or 282 M. per head. This would imply an increase of 25% in the real income. This figure is, however, very doubtful considering that the cereal production, livestock and industrial output were all below the pre-war level.

The League of Nation's Statistical Office[2] has published the figures of Roumania's national income, shown in the first line of the following table. We have added the official wholesale index and income figures at price level 1929 according to this index:—

('000,000 lei)

	1929.	1930.	1931.	1932.	1933.
Nominal income .	201	150	110	103·5	99·3
Wholesale index .	100	78·4	60·2	54·0	52·3
Real income .	201	191	183	192	189

If the figure for 1929 is converted into gold lei the national income for 1929 was equivalent to 6·23 milliard gold lei (francs) or to 5·06 milliard M. This would appear to be the same figure as stated by the Dresdener Bank, but this is a mistake. It must not be overlooked that in 1929 the price level on a gold basis was above the pre-war level by about 26%. Allowing for this rise, it is

[1] Cf. Dresdener Bank, *The Economic Forces of the World*, 1930.
[2] Cf. League of Nations, *World Economic Survey, 1938–1939*, p. 84.

obvious that the real national income in 1929 was not higher than that for 1913. In the following years it decreased, though no figures are available beyond 1933.

The general standard of living in the country was rather lower than before the war.[1] The Trade Cycle Institute of Bucharest calculated that between 1911–1913 and 1931–1937 the annual consumption per head of cotton fell from 3·1 to 2·1 kg., and that of tobacco from 0·930 to 0·595 kg. This seems also to indicate a decrease in the national income.

[1] Cf. *South-Eastern Europe*, published by the Royal Institute of International Affairs, 1939, p. 127.

EPILOGUE

THE AIM of this study has been defined in the first chapter as an empirical investigation into certain powerful economic tendencies of our time in the light of the experience of the Danubian area. Its subjects are in the first place economic nationalism, and in the second a certain economic ideology which is everywhere working in the same direction, though it is not always inspired by conscious nationalism. The field of our investigation was the area formerly united in Austria-Hungary, and later divided into a number of Succession States. This process formed an historic experiment of great significance.

We began by studying the development of the national income in the former Empire. Careful calculations led to the conclusion that in the last ten years before the First World War the national income rose in Austria by 86% and in Hungary by 92%. If allowance is made for the rise in prices, the increase in real income was in Austria 69% and in Hungary 75%. The calculation was based mainly on the statistics of agricultural output and of wages and profits in the industries, etc. Its result was then checked by figures showing the increase in the factors of production, such as the number of workers employed, the quantity of raw materials used, the rate of technical efficiency and, lastly, by figures showing the progress in wealth.

The pace of the increase in national income was much quicker than in Britain, or even in Germany. All nationalities of old Austria showed an almost equal percentual increase in wages and other income, except the most backward parts, where wages rose more quickly than in the more advanced parts. The number of unemployed was exceedingly low. There was actually no problem of unemployment on a large scale.

The particular significance of this development was that it was not due to the favours of Nature or history—Austria-Hungary could not compare in mineral resources with the other great industrial countries; in a large area transport was difficult and expensive owing mainly to the remoteness from the sea and the

218

mountainous character of the country. The historical background and social structure of the peoples concerned, moreover, were not propitious for a rapid increase of wealth. These grave disadvantages were, however, more than counterbalanced by the advantages of the great internal market, of the natural division of labour between the different parts of the Empire and of the organic integration into a well-balanced whole. To this were added a comparatively liberal policy in regard to foreign trade, a sound currency and a high international credit for financial trustworthiness. Lastly, there was a firmly established Reign of Law, and—at least in the Austrian half of the Empire—the striving to overcome the dangerous instincts of nationalism, to give everyone a chance and to encourage co-operation between all the nationalities as equal members in a community. These advantageous forces were partly checked by bitter rivalries between the nationalists among all the peoples, by the shortcomings of governments and parties, by deep-rooted historical inequalities, and widespread backwardness and poverty. Nevertheless the positive factors prevailed, and rendered possible a rapid rise in wealth.

This promising development came to an abrupt end through the First World War, which sprang out of national fanaticism and militaristic blindness.[1] The community of the greater part of the Danubian area, the outcome of a long historical growth, was hacked to pieces. The dictated peace settlement paid little regard to economic necessities. It was almost exclusively concerned with political questions. Except in a few minor points no attempt was made to achieve a far-sighted and fair compromise between the claims of the twelve nationalities concerned. In most cases the scales were heavily weighted in favour of certain nations, to the detriment of others. The result of all this was that the new States were separated from one another by high barriers of resentment, jealousy and hatred; that the seeds of new wars were widely scattered over the Danubian area, and that the nationalists and militarists gained in many countries the upper hand over the more peaceable elements. It was, in brief, the Balkanisation of the

[1] The immediate and overwhelming responsibility must certainly be ascribed to General Conrad von Hötzendorff and to Count Berchtold. But it would be a long story—quite outside the scope of this study—to trace the contribution of all the numerous militarists and nationalists of other countries.

Danubian countries, which soon spread far beyond that region. Almost everywhere fascist or semi-fascist governments were set up. It is clear that this system was irreconcilable with close economic co-operation; it naturally aimed at the greatest possible self-sufficiency, and was bound up with open, or concealed, economic warfare of all against all.

We need not repeat here the story of the attempts to find a way out of the morass. They were all in vain. Nor need we here record again the destructive influence of this system on State finances, currencies and international trade. But it is necessary to warn against the cheap argument that all this was merely due to the world crisis. This event had certainly a disastrous influence in bringing about the collapse and the protracted depression, but its effects would never have been so devastating if the Danubian States had been able to co-operate. Moreover, the world crisis itself was to a very great extent the fruit of economic nationalism.

Our study examines the economic development in the new States by means of copious statistical material. It shows that all the efforts to foster, by an extreme protectionism, either the rapid increase of agricultural production or that of industrial output had only a very limited success. Increases of production were smaller than the progress under the former conditions of free trade within the Austro-Hungarian Customs Union. Moreover, the progress achieved in one field was as a rule offset by retrogression in another. Austria increased her production of foodstuffs—but at the expense of her industries. Hungary forced by every means the rapid development of her industries—but at the expense of her agriculture. In Czechoslovakia agriculture remained stationary, though its financial returns greatly declined. But the great industries which had developed in Bohemia, Moravia and Silesia under the Austrian regime went down and a large part had to be scrapped. In Yugoslavia and Roumania the forcing of industrial development had also very unfavourable effects on agriculture. It is characteristic that in most countries the pre-war number of cattle was not reached again for good, and that mostly not even the number reached a few years after the war could be maintained. This shows that it was not the reduction of livestock owing to the war that caused the decline.

The most striking symptom of the economic disorganisation was the rise in unemployment. After the worst had passed it became almost normal that a third of the workers should be idle, though sometimes the statistics did not tell the whole truth. In certain countries there was very widespread undisclosed unemployment, especially in agriculture. In Czechoslovakia the German population had to suffer much more from unemployment than the Czechs had, and this played a great part in driving them into violent opposition.

This study further investigates the development of the national income after the war. It shows that the pre-war amount of income was scarcely ever reached in any country—not even at the peak of the fallacious boom of the late 'twenties. In the subsequent years the national income everywhere fell rapidly to unprecedented depths, far below the pre-war level, and then only slowly recovered. It can be said that twenty or more years after the outbreak of the Great War the national income per head was everywhere much smaller than before, in spite of the fact that greatly improved methods of production were available owing to new inventions.

This finding is confirmed by the study of the consumption of the essential foodstuffs and other articles. We need hardly mention Austria, which suffered most through the peace settlement. But even in Czechoslovakia, which had been given the richest agricultural and industrial assets of former Austria, the per head consumption of the principal necessities of life was in 1936 lower than ten years before, and also lower than before the World War. The same decline in the standard of life can be observed in Hungary, Yugoslavia and Roumania.

The decline, or standstill, in demand, and consequently in employment, has often been ascribed either to an excessive increase in prices or to an excessive rise in wages. Our study presents a great deal of new material referring to this question. It cannot be denied that in certain cases prices or wages were too high. But in a world of economic nationalism their level is not decisive. A comparison of the Danubian States proves that countries with low prices or wages were not better off in international competition or in maintaining a high internal demand than others with a high level of prices and wages. Under economic nationalism a country trying to lower its prices and wages in order to undersell competitors on foreign markets would immediately be faced by rising tariffs against its goods, and the advantages gained in the beginning would soon be lost, and even be turned into losses.

The new States therefore used another device. One of the most vicious features of economic nationalism was the development of an aggressive trade policy on external markets. Tariffs and State regulations were used to keep prices high on the home market, and the profits were employed for subsidising exports at prices far below the cost of production. Most Danubian States indulged in these practices, which naturally provoked further rises in protection in the other countries.

Economic nationalism has often been defended also on the ground that it was the only means of accumulating sufficient capital for the further development of a country's economic resources and the employment of an increasing population. This argument, however, is not confirmed by the facts. The Danubian States were driving protectionism to extremes. But the formation of capital was everywhere extremely slow and insufficient, and industries as a whole showed a very low rate of profit. Besides, after the collapse international loans also came to an almost complete standstill because of the economic and political insecurity in the Danubian countries.

It has not yet been sufficiently realised that this whole situation was one of the main causes of Hitler's triumph, and of the Second World War. The disruption of the former Empire, and the inability of the new States to co-operate, led to terrible mass unemployment, to the impoverishment of wide sections of the people and to the rise of the spirit of violence and cynical disregard of the rights of others. Hitler cleverly exploited this opportunity. When trade between the Danubian States had shrunk to a minimum Germany offered to take large amounts of their products on favourable terms in exchange for her goods. This exchange was greatly welcomed by the States concerned, and for a time was certainly a considerable advantage.[1] Later on, however, the cloven hoof became visible. Hitler used those benefits for his political purposes. The misery of wide sections and their de-

[1] Cf. in this regard *South-Eastern Europe, a Political and Economic Survey*, published by the Royal Institute of International Affairs, 1939, p. 198.

moralisation made it very easy for the Nazis everywhere to win large numbers of supporters, who were quite willing to serve them for the prospect of getting a post, or for the expected permission to loot the Jews. The predominant political passions worked in the same direction as the economic distress. The Peace Treaties had brought no appeasement in the Danubian area, but had greatly aggravated national and social hatred. It was the lack of any real solution of the Danubian problem which paved the way for Hitler, and it is very questionable whether there would ever have been a Second World War if the community of the Danubian nations had been maintained and reformed instead of being destroyed.

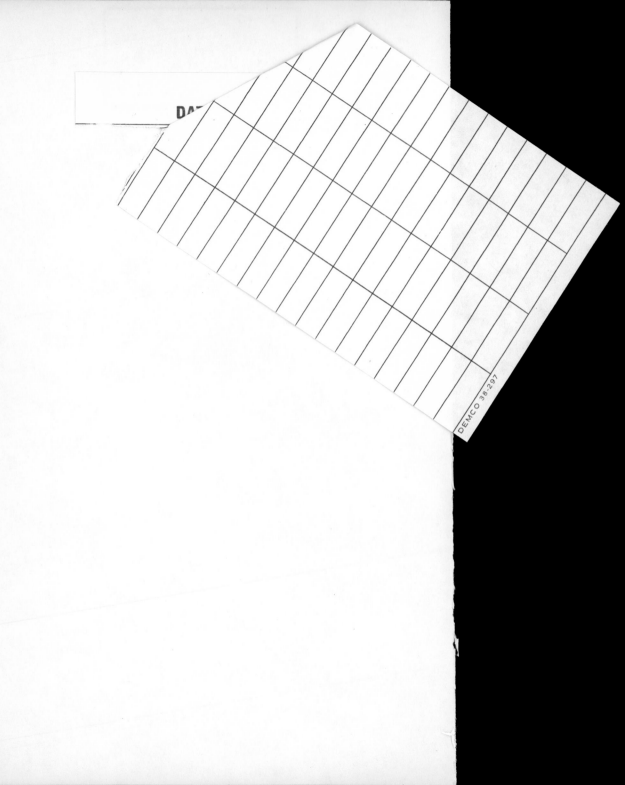